REPUTATIONS

Already published

THOMAS MOORE	John Guy
OLIVER CROMWELL	J.C. Davis
LOUIS XVI	John Hardman
NAPOLEON	R.S. Alexander
DISRAELI	Edgar Feuchtwanger
NEVILLE CHAMBERLAIN	David Dutton
NIXON	Iwan Morgan
EDWARD IV	Michael Hicks

Titles in preparation include

HENRY II	John Gillingham
THOMAS BECKET	Anne Duggan
CAVOUR	Eugenio Biagini
GLADSTONE	David Bebbington
J.F. KENNEDY	Robert David Johnson
THATCHER	E.H.H. Green
GORBACHEV	Mark Sandle
JEFFERSON	Frank Cogliano

EDWARD IV

Michael Hicks

*Professor of Medieval History,
King Alfred's University College, Winchester*

A member of the Hodder Headline Group
LONDON
Distributed in the United States of America by
Oxford University Press Inc., New York

First published in Great Britain in 2004 by
Arnold, a member of the Hodder Headline Group,
338 Euston Road, London NW1 3BH

http://www.arnoldpublishers.com

Distributed in the United States of America by
Oxford University Press Inc.
198 Madison Avenue, New York, NY10016

British Library Cataloguing in Publication Data
A catalogue record for this book is available from the British Library

Library of Congress Cataloging-in-Publication Data
A catalog record for this book is available from the Library of Congress

ISBN 0 340 76005 2 (hb)
ISBN 0 340 76006 0 (pb)

1 2 3 4 5 6 7 8 9 10

Typeset in 10 on 13pt Sabon by Phoenix Photosetting, Chatham, Kent
Printed and bound in Great Britain by CPI, Bath.

What do you think about this book? Or any other Arnold title?
Please send your comments to feedback.arnold@hodder.co.uk

Contents

List of pedigrees   vi
General editorial preface   vii
Preface   ix
Abbreviations   xi

1 Placing Edward IV in English history   1
2 The shaping of Edward IV   11
3 Alternative images of Edward IV   27
4 The degeneration of Edward IV   55
5 The rehabilitation of Edward IV   81
6 Edward's first reign   103
7 The king's wars   123
8 The 'New Monarchy': government and finance   149
9 The king's peace   165
10 Edward IV and the nobility   185
11 Territorial reordering   205
12 The collapse of the regime   223
13 Conclusion   229

Notes   231
Select bibliography   255
Chronology of events   263
Index   269

List of pedigrees

1 The Lancastrian and Yorkist titles to the English Crown 3
2 Simplified pedigree of the House of York 12
3 The royal family of Edward IV 24

General editorial preface

Hero or villain? Charlatan or true prophet? Sinner or saint? The volumes in the Reputations series examine the reputations of some of history's most conspicuous, powerful and influential individuals, considering a range of representations, some of striking incompatibility. The aim is not merely to demonstrate that history is indeed, in Pieter Geyl's phrase, 'argument without end', but that the study even of contradictory conceptions can be fruitful: that the jettisoning of one thesis or presentation leaves behind something of value.

In Iago's self-serving denunciation of it, reputation is 'an idle and most false imposition; oft got without merit, and lost without deserving', but a more generous definition would allow its use as one of the principal currencies of historical understanding. In seeking to analyse the cultivation, creation and deconstruction of reputation, we can understand better the wellsprings of action, the workings-out of competing claims to power, the different purposes of rival ideologies – in short, see more clearly ways in which the past becomes history.

There is a commitment in each volume to showing how understanding of an individual develops (sometimes in uneven and divergent ways), whether in response to fresh evidence, the emergence or waning of dominant ideologies, changing attitudes and preoccupations of the age in which an author writes, or the creation of new historical paradigms. Will Hitler ever seem *quite* the same after the evidence of a recent study revealing the extent of his Jewish connections during the Vienna years? Reassessment of Lenin and Stalin has been given fresh impetus by the collapse of the Soviet

Union and the opening of many of its archives; and the end of the Cold War and its attendant assumptions must alter our views of Eisenhower and Kennedy. How will our perceptions of Elizabeth I change in the presence of a new awareness of 'gendered history'?

There is more to the series than illumination of ways in which recent discoveries or trends have refashioned identities or given actions new meaning – though that is an important part. The corresponding aim is to provide readers with a strong sense of the channels and course of debate from the outset: not a Cook's Tour of the historiography, but identification of the key interpretative issues and guidance as to how commentators of different eras and persuasions have tackled them.

Preface

Edward IV has always been a controversial king. Today, of course, as non-participants in long-forgotten causes, we find it hard to share past passions. We need to recall that in *his* day it was Christian morality against which he was implicitly and explicitly measured – the touchstone of contemporary historians, even if they are not our standards and will seldom figure in the pages that follow.

Our criteria and our interpretations, which we fondly believe to be the judgements of History and hence eternal, are bound to differ. Our notions of what constitutes history and what is acceptable in politics are very different. Our own democratic, egalitarian, feminist and multicultural expectations inevitably colour our historical interpretations. We are better researchers than our predecessors, possess all the advantages of hindsight and perspective that our forerunners lacked. Dividing lines need to be drawn between such helpful vantage points and anachronism. Historians have to present the past in our own language for today's audiences and yet do so in terms that would have made sense at the time. We cannot legitimately condemn Edward IV for faults that neither he nor his contemporaries recognized or could have conceived. Too often we do so. Not all interpretations are equal, moreover, and this book seeks critically to discriminate between them, and to make balanced judgements, *for* and *against* Edward IV.

This book is concerned with what others have written of Edward IV from his own time to date. That survey complete (Chapters 1–5), it devotes the next seven chapters to his two reigns and the key themes within them. It is concerned with the controversial, not with his victories or personal morality, which are not in debate. Much is therefore omitted that is available elsewhere. Rereading past histories uncovers some data and many perceptions otherwise overlooked. Many past historians were much closer to the social and ethical climate of Yorkist England than ourselves and could more readily appreciate eras that, like their own, were rightly monarchical, aristocratic, inegalitarian and, in so many ways, alien to us.

If not researched in the archives, this book is informed by them. It draws on many historians, most of them now dead, who have created the raw material. How much excellent history has been written about Edward IV! When I began, I expected the Second Crowland Continuator, Cora L. Scofield, Jack Lander, Bertram Wolffe and Charles Ross to be my principal guides. Closer examination, not for the first time, has changed my perspective. As I finish, I find that Philippe de Commynes, William Habington, Scofield and, above all, Ross excite my admiration the most. The most recent work is (and indeed ought to be) more fully researched, and more stridently and cogently argued, but it often devotes itself to issues that Edward and his contemporaries could not have recognized and policies that they never intended. I also acknowledge the influence of my mentors Charles Ross and John Armstrong, and in alphabetical order Margaret Condon, Barrie Dobson, Keith Dockray, Ralph Griffiths, Rosemary Horrox, Hannes Kleineke, Jack Lander, Tony Pollard and Brynmor Pugh. None of them will approve of all that is written here, which is obviously my responsibility and mine alone. The actual research, the writing and especially the checking are solitary tasks that isolate the writer from the family who sustain him, but without Cynthia, this book could not have been written, so my principal thanks are to her.

All quotations, in whatever language, have been rendered into modern English. Unless otherwise stated, all works cited were published in London.

Winchester, December 2003

Abbreviations

Arrival	*The Historie of the Arrivall of Edward IV in England and the Finall Recouerye of his Kingdomes from Henry VI,* Camden Society I (1836)
Bellamy	J.G. Bellamy, 'Justice under the Yorkist Kings', *American Journal of Legal History* IX (1965)
Carpenter	C. Carpenter, *The Wars of the Roses: Politics and the Constitution in England c.1437–1509* (Cambridge, 1996)
Chrimes	S.B. Chrimes, *Lancastrians, Yorkists and Henry VII* (1964)
Commynes	P. de Commynes, *Mémoires,* ed. J. Calmette and G. Durville (3 vols, Paris, 1924–6)
Crowland	*The Crowland Chronicle Continuations 1459–86,* eds N. Pronay and J.C. Cox (Gloucester, 1986)
Death and Dissent	*Death and Dissent: The Dethe of the King of Scots and Warkworth's Chronicle,* ed. L. Matheson (Woodbridge, 1999)
Dockray	K.R. Dockray, *Edward IV: A Sourcebook* (Stroud, 1999)
EHD	*English Historical Documents IV, 1327–1485,* ed. A.R. Myers (1969)
EHR	*English Historical Review*

GEC	G.E. C[okayne], *Complete Peerage of England, Scotland, Ireland, Great Britain and the United Kingdom*, eds H.V. Gibbs *et al.*, (13 vols, 1910–59)
Habington	W. Habington, *History of the Reign of King Edward the Fourth* (1640)
Hicks, *Clarence*	M.A. Hicks, *False, Fleeting, Perjur'd Clarence* (Gloucester, 1980)
Hicks, *EPC*	M.A. Hicks, *English Political Culture in the Fifteenth Century* (2002)
Hicks, *Richard III*	M.A. Hicks, *Richard III* (2000)
Hicks, *Rivals*	M.A. Hicks, *Richard III and his Rivals* (1991)
Hicks, *Warwick*	M.A. Hicks, *Warwick the Kingmaker* (1998)
Horrox	R.E. Horrox, *Richard III: A Study of Service* (Cambridge, 1989)
HR	*Historical Research*
Hughes	J. Hughes, *Arthurian Myths and Alchemy: The Kingship of Edward IV* (Stroud, 2002)
Ingulph's Chronicle	*Ingulph's Chronicle of the Abbey of Croyland*, ed. H.T. Riley (1859)
JMH	*Journal of Medieval History*
Jones	M.K. Jones, *Bosworth 1485: Psychology of a Battle* (Stroud, 2002)
Jurkowski	M. Jurkowski, C.L. Smith and D. Crook, eds, *Lay Taxes in England and Wales 1188–1688* (1998)
Kingsford	C.L. Kingsford, *English Historical Literature in the Fifteenth Century* (1913)
Lander	J.R. Lander, *Crown and Nobility 1450–1509* (1976)
Mancini	D. Mancini, *The Usurpation of Richard III*, ed. C.A.J. Armstrong (2nd edn, Oxford, 1969)
More	T. More, *History of King Richard III*, ed. R. Sylvester (Yale, 1963)

Pollard	A.J. Pollard, *Late Medieval England 1399–1509* (Harlow, 2003)
RP	*Rolls of Parliament* (6 vols, 1832)
Ross, *Edward IV*	C.D. Ross, *Edward IV* (2nd edn, 1997)
Ross, *Reign*	C.D. Ross, 'The Reign of Edward IV', *Fifteenth-century England, 1399–1509: Studies in Politics and Society,* eds S.B. Chrimes, C.D. Ross and R.A. Griffiths (Manchester, 1972)
Ross, *Richard III*	C.D. Ross, *Richard III* (2nd edn, 1999)
Scofield	C.L. Scofield, *The Life and Reign of Edward IV* (2 vols, 1923)
Vale	*The Politics of Fifteenth-Century England: John Vale's Book*, eds M.L. Kekewich, C.F. Richmond, A.F. Sutton, L. Visser-Fuchs and J.L. Watts (Stroud, 1995)
Vergil	*Three Books of Polydore Vergil's English History*, ed. H. Ellis, Camden Society XXXIX (1844)
Warkworth's Chronicle	*A Chronicle of the First Thirteen Years of Edward the Fourth*, ed. J.O. Halliwell, Camden Society VI (1839)
Wolffe	B.P. Wolffe, *The Royal Demesne in English History* (1971)

1

Placing Edward IV in English history

Edward IV

This book is about the historical reputation of one of the least known of English kings. Out of the eight King Edwards since the Norman Conquest, Edward IV (1461–83) is much the least familiar, even though two of them never grew up, two lasted for only a few months within a single calendar year, one abdicated and two were never crowned. King Edward IV impinges less on our memories than any other fifteenth-century English king. Most people know more about his three Lancastrian predecessors Henry IV, Henry V and Henry VI, about Edward IV's own teenaged son Edward V (best known as the elder of the little princes in the Tower), about his own youngest brother, that wickedest of uncles, Richard III and, indeed, about his Tudor successors. Tudor history, part of Key Stage 2 and a common focus for A-level history, commences two years after Edward IV's death. Here, as elsewhere, Shakespeare has much to answer for. Although Edward IV does feature in two of Shakespeare's history plays, he takes centre stage in neither – there is no Shakespearean *King Edward IV*. He features merely as a boy in *Henry VI* and as the time-expired outgoing monarch in *Richard III*.[1] History has done us all a disservice in so neglecting the real success story of the Wars of the Roses.

Edward IV was not born to be king of England. He was still only a teenager in 1461 when he was propelled to the leadership of the Yorkists and declared himself King Edward IV. To a remarkable extent he created his kingship himself, on the battlefield and by declaring each success to be God's affirmation of his cause. It has recently been argued that he may even have believed himself divinely

inspired and predestined to rule.[2] Edward won the decisive victory
at Towton that deposed Henry VI – an incumbent king of almost
forty years standing – and displaced the Lancastrian dynasty that
had ruled for over sixty years. Edward made himself king and
inaugurated his new, Yorkist, dynasty. The winner of the first phase
of the Wars of the Roses (1459–61) was also the winner of the
second (1469–71). After briefly losing his throne, he recovered it –
only the second post-conquest English king to rule more than once
– and was again the victorious commander in battle. Edward was
the most successful general of the Wars of the Roses. Modern
historians have credited him also with the regeneration of the discredited English monarchy for the ultimate benefit of the Tudors.
He re-established royal prestige, a splendid court and royal
authority, through his reconstruction of royal finances and solvency,
by restoring law and order and by inaugurating the devolved
governments for Wales and the North that the Tudors were to carry
much further.[3] He kept his throne at a time when mere survival was
exceptionally difficult for English kings. It was Edward IV who
finally defeated Warwick the Kingmaker. He reigned for twenty-
three years, the last twelve without challenge, and died naturally in
his bed. The Crown that he had won by force of arms was transmitted naturally and peacefully to his son Edward V. These are
impressive credits for Edward IV.

Whether Edward intended all that he achieved is doubtful. It had
been his father who had asserted the Yorkist claim to the throne and
secured its acceptance at the parliament of 1460. It was York's
defeat and death that provoked his son's bid for the throne – an out-
rageous gamble undertaken only because Edward had no other
option. Any self-confidence, self-belief and sense of mission were
surely secondary to his need to fight. Edward did not make himself
king by himself nor rule on his own: his cousin Warwick was much
more than his right-hand man in the early years. There were two
rulers in England, joked the Calais garrison, one being Warwick and
another, whose name they had forgotten.[4] Obviously Edward never
planned to be deposed in 1470, his third consecutive disastrous
political miscalculation, and he fully accepted how unfavourable
were the odds that he had overcome. Edward was not a natural
reformer. A traditional rather than an original ruler, content to
survive and continue rather than to introduce or reform, it is

Pedigree 1: The Lancastrian and Yorkist titles to the English Crown

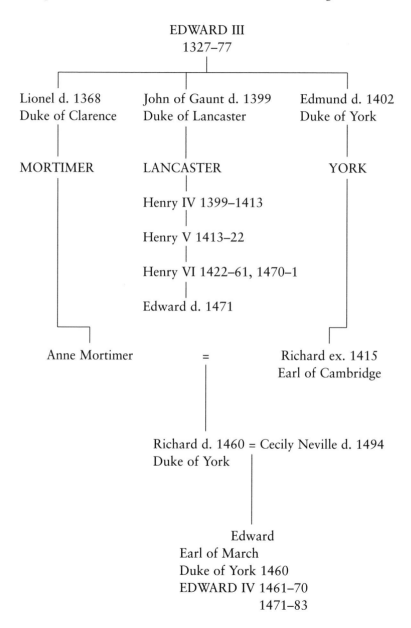

EDWARD III
1327–77

| Lionel d. 1368 | John of Gaunt d. 1399 | Edmund d. 1402 |
| Duke of Clarence | Duke of Lancaster | Duke of York |

MORTIMER   LANCASTER   YORK

Henry IV 1399–1413

Henry V 1413–22

Henry VI 1422–61, 1470–1

Edward d. 1471

Anne Mortimer   =   Richard ex. 1415
Earl of Cambridge

Richard d. 1460 = Cecily Neville d. 1494
Duke of York

Edward
Earl of March
Duke of York 1460
EDWARD IV 1461–70
1471–83

questionable whether he consciously intended the changes with which he is credited or the extent to which they worked. He was an effective medieval monarch rather than the inaugurator of a new way of ruling.

Against Edward, there is also much to be said. Like all usurpers, he was a controversial figure in his own day with more than his share of enemies. Many sought to defeat, destroy, dethrone and slay him. Twice he was driven abroad and twice he was attainted as a traitor by his Lancastrian foes. Twice, to their perception, he usurped Henry VI's throne. Twice at least enemies amongst his kindred labelled him a bastard, not the son of his father York, and hence disqualified him from ruling.

Catastrophe followed Edward's death in 1483. Arguably it overturned all his achievements. Arguably also it was all Edward's fault. His son, namesake and unquestioned successor, Edward V, still under age, was deposed by his uncle, Edward IV's own brother, Richard Duke of Gloucester, who made himself King Richard III. Many disapproved of Richard's actions, perhaps including the majority of the Yorkist establishment of southern England, who, stiffened by French and Scottish support, destroyed Richard and the Yorkist dynasty and placed Henry Tudor on the throne as King Henry VII. Although some Yorkists plotted on for another forty years, Henry VII married Edward IV's eldest daughter, Elizabeth of York: Edward IV was thus grandfather of Henry VIII, great-grandfather to Edward VI, Mary I and Elizabeth I, and ancestor of every English monarch since. Ever present on all their family trees, it is not Edward IV that historians have traditionally chosen to develop. He has been the forgotten king of what, until recently, could be dubbed a dark age of English history.

Historians of his own age and immediately after disagreed about him, just as subsequent historians have done. 'Over the last five hundred years', writes Keith Dockray, 'Edward IV's reputation has fluctuated widely: the king has attracted both powerful criticism and fulsome praise'.[5] Never, however, have the verdicts been further apart than today. For Christine Carpenter, Edward IV 'should be acknowledged as one of the greatest of English kings'.[6] Jonathan Hughes presents him as a charismatic and adventurous youthful hero – the fulfilment of prophecy and the hope of the future – who degenerated in his early middle age into ineffective indulgence, indolence and inertia.[7] For Colin Richmond, on the other hand, Edward IV was responsible not only for the loss of his throne in 1470, which he was fortunate to be able to regain, but also for the abyss of 1483–5 that engulfed his son and his dynasty[8] and which he should have foreseen and averted. Edward must have supposed that he had brought an end to the Wars of the Roses in 1471. Instead he had merely postponed – or perhaps even provoked – phase III (1483–5). What happened in those years has become one of the fiercest debates in English history, one known to everybody, interested or not, although it is usually conceived in terms of the sons, brother, queen, chamberlain and in-laws that Edward IV left behind. How far he overcame almost insuperable odds or created them for his heirs are key issues that no study of him can ignore.

The Wars of the Roses

Edward IV and Henry VII were the true victors of the Wars of the Roses. Without the Wars of the Roses, neither could have reigned. Edward was the eldest son and heir of the wealthiest English nobleman of his day, Richard Duke of York, Earl of March and Ulster (d. 1460). York had high aspirations both for himself and his son: lieutenant to Henry VI in both France and Ireland, he coveted the Crown of Castile, to which he had an arguable title, and pursued the King of France's daughter as consort to his son. Young Edward himself was not predestined to reign in England, no matter what pedlars of pedigrees and prophecies may have forecast,[9] for that was the privilege of his cousin King Henry VI (1422–61) and his issue. It was Edward's pre-ordained future to succeed his father as the greatest of Henry's subjects. Only when the House of York became ranged against the ruling dynasty did Edward's prospects alter. Only after this opposition had generated the Wars of Roses and destroyed his father was Edward prompted to claim the Crown for himself and for his family and then, in battle at Towton, to make his title good. It was the perjury of Henry VI, who involuntarily broke the Accord of 1460, that excused Edward of any perjury for his own breach of allegiance. How Edward secured the Crown, by victory over Lancaster and through the blood of the Lancastrians, many of whom did not give up for years, was to colour his first reign (1461–70), which culminated in his own defeat and flight into exile.

Henry VI reigned again (his readeption of 1470–1), albeit only for six months, before Edward's much more complete and final triumphs at Barnet and Tewkesbury in 1471. Henceforth he held the throne securely and transmitted it on his death, peacefully and as planned, to his eldest son, Prince Edward, as Edward V. No prophet, Edward IV did not expect his son to be deposed within three months, nor his loyal and trusted brother, Richard Duke of Gloucester, to be transformed into King Richard III (1483–5), nor for internecine strife to resume, nor for the Wars of the Roses to enter a third phase, nor indeed that within three years his own sons and his own Yorkist dynasty should have been supplanted by that obscure exile Henry Tudor.

The preceding paragraph outlines history through the individuals – who they were and what they did – and has overstressed perhaps the importance of individual motives and personal ambition. Indeed it is hard to explain what happened in 1483 other than through the personal frictions and animosities that caused Richard III to reignite embers that had died down almost to ashes. Dynasticism, the rival hereditary claims of rival dynasties, came to be the main reason for conspiracy and conflict. It was as a dynastic struggle that the Wars of the Roses were presented by the Tudor victors, who traced their origins to the deposition in 1399 of Richard II, undoubtedly a legitimate king and also the Lord's anointed, from which sin the whole providential cycle of punishment logically unfolded. This orthodoxy was codified most elegantly and memorably, and was popularized by Shakespeare in his fifteenth-century history plays and hence in art, history, literature, school textbooks and public imagination up to this third millennium.

Yet it had not always been so. Admittedly it was because of their royal blood and royal descent, as heirs through Mortimer of Lionel Duke of Clarence, the second son of King Edward III (1327–77), that first Richard Duke of York in 1460 and then his son in 1461 became the rival claimants to the reigning King Henry VI, whose title emanated only from Edward III's third son. Their genealogy and the ominous surname of Mortimer were known to them and a few others, who asserted – or denied – York's claim to the Crown as early as 1450. Possibly, but not certainly, hereditary right was motive enough for York and Edward themselves.

It was not sufficient for their backers, who had much more to lose from treason and civil war than to gain from the accession of their claimant. Most of these had sworn allegiance to Henry VI. As late as 1460, whilst regarding York's hereditary title to be unquestionable, even the Yorkist Lords declined to set aside King Henry. Dynastic legitimacy was critical for Edward's Yorkist propagandists, who were encouraged as much by prophecies and genealogies recycled from Arthurian and Trojan myths as by descent from Edward III, but lineage scarcely features in the propaganda designed to win over the uncommitted to the cause of the aggressors. Other, far more powerful, grievances created the movement that swept the Lancastrians away and installed in lieu Edward IV, its figurehead and instrument. Nor was it mere personalities and the respective merits of different dynastic titles that first dislodged Edward in 1470 and then astonishingly restored him to his throne. Edward V, Richard III and Henry VII sat uneasy on their thrones for reasons other than the dubious titles their rivals paraded as justifications for revolution, which in each case identified particular nobles as the alternative dynastic candidates. Five times during the Wars of the Roses new kings overthrew their incumbent rivals. At least another six attempts foundered. Such instability has no parallel in English history. Never before and never again in England have governments so easily been overthrown and replaced.

The Wars of the Roses broke out more than thirty years after the accession of King Henry VI. Most of the causes, certainly the short-term factors, the immediate triggers and the alignment of sides are properly located in his reign. Henry presided over a dispiriting sequence of reverses and lost in turn his kingdoms of France and England, the latter twice. Enormous external challenges and pressures were compounded by his own personal inadequacies. First a child, then a simpleton, once mad, he was surely the least suited of any medieval English monarch to rule. It was the 'inanity' of Henry VI that was blamed by K.B. McFarlane for the outbreak of the Wars of the Roses.[10] Apparently uninterested in government or military leadership, Henry was at best erratically involved in ruling. If ever more than the vacuum that John Watts and Christine Carpenter perceive,[11] he was rarely moved to intervene in politics and always, so Anthony Pollard has suggested, did so incompetently and counter-productively. Even his pacific inclinations proved disastrously misplaced.

By the late 1430s, when Henry VI came of age, any chance of implementing the Treaty of Troyes and making himself king of a united France had passed. Now unwinnable, the Hundred Years War was also to become, for England, financially insupportable. To search for an alternative that retained some territorial gains in return for renunciation of the French Crown was both sensible and honourable. Henry was right therefore to override the opposition of those diehard warmongers who postured as Henry V's political heirs, notably his uncle, Humphrey Duke of Gloucester (Good Duke Humphrey, d. 1447), but he stopped short of abandoning his title, which alone, surely, offered any hope for a permanent settlement. Without this concession, no lasting peace was possible, merely truces. To surrender Maine unnecessarily, as Henry decided, was to make too much of the peace dividend; to do it too prematurely, so that English possessions in France lay exposed; and finally to break the truce that alone offered protection, were three foolish errors, all historians are agreed, that had the direst consequences. It was impractical idealism that ranged veterans like Sir John Fastolf behind York and urged the aggressive strategies that King Henry wisely ignored. Between 1449 and 1453 all the English territories were lost except Calais. England itself suffered from French raids and was threatened with invasion. Hence the upsurge of fury amongst the English nobility, parliamentary Commons and the commons alike, who liquidated the king's ministers in 1450 and committed themselves to radical reforms that were repeatedly expressed in violence. Maybe Henry VI was unusual in his reliance on a succession of ministers and favourites, from Suffolk (k. 1450) to Somerset (k. 1455) and Buckingham (k. 1460), who were perhaps (but not certainly) more self-interested than their counterparts in other reigns; but it was the repeated resort to force of York, as champion of reform, that disrupted the government's attempts to restore order and rule effectively. It was the responsibility of all kings to quash the quarrels of the nobility before they got out of hand and to impose peace on the contenders, yet a series of such provincial disputes escalated in the 1450s into private war and became enmeshed in national politics.[12] York himself rejected the king's attempts to draw a line under the past, repeatedly broke the oaths of obedience that he swore and twice eliminated his opponents in cold blood. The king's willingness to forgive three times allowed the duke to escape the penalties of treason. Henry's lunacy in 1453–5 enabled York to recover from apparently terminal defeat. If Henry failed to rule effectively, York certainly impeded him and continued to mobilize popular support for reforms that had perhaps already been achieved. From a Lancastrian point of view, as the 1459 parliament frankly admitted, York was an incorrigible fomentor of discord.[13]

Maybe King Henry was too willing to treat York as his cousin and near equal and to allow him privileges and immunities beyond any of his peers. Henry's weakness as king resulted not merely from his own personal inadequacies and the failures of his regime, but also from the lack of resources at his command. The French wars had plunged him into debt, forcing him to cut back in the ways outlined above, and destroyed his credit rating. Stringent economies late in the 1440s brought current income and expenditure nearly into balance, without reducing his debts,[14] but plunging revenues thereafter, especially customs revenues, slashed his income to a third or even a quarter of that of his predecessors. The king should live of his own, reformers declared, at a time when it was frankly unattainable and sensible taxes were refused. Scarcely able to find the everyday costs of government, Henry could not finance anything exceptional, whether against the French or his English opponents. His greatest subjects, such as York and Warwick, whose resources were normally dwarfed by the Crown's, found themselves able to contend with the king almost on equal terms and therefore to be overmighty. Nor did this weakness end with Henry VI. Professor Hatcher's 'Great Slump' of *c*.1440–80, which was the root cause, continued during the next reign, denied Edward IV the assets of his predecessors and successors, and disadvantaged him in international and domestic politics. Though neither Edward IV nor Richard III were personally unfitted to rule, both lost their thrones, in Edward's case temporarily. Starting with 'an extremely difficult situation,' writes Carpenter, then contending with one that 'was simply impossible',[15] Edward was nevertheless able to manage on and off for twenty-three years.

Besides the weakness of the Crown, there were two other reasons why Henry VI, Edward IV and the other English rulers of this era were so susceptible to overthrow. One was domestic, the engagement of the populace, at least of southern England, from Jack

Cade's Kentishmen in 1450 to the Cornishmen in 1497, in politics and their willingness to resort to force when summoned by aristocratic champions of reform. Several times, in 1450, 1460 and 1470, they turned out in numbers that the governments of the day could not withstand. Second, the rival great powers of northern Europe, the King of France and Duke of Burgundy, actively intervened in English politics, sheltering exiles and supporting their raids and invasions with money, shipping and highly trained manpower. Again and again the kingdom was attacked from without, several times successfully.[16] If the Wars of the Roses were precipitated during the reign of Henry VI and due, at least in part, to his deficiencies, it was the unprecedented weakness of the Crown against its greatest subjects, its people and foreign neighbours that permitted the wars to continue and repeatedly resume. Only after Edward IV's death did the recovery of the economy, royal finances and national prosperity, and the end of popular revolution and foreign intervention, surely causally connected, enable his Tudor successors to outlast the wars. Though dynastic rivalries endured and indeed dynastic rivals proliferated, they could not prolong the conflict.

2

The shaping of Edward IV

Contexts

Edward IV must be seen in context – or rather in contexts. Not only did he have nineteen years of life before he became king, but those nineteen years were shaped by who he was and what he was destined to be – by his pedigree, hereditary estate and expectations, and also by the family traditions and honour that were his heritage, which he was expected to continue and ideally to enhance. Edward needs to be perceived as heir to the Houses of Clare, Mortimer and York. All such antecedents were to be superseded, transcended and transmuted after his accession into a Yorkist myth, which sadly failed to last. The short twenty-three years of Edward's reign almost exsanguinated the House of York. The years immediately after Edward's demise saw a re-evaluation of his place in history. King Edward IV and his Yorkists had to be downsized and refashioned for futures different from any that Edward – or anyone else during his lifetime – could have foreseen. This chapter therefore discusses three contexts: the traditions of Clarence, Mortimer and York; the specific contribution of Edward's father, Richard Duke of York; and the Yorkist myth.[1]

Ancestral traditions

Edward IV succeeded to the Crown of England because of his royal descent. His father, Duke Richard, was heir to two sons of King Edward III: Lionel of Antwerp, from whom he was descended in the female line and from whom he claimed his Crown, and Edmund of Langley, to whom he was heir male. It was his paternal pedigree, the coat of arms and livery of York alone, that he sported until 1460, when those of Clarence were given priority. Through his wife, Duke

Pedigree 2: Simplified pedigree of the House of York

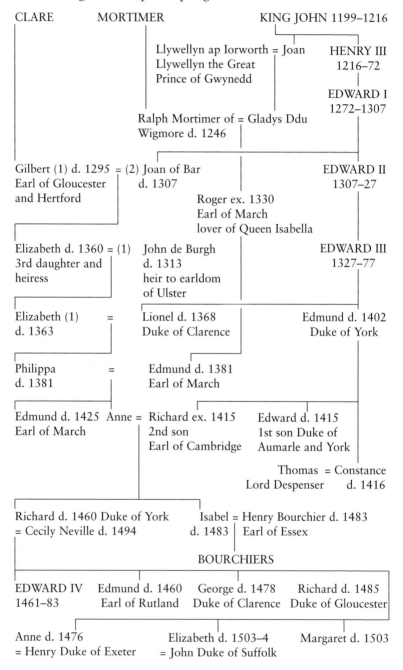

CLARE   MORTIMER   KING JOHN 1199–1216

Llywellyn ap Iorworth = Joan   HENRY III
Llywellyn the Great   1216–72
Prince of Gwynedd

EDWARD I
1272–1307

Ralph Mortimer of = Gladys Ddu
Wigmore d. 1246

Gilbert (1) d. 1295 = (2) Joan of Bar   EDWARD II
Earl of Gloucester   d. 1307   1307–27
and Hertford

Roger ex. 1330
Earl of March
lover of Queen Isabella

Elizabeth d. 1360 = (1) John de Burgh   EDWARD III
3rd daughter and   d. 1313   1327–77
heiress   heir to earldom
                                      of Ulster

Elizabeth (1)   =   Lionel d. 1368   Edmund d. 1402
d. 1363   Duke of Clarence   Duke of York

Philippa   =   Edmund d. 1381
d. 1381   Earl of March

Edmund d. 1425 Anne = Richard ex. 1415   Edward d. 1415
Earl of March   2nd son   1st son Duke of
                                  Earl of Cambridge Aumarle and York

                                                            Thomas = Constance
                                                        Lord Despenser   d. 1416

Richard d. 1460 Duke of York   Isabel = Henry Bourchier d. 1483
= Cecily Neville d. 1494   d. 1483 | Earl of Essex

                                      BOURCHIERS

EDWARD IV   Edmund d. 1460   George d. 1478   Richard d. 1485
1461–83   Earl of Rutland Duke of Clarence Duke of Gloucester

Anne d. 1476   Elizabeth d. 1503–4   Margaret d. 1503
= Henry Duke of Exeter   = John Duke of Suffolk

Richard traced himself back to yet another son of Edward III, John of Gaunt. York was also descended independently through two lines from Joan of Acre, a daughter of King Edward I, from the latter's younger brother and from a daughter of King John. Edward IV was thus living demonstration that the blood royal of medieval England tended to marry one another. Such luxuriant interconnections defeated the compilers of the splendid illuminated genealogies that were commercially produced in Henry VI's London. Necessarily selective in what they recorded, they cautiously underplayed the Mortimer line that was to take pride of place after Edward IV's accession.[2]

If Edward's royal lineage was ancient, the House of York, in contrast, was relatively recent. Its founder was Edmund Duke of York (d. 1402), the fourth surviving and penultimate son of King Edward III. Made Earl of Cambridge by his father, he was created Duke of York by his nephew Richard II, but without either the generous endowment or the fortunate marriage of his four brothers. It was a poor duchy, heavily reliant on uncertain exchequer annuities, that he passed to his son and grandson. Edmund's marriage to a Spanish princess, Isabel (d. 1392), the youngest daughter of King Pedro the Cruel of Castile by his mistress, brought him neither a crown nor wealth, but it did infuse his line with the blood royal and also claims to the Crown of Castile, which they cherished to little constructive effect.[3] Unlike his brother, York had not inherited a family mausoleum as a focus for the family traditions that had become de rigueur. Edmund himself was buried at Langley where he was born, but in 1412 his son founded the college at Fotheringhay (Northants), where future dukes were to be laid to rest. That Edmund's eldest son Edward, in turn Earl of Rutland and Duke of Aumarle, was the most intimate favourite of Richard II, proved counter-productive after the latter's deposition in 1399 and Henry IV's accession. Duke Edward perished at Agincourt soon after his younger brother, Richard Earl of Cambridge, had been executed. Again there was no ancestral lustre to inherit for Cambridge's son, Richard, henceforth Duke of York, his uncle's heir male and predestined to father Edward IV. Consigned to the care of Ralph Neville, Earl of Westmorland and his countess Joan Beaufort, half-sister of Henry IV, he was matched as a minor to their youngest daughter, Cecily Neville, 'the Rose of Raby'. Thus rehabilitated as a

member of the house of Lancaster and connected to the most extensive of noble clans, young Richard – now premier duke – acquired
no addition to his modest estates. What transformed his fortunes to
match his rank was his succession via his mother Anne Mortimer to
the vast inheritance of his uncle Edmund (d. 1425), the last
Mortimer Earl of March.

Anne Mortimer too had been descended from Edward III,
through the female line from his second son, the short-lived Lionel
Duke of Clarence (d. 1368), but also from Edward I (1272–1307)
via his daughter Joan of Acre (d. 1307), the wife of the penultimate
de Clare Earl of Gloucester and Hertford. Joan's daughter and
co-heiress Elizabeth (d. 1360), the Lady of Clare, married John de
Burgh (d. 1313), heir to the earldom of Ulster. It was their grand-
daughter and heiress, Elizabeth de Burgh (d. 1363) who married
Duke Lionel. Their only child, Philippa, married Edmund Mortimer,
Earl of March (d. 1381), combining the Clare, Clarence, De Burgh
and Mortimer inheritances and the earldoms of March and Ulster
for Anne Mortimer to transmit to Richard Duke of York. It was not
just great wealth and estates in England, Wales and Ireland,
therefore, to which Duke Richard succeeded, but also the long-
standing traditions of the ancient houses of de Clare, de Burgh and
Mortimer.

The last Earl of March was interred not at Wigmore Abbey
(Salop), but at the Austin friary at Clare in Suffolk, the source of the
title of Clarence that Edward III coined for Duke Lionel. A Norman
family and lords of Clare, whence they took their name, the Clares
had been earls of Hertford since Stephen's reign and earls of
Gloucester from 1217. By 1314 the Clares were the second
wealthiest English noble house. They had distinguished themselves
both against the Scots and in the political crises of Henry III. At
their Austin friary at Clare, the first English house of the order
established by Earl Richard in 1248, there lay buried Joan of Acre,
the Duchess of Clarence, and the Duke himself, 'for such a prince,
too simply'. Although the Clares, Mortimers and York seldom
resided at Clare and reposed elsewhere, at Tewkesbury, Wigmore
and Fotheringhay, the friars evidently so cherished the memory of
their prestigious patrons that one of them, the author Osbert
Bokenham (d. *c.*1467), developed it in the mid-fifteenth century.
Bokenham was apparently author of the surviving Clare Roll that in

1456 celebrated their patrons from Joan of Acre to Duke Richard and his children. A 'dialogue betwixt a secular asking and a friar answering at the grave of Dame Joan of Acre', the Roll takes the form of three columns of eighteen English stanzas, eleven identified coats of arms, and Latin verses. Bokenham stressed his patrons' royal lineage. The Mortimers were traced rapidly through to Richard Duke of York, 'this Prince mighty' and his 'progeny gracious', eleven being born and four having already died. Whereas the Latin version records Duke Richard's 'war triumphs' and 'many talents', the English stanza merely looks to the future:

> Long may he live in God's pleasure,
> This high and mighty prince in prosperity.
> With virtue and victory God advance him
> Over all his enemies, and grant that he
> And the noble Princess [Cecily] his wife may see
> Her children's children ere they depart hence ...

Probably originally for display by Joan's tomb at St Vincent's altar (and an excellent advertisement there for the House of York),[4] a copy may have been presented to Duke Richard, since Bokenham had apparently designated some of his other works for him in the mid-1440s. Bokenham's verse translation of Claudian's *Of the Consulate of Stilicho* drew parallels between York and the fifth-century consul, last hope of the decaying Roman empire, and even his recital of the legends of thirteen female saints and St Mary Magdalene mentioned York's title to the Castilian throne.

> For now the parliament peers, whether they go or ride,
> Say the Duke of York has God upon his side.[5]

Also originally from Normandy, the Mortimers of Wigmore were established in the central marches of Wales, and indeed in English politics, long before Roger Mortimer was created Earl of March in 1327. Eventually they held no less than seventeen marcher lordships. Wigmore Abbey, their house of Victorine canons, was the Mortimer mausoleum, sadly now destroyed. Like the friars of Clare, the canons of Wigmore saw themselves as highly sympathetic custodians of the Mortimers' memory. Their foundation chronicle described their founder, Sir Hugh Mortimer as 'the most glorious knight renowned and endowed above all then living in England'.[6] A

Latin chronicle, which reached back to the Norman conquest, recited all the lords of Wigmore, their consorts, children and their marriages and their achievements down to the last Earl Edmund. Mortimer marriages, the resultant offspring and their marital alliances, feats of arms and religious foundations, dates and modes of death where interesting (as in tournaments) and places of burial were recorded. Successive generations of warlike and chivalrous Mortimers enhanced the family's renown against the Welsh at first, abroad and increasingly in English affairs, culminating in the overthrow of Edward II by the first earl. The marriage of Ralph Mortimer (d. 1282) to Gladys Ddu, daughter of Llewellyn the Great by Joan, bastard daughter of King John, linked the Yorkist kings to the Welsh princes.[7]

Their descendants married into many of the principal English houses. Much more attention is given to the match of Edmund, the third earl, with Philippa, sole daughter and heiress of Lionel Duke of Clarence (d. 1368), second son of Edward III. She brought him the honour of Clare and other English lands and the earldom of Ulster, which justified the appointments of Edmund 'the glorious' (d. 1381), Roger (d. 1398), Edmund 'the good' (d. 1425) and Richard Duke of York as lieutenants of Ireland, where the first two died. Philippa also brought a claim on the death of Richard II to inherit the kingdoms of both England and France: in popular parlance, the chronicler daringly reports that Edmund the fifth earl 'stands unjustly excluded from the crown of the kingdom of England in right of the said lord Lionel the second-born'. Hence Lady Despenser carried away the last earl as a child, but her plot was foiled.[8] The Mortimers' chivalric renown occurs even in the widely circulated popular chonicle the *Brut*. A deluxe Wigmore roll stresses the Mortimers' Welsh ancestry, tracing them back to Cadwallader and even King Arthur and the Trojan Brutus who founded Britain.[9] One Mortimer badge was the white rose, which York included on his seal and which featured on the rich collar worth 4,000 marks (£2,666 13s. 4d.) that he commissioned, although the falcon and fetterlock remained his preferred livery badge. The duke himself was identified in prophecy as the heir of Cadwallader from 1451, admittedly by those anxious for political change, and sometimes features as the heir of Brutus in contemporary genealogies.[10]

Such was the tradition into which Edward IV was born and which should have shaped his view of his family's heritage. That it was favourable must be expected of history written by clients *of* the family *for* the family: it presents their case. Other versions of the past were possible. Some ancestral legacies were adverse, even dishonourable. The earls of March and dukes of York had plenty of critics. It was his adulterous liaison with Queen Isabella, the 'She-wolf of France', that brought Roger Mortimer to the earldom of March. He quickly proved himself to be as grasping and tyrannical as the Despensers whom he supplanted. He was equally hated and likewise perished on the block, which the Wigmore chronicler carefully overlooks. Edmund Duke of York was 'as much of a nonentity as any royal duke could be in late-medieval England,' declared T.B. Pugh.[11] He was not a military hero like his eldest brother the Black Prince, nor did he dominate English affairs even briefly, like his senior, John of Gaunt, and junior, Thomas of Woodstock. As keeper of the realm for his nephew, Richard II, then in Ireland, he did not stop the revolution that resulted in Henry IV's usurpation. 'Despite the strictures of recent historians, who have been unsparing in their censures on "wretched Regent York"', Pugh objects, 'it must be noted that Edmund of Langley's judicious conduct in the greatest crisis of his career was not criticized by any contemporary English writer'. Faced with inevitable defeat, it was 'shrewd and timely' to submit as he did, and thereby he 'rescued the House of York from impending disaster and he saved England from an outbreak of civil war'. From his consort may have been inherited the sexual immorality for which his house became notorious: his daughter Constance Lady Despenser bore a bastard in her widowhood. Fatefully, Duke Edward advised Richard II to divide his army in two, counsel which the chronicler Creton thought treacherous rather than merely mistaken. He was traitor both to Richard II and to Henry IV. Henry IV had justifiable doubts about the allegiance both of him and 'the king's disreputable cousin', Lady Constance. Their brother, Richard Earl of Cambridge, was implicated in the Southampton Plot and executed in 1415; Edmund Earl of March, now adult, the intended beneficiary of the plot, retained his head but not his reputation. The Wigmore chronicles pass lightly over him. The Clare Roll mentions him not at all. Duke Edward's suffocation in his armour at Agincourt – for he was a fat man – was decidedly unheroic.[12]

What had to be lived down by Richard Duke of York was thus rather more obvious than any accrual of ancestral renown. In and after 1460, Duke Richard himself, Edward IV and their spin doctors reinterpreted these unfortunate antecedents more positively into consistent loyalty to Richard II, the last legitimate king, and to his rightful heirs the Mortimers, and consecrated them with memories of St Richard, the martyred Archbishop Scrope.[13] We cannot tell how early this process commenced. Whilst little is known of the movements of the future Edward IV as a child, we know of those of his parents and the birthplaces of his siblings. Apart from France, where he was born, Edward was surely at Dublin in 1449 and at Fotheringhay in 1452 to encounter different aspects of his heritage. We cannot locate him at Clare, however, or know whether he ever saw a copy of the Clare Roll: naturally he was aware of the lineage that it celebrated. From the mid-1450s, Edward and his next brother, Edmund (significantly a Mortimer name!) Earl of Rutland were based at Ludlow in the Shropshire marches. Therefore they must have known the Wigmore mausoleum and the Mortimer traditions first-hand. They were still there in 1459 for the disaster of Ludford. It was nearby, in 1461, that Edward won his first victory of Mortimer's Cross, a location that he may well have selected. It was from his Mortimer affinity that he plucked William Herbert and Walter Devereux during his first reign. It was at Ludlow, from 1473, that he settled his own son to rule the marches. Edward was to promote his next brother (and next heir), George Duke of Clarence and his own son, Richard, Duke of York. It was Edward who had his father York and brother Edmund reinterred at Fotheringhay in 1476. The Mortimer earldom of March, the most concrete and least symbolic part of his inheritance, he annexed to the Crown in 1479.

The political legacy of Richard Duke of York

Richard Duke of York was the premier duke, a prince of the blood royal and the greatest of English noblemen under Henry VI. He saw himself as a member of the European nobility, with royal blood and royal titles to crowns other than England. He had explored his rights to the Crown of Castile.[14] He served his king in the highest available offices, as his lieutenant – commander-in-chief – both in France and Ireland and three times as lord protector. If there was little scope for glory in France by the time he went there, for the English were decidedly in retreat, and if Chester heralds' portrayal of him in 1476 as 'the flower of nobility' is somewhat exaggerated, nevertheless York deserves credit for his skilful orchestration of English defence against the resurgent France. In retrospect, his finest hour was his relief of Pontoise in 1441. A significant achievement at the time, it was not decisive, obviously inconsiderable when compared with Agincourt or Verneuil, and at best one of the minor episodes of the Hundred Years War. The most was made of it much later, when his epitaph (1476) asserted that he had routed Charles VII and the Dauphin Louis.[15] York's lieutenancy ended somewhat under a cloud, with aspersions of favouritism and corruption that 'should be cause of the loss of your said duchy', which York vehemently denied.[16] He remained popular with his captains and old soldiers such as Sir John Fastolf, who saw him as the chosen instrument for recovery and the principal mouthpiece of advocates of an aggressive anti-French policy. It was to York that Fastolf addressed his call for united efforts against France in 1449.[17] Like other disaffected veterans who suffered financially when Normandy was lost, York was convinced he could have done better. He attributed the French triumph to betrayal by the English commander and relentlessly sought Somerset's trial, long after he had been exculpated by the king.[18] York also made himself popular during his brief sojourn in Ireland, where he was allowed to take refuge in 1459–60, where his son, George Duke of Clarence, was also apparently a popular lieutenant and where his supposed heirs, Lambert Simnel and Perkin Warbeck, were accepted as Edward VI and Richard IV. York was the rightful king, according to an epitaph written fifteen years into his son's reign rather than at the time, and 'a warrior of renown, wise, valiant, of virtuous life'. 'Of England he was protector for a long time: he loved the people and was their defender'. It was when 'treating for peace [that] misfortune overtook him' at Wakefield in 1460.[19]

How much of this eulogy was recognizable before 1461 is hard to say. Duke Richard's public stance on the major issues of his day is revealed in his open letters of 1450, 1452 and 1459, his manifestos of 1459 and 1460, Yorkist versions of events from 1455, 1460 and 1461,[20] and from the narratives of his contemporaries. That most narrators became his partisans suggests that his projection of himself was widely believed. Until 1450, Richard Duke of York made little impact on domestic politics. His rank required attendance at parliaments, councils and formal audiences, and important military commands. He was a loyal subject. So too he continued to claim until 1459, but with a difference. From his unlicensed return from Ireland in 1450 onwards, he claimed to know the king's best interests better than Henry VI himself. York contrasted himself with the king's other councillors, by definition untrue and evil, who were causing Henry to perjure himself.[21] He 'loved loyalty without malice', his epitaph declared.[22] York was the true successor of 'Good Duke Humphrey' to the legacy of Henry V in France. He urged the reconquest of the English possessions. In succession to the popular rebel, Jack Cade (d. 1450), and in defiance of the memory of the disgraced minister, William Duke of Suffolk, who had been lynched earlier the same year, York advanced himself as the champion of a reform movement committed to the restoration of respect, solvency and good governance to king and realm.[23] The English defeat abroad and the weakness of government at home owed nothing, to York's eyes, to the strength of a rejuvenated France or to the Great Slump, and everything to the incompetence, corruption, cowardice and collusion with the French of the king's ministers and commanders. York's stance obliged him to oppose, correct, overcome and even try the king's evil councillors (and their successors as evil councillors) and replace them with himself. The duke was, after all, a royal prince, the king's senior cousin and the premier duke, whose very birth placed him on a different plane to his fellow subjects – not that any were really his equals – and entitled him to counsel and even forcefully correct the king. His status exempted him from the treason laws and even the oaths of obedience that he had sworn reluctantly.[24] Duke Richard did not permit even the king's acquittal to impede his pursuit of Somerset. He appealed over the king's head to the people in 1452, portrayed the victims of his ambush at the first battle of St Albans in 1455 as the aggressors and guilty parties, and continued to demand a thoroughgoing resumption of royal grants even after this had been fulfilled. York's exculpation for his Dartford uprising in 1452 and for the first battle of St Albans were duly confirmed by favourable parliaments and registered on the parliament roll;[25] the parliament of 1459 that condemned him was dubbed the 'Parliament of Devils' and annulled. Earlier that year, when the king offered the duke an olive branch – the chance to escape the certain defeat with which he was faced – York insisted on the dismissal of the government that had been the objective he would have forced on the king had he actually won. His son, Edward, therefore, found himself the designated leader of protagonists of the Hundred Years War, among them the handful of surviving veterans, and of root-and-branch reform of the government. Neither was an easy challenge to fulfil, nor was either in fact fulfilled.

Yorkist propaganda was highly successful and has been transmitted down to us as the truth in almost all the chronicles of the 1450s. Those who opposed York – Edmund Beaufort, Duke of Somerset, Humphrey Stafford, Duke of Buckingham, and Queen Margaret of Anjou – supposedly opposed reform and did not receive sympathetic treatment. Yet York's reforming stance, the thinly veiled threats of punishment that he made against any councillors who were not in his parlance 'true', his failure to keep the peace or to honour his repeated oaths not to resort to force, his insurrections and his ruthless elimination of those who stood in his way made possible very different interpretations. He was unwilling to obey the king's commands or accept the judgements of his peers. When he was protector, he was far from disinterested and impartial in his exercise of authority. He did not acknowledge the problems of government in the crises of the 1450s and indeed made ruling more difficult and more hazardous. Henry VI's councillors feared for their lives. Some certainly wanted the duke out of the picture much earlier than he was. The patience and mercy of Henry VI was repeatedly flouted. Finally, in 1459, a statute of attainder spelt out the duke's repeated offences and pardons, and revealed him as utterly incorrigible. But the Lancastrians failed to promulgate their version as widely or convincingly as York's own propaganda. Next year, moreover, victorious again, the Yorkists had the acts of the parliament of 1459 revoked and their own account of events henceforth prevailed.

Perhaps York had long thought himself to be the rightful king of England. Whilst he cannot have been unaware of his descent via the

Mortimers from a royal line senior to that of the ruling house of
Lancaster, he kept quiet about it and repudiated those who raised it,
even perhaps at his instigation. It was the coat of arms and livery of
York that he wore – until 1460. Only then, following the defeat of
Henry VI at Northampton, the capture of the government and the
elimination of his noble rivals for the third time, did York don the
murrey and blue livery and the coat of arms of Clarence and lay
claim to the throne for himself. The pedigree that he presented to
the Lords, which demonstrated his seniority to Henry VI, could not
be denied, declared the Lords, who nevertheless refused to unseat
their king. Henry VI was to reign for life and after him York, who
was to rule nevertheless in the meantime. So stated the Accord that
was agreed amongst the Yorkists and registered (but never confirmed) by parliament.[26] When it was rejected by the Lancastrians,
York was slain and Henry VI was removed like mere baggage from
Yorkist into Lancastrian hands. The fiction was promulgated that
by his recapture Henry had broken the Accord and that Edward IV,
as heir of York, was now rightly king. This was how it was to
restore peace that York proceeded to Wakefield: a perverse interpretation of peace which presumed that his opponents should
abandon their principles and surrender unconditionally. God, it was
later claimed, had dismissed King Henry as his representative on
earth and had set up King Edward in his place.[27] However popular
he was, 'Edward was made king by a faction' on 4 March 1461, as
Jack Lander observed.[28] Edward quickly changed the fiction into
reality.

The Yorkist myth

To Yorkist eyes, 1461 marked the beginning of a new era. The
parliament roll of the first Yorkist parliament duly confirmed this
tendentious Yorkist view of events. Lancastrian rule had been both
illegitimate and bad. Henry VI and his family, the slayers at
Wakefield of York himself – now regarded as the rightful king – and
the Lancastrian leaders at Towton were attainted as traitors.
Moreover the history of the preceding sixty years was rewritten, so
that those domestic rebels who had risen against the Lancastrians
were rehabilitated and their forfeitures annulled. Top of the list was
York's father (and Edward's grandfather), Richard Earl of

Cambridge and the other Southampton plotters executed in 1415. Also included were the four Ricardian earls who had perished in 1400: Warwick the Kingmaker, heir to three of them, was the principal beneficiary.[29] Archbishop Scrope, the martyred rebel of 1405 popularly venerated in York Minster as St Richard, was officially rehabilitated. Most of the not very impressive chronicles of the 1450s, notably Davies' *English Chronicle*, subscribed to this version of events. So, too, did the authors of *Warkworth's Chronicle* and the historical digest included in *John Vale's Book*, both of which some time after 1471 (and hence after the disasters and disappointments of Edward IV's first reign) subscribed to the legend that Duke Humphrey had been murdered and still attributed the sequence of foreign and domestic disasters to Henry VI's 'insatiable covetous persons and diabolic councillors'.[30]

Inevitably Edward's accession was presented as divinely providential. Not only had God bestowed his verdict in battle, but he was seen to have done so. The three suns that appeared on the morning of Mortimer's Cross, the astronomical phenomenon called a parhelion, were unequivocally a mark of divine favour reminiscent of the Trinity. They were mentioned in chronicles; they were actually depicted in one historical roll as three suns shining through three crowns; and they were exploited by Yorkist genealogists and alchemists. No wonder Edward took as one of his badges the sun in splendour, the sun with rays or sunburst. Since Edward's title was hereditary, it was best presented via the pedigrees that were such potent symbols of an aristocratic age. Not only was he descended from Edward III, but via Gladys Ddu from the Welsh princes. Edward's accession fulfilled Merlin's prophecy of the defeat of the usurping Saxons. Edward was equated with Taurus, the British king foretold by John of Bridlington. He was the true stock of Brutus. Even before his coronation the expensive and elaborate pedigree rolls produced commercially were amended to locate the new king and his line centre stage, to incorporate his Welsh ancestry and to display his various emblems – suns, roses, falcon and the red dragon of Wales – and cognomens like Brutus and Sol. By commencing with God and Adam, the so-called Philadelphia Roll demonstrates Edward's accession as God's will. Two early Welsh calendars placed England and indeed Britain in the context of prophecies about the fate of Britain that Edward fulfilled. Edward was the first true

Pedigree 3: The royal family of Edward IV

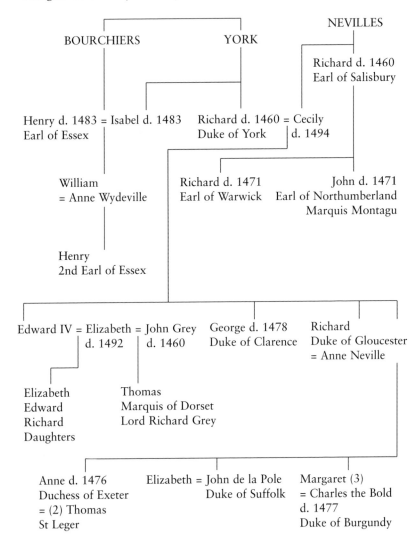

British king from Cadwallader. He was predestined to redeem the corruption of Britain and to restore the mythical golden age out of confusion and civil war, and also Britain's ancient hegemony. He was the liberator of Troy against the foreign intruders of Queen Margaret.

Edward was well suited to such propagandist portrayal, not just by descent but as a person. He was a most prepossessing youth – immensely tall, exceptionally handsome by the standards of the day, valiant and militarily successful, a good public speaker, charming and – as Hughes has rightly emphasized – genuinely charismatic. He was everything that a king was expected to be. Comparisons with Hector and Achilles and King David came naturally. It was not unrealistic to hope for the statesmanship of Julius Caesar and the Emperor Augustus. His accession was optimistically likened to the new flowers of the spring.[31] He offered a fresh start. Whether or not Edward believed all this or was impelled by a sense of destiny and mission, as Hughes has inferred,[32] he and/or his advisers certainly saw propaganda value in such material and made the most of it. Temperamentally Edward was attracted to the revival of Arthurianism at his court and the cult of St George at the Garter chapel at Windsor that he was to refound.

However, Edward was not to add much lustre to his escutcheon. Neither in the 1460s nor the 1470s was he able to vanquish the French, which both he and his subjects valued most highly, nor to conquer even a fragment of France. Edward's Picquigny campaign ended tamely in a bloodless retreat. Several victories against domestic enemies, in 1470 at Losecote Field and in 1471 at Barnet, Tewkesbury and London, were written up properly in two official chronicles, the *Chronicle of the Lincolnshire Rebellion* and the *Arrival of Edward IV* (a French version of the latter was distributed abroad) and in verse. The aged Sir John Fortescue, chancellor-in-exile to the Lancastrians and their principal propagandist, was induced to refute those works in which he had promoted their title. Parliament exulted in the recapture of Berwick.[33] Landmarks in royal history – coronations, baptisms, peerage creations, tournaments, funerals and marriages – were celebrated with great splendour and written up by heralds, whose narratives (judging from surviving copies of copies) achieved significant circulations. High on the list in 1476 was the reinterment of Richard Duke of

York and his second son, Edmund, in the Yorkist mausoleum at Fotheringhay in fulfilment of his wishes and dynastic tradition. For himself, his offspring and such committed adherents as Lord Hastings, the king embarked self-consciously instead on a new royal mausoleum at Windsor as the spiritual focus of the new Yorkist royal dynasty.

Edward's son, Edward V, was heir to the Yorkist myth, which Richard III sought to adapt by reverting to his father, York, discrediting the rights of Edward IV and his offspring, and by posing himself as the champion of reform set to remedy the misgovernment of Edward IV's evil councillors. Richard's version (*Titulus Regius*) was confirmed and enrolled by parliament. Elizabeth of York, queen to his conqueror, and their Tudor descendants were heirs to the Yorkists and hence their myths, but these were superseded by the Tudor myth and forgotten. Yorkist propaganda even before Henry VI's demise had depicted the usurpation of King Henry IV as a sin – for which the perpetrator suffered horrible physical afflictions[34] – and which was expiated by the punishment of his grandson Henry VI and great-grandson. Edward IV here acted as God's instrument. *The Illustrated Life of Edward IV* shows in 1461 that the wheel of Fortune had ceased to turn because Reason decisively stuck his rod in its spoke.[35] Evidently, however, Reason had not. This Yorkist interpretation was rendered obsolete by the disasters that befell the House of York – clearly they could not be God's end purpose. No historian after 1485 could possibly subscribe to that notion and none indeed did promote it. Long forgotten, it has required exceptional efforts from modern historians – Glanmor Williams, Alison Allan and Jonathan Hughes – to reveal the Yorkist myth as it once was.

3

Alternative images of Edward IV

Which contemporaries wrote

Who King Edward IV was and what King Edward IV became were determined, at least in part, by the pre-existing histories of his families, their traditions and myths, which the king exploited, imitated, enhanced and subconsciously or self-consciously reshaped, often with the assistance of astrologers, heralds, historians, poets, servants and well-wishers, whether in his pay, aspiring to be so or merely committed to what they perceived to be his cause. How Edward IV was spun is a subject that merits and has recently received its own historian;[1] how universally his message was transmitted and how effectively it was imparted is certainly a phenomenon deserving of proper study elsewhere. Somewhere in between the recording and the spinning, however, history has become the story of how past futures were shaped rather than a register of what Edward IV actually did, the events and processes of his reign, and what they meant to his own contemporaries and immediate successors. It is to this record and its meaning that this chapter now turns.

The histories of Edward IV that survive from his own day are frankly inadequate for most historical purposes. There also survives in the Public Record Office (now the National Archives) a mass of records of what his government did and how it did it: too much, by far, for any individual to peruse or assimilate. Not much of it reveals why Edward acted as he did or how successful his actions were. Great and perhaps undue attention has to be paid to occasional letters of random relevance written by native correspondents, to the diplomatic machinations of Warwick and Louis XI in the 1460s, and to the relaying of news and rumour by Italian ambassadors abroad to their employers. How very different Yorkist history would appear had there survived more than odd fragments of the state papers that once existed and which from the 1530s almost remove the medievalists' obligation to trawl the most humdrum administrative records and extract every last fact from the most paltry contemporary narratives. For historians of Edward IV, like all their medieval predecessors, what chronicles there are enjoy an exaggerated respect, even though those of the Yorkist age are admitted to be far inferior to those of Thomas Walsingham, Henry Knighton, Adam of Usk, Jean Creton and their anonymous counterparts of less than a century earlier.

Our contemporary narratives fall into five principal categories.

First come the contemporary chronicles. The best of these carry the names of William Gregory, John Warkworth, William Worcester, John Stone and Robert Fabian, yet they consist of little more than a few dozen pages of annals – selections of facts – that were loosely assembled according to the chronicler's prejudices.[2] Who the chronicler was, and hence how well informed he was and how trustworthy a source, is seldom known. Gregory did not live to finish his chronicle and the *Great Chronicle of London* cannot be wholly the work of Fabian. Neither Warkworth nor Worcester need have contributed much to the chronicles that currently bear their names.[3] Less valuable yet (as their modern names so often indicate) are the the anonymous *First Crowland Continuation*, the *Tewkesbury Abbey Chronicles*, the *Brief Latin Chronicles* and the *Short English Chronicles*, amongst others.[4] Relatively numerous in the 1450s, several chronicles expire with *John Benet's Chronicle* and Davies' *English Chronicle* at the start of Edward IV's reign and all the others before his second reign bar *Warkworth's Chronicle*, which terminates in 1473.[5] The two principal exceptions are the London chronicles, which survive in myriad inter-related short annals,[6] and the *Second Anonymous Crowland Continuation* (henceforth Crowland),[7] which is discussed at greater length below.

Second come the official accounts of events penned by civil servants, heralds and poets. Chronologically and thematically highly focused, sometimes surviving in several versions and in multiple copies, these are the fullest and most circumstantial narratives of particular events that we possess, if also the most obviously biased. They were written for short-term effect, composed deliberately to secure that result and can seldom be checked against alternative sources of equal quality. They include the *Chronicle of the Rebellion in Lincolnshire* (1470); *The Arrival of Edward IV* (1471), probably by Nicholas Harpsfield;[8] celebratory verses; descriptions of the coronation of Queen Elizabeth Wydeville (1465); the tournament of Lord Scales against the Bastard of Burgundy (1467); the marriages of Princess Margaret (1468) and Prince Richard (1478); the visit of Lord Gruthuyse (1472); the reinterment of the king's father, Richard Duke of York (1476); the king's own funeral (1483); knightings and baptisms; the king's epitaphs (1483);[9] and royal proclamations and preambles to acts of parliament. Thanks to the work of Drs Anne Sutton and Livia Visser-Fuchs, these are rightly much better known than they used to be, but they nevertheless amount to disappointingly little.

Third, hostile manifestos, dating from 1469–70 and 1483, justified new regimes by denigrating the failings of Edward IV.[10] Since ulterior motives take primacy in what are essentially propaganda pieces, these need the most careful handling. If Warwick's manifestos struck home at least sometimes, Richard III's *Titulus Regius* was almost without foundation.

Fourth, Edward IV and his reign appear briefly and uncritically as scene-setting for what followed in the histories of Dominic Mancini (1483), Polydore Vergil and Thomas More (c.1516).[11]

Fifth are the continental chronicles, mainly from France and Burgundy, such as those of Basin, Commynes, De Roye and Waurin, but also including, for instance, narratives from Danzig and Spain.[12] Only Waurin showed a sustained interest in English affairs, up to 1471, but Commynes, as we shall see, has exercised a far greater influence.

Most of these sources took Edward's side – the official narratives necessarily so – but surprisingly many were produced by enemies or critics. Albeit individually and collectively somewhat sparse, the data provided by these sources when combined have enabled historians to construct satisfactory accounts of the principal events of Edward IV's reign. There are regrettably many events that either we cannot retrieve or that we know almost nothing about, such as the factional infighting at court in Edward's last years. Understanding and interpreting what was happening has become ever more difficult. Often more than one interpretation is compatible with a given sequence of events. We need to recall that Edward IV was the victor in two phases of the Wars of the Roses. Civil wars were the gravest type of political disagreement, when compromise and negotiation gave way to force and all parties hazarded their lives. Attitudes remained polarized long after the events. A succession of views can be identified – the products both of the twists and turns of Yorkist politics and the changing identity, affiliations and objectives of our writers.

What contemporaries wrote

The last years of the Lancastrian dynasty are presented to us primarily through hostile eyes. York won the propaganda war after 1450. It was also the Yorkists who survived his victory and who wished to record it for posterity.

And not only the Yorkists. The First Crowland Continuator, relieved to have escaped from Queen Margaret's northerners, saw Edward – 'now in the flower of his age' – as God's instrument against their wickednesses. 'In these days, however, the kingdom enjoyed peace, and all the people returned thanks to Almighty God for the triumph granted by heaven over their enemies'. The new king repaid many of his obligations at once. He curried favour through his promotion of peers, knights and gentlemen 'as they had deserved', his ratification and enlargement of franchises and charters 'to have the more goodwill and love of the land'.[13] His regime promoted its achievements at key moments, often coinciding with sessions of the great council or parliament, such as the king's marriage, the churching of his queen, the defeat of the northern Lancastrians and the capture of King Henry, and publicly commended and promoted those responsible. Heraldic tracts preserve the official view of such events as the queen's coronation, the tournament of her brother against the Bastard of Burgundy and the wedding of Princess Margaret.

Much indeed was expected of the new dynasty, but any benefits were slow in coming. Every year, it seemed, there were Lancastrian rebellions to be crushed and conspiracies to be foiled. *Warkworth's Chronicle* records general disenchantment and hostility. 'The people grudged sore' about taxes. It was not Henry VI himself that people had wished to remove in 1461, it recalled, but his evil councillors.

Nevertheless, when King Edward IV reigned, the people looked after all the foresaid prosperities and peace, but it came not, but ever one battle after another, and much trouble and great loss of goods among the common people [including taxes] . . . And yet at every battle [they had] to come far out of their countries &c at their own cost; and these and such other brought England right low. And men said that King Edward had great blame for hurting of trade, for in his days they [English merchandise] neither in other lands nor within England were taken in such reputation & credence as they were before &c.

Warkworth was writing in retrospect rather than at the time of the events through which he had lived, but 'the great hurt and grudge of all this land' and 'the great grudge and impoverishing of them, which caused all the people of this land to grudge' arising from government actions also feature in Robin of Redesdale's manifesto of 1469. Although biased and tendentious, this needed to focus on real grievances to be effective. Significantly, it also complains of taxation and the recoinage and indeed much else, which it blames on the new king's evil councillors; so does the *First Crowland Continuation* of 1470. Moreover the manifesto stresses Edward's failure to live up to his 'golden speech' of the 1467 parliament 'to live of his own except in great and urgent causes'. Hence Edward found himself deserted late in 1470, when Henry VI was swept back to his throne by popular enthusiasm: 'all his good lovers were full glad', reports *Warkworth's Chronicle*, 'and the most part of the people'.[14]

The reports in *Warkworth's Chronicle* of Edward's counter-measures are not uncritical, whether overtly as with the de Veres, 'wherof the most people were sorry', or by implication. Sir Thomas Cook in 1468 was acquitted, yet fined. 'And men said that the Lord Stafford of Southwick was cause of Henry Courtenay's death, for he would be Earl of Devonshire, and so the king made him afterwards'. The chronicler disapproved of the 'disordinate death' introduced by Lord Constable Tiptoft, who added to already horrible rites of execution the impaling that he had supposedly imported from Padua. Moreover the king's marriage angered Warwick:

then was he greatly displeased with the king, and after that rose great dissension every year after more and more between the king and him for that and other &c … And yet they were accorded divers times, but they never loved together after &c.[15]

Almost certainly Warwick was behind Redesdale's 1469 manifesto, in which all the evils of Edward's first reign – including a breakdown of order, maintenance and the pillaging of the royal demesne – were blamed on the Wydevilles and Herberts, a new set of evil councillors, who feathered their own nests at royal and public expense, and who again estranged their king from the great lords of his blood.

Warkworth's Chronicle traces the rift back to the king's ill-considered marriage.[16] So indeed did most other historians writing then or soon after: the _First Crowland Continuation_, Waurin, Mancini, _Hearne's Fragment_, Vergil and More.[17] We know that Edward's unexpected marriage was a shock and controversial at the time. Initially opposed, according to a Venetian ambassador, Mancini, and More, it had to be accepted as inescapable, but it was questioned again in 1483 and perhaps also in 1469.[18] 'This the nobility and chief men of the kingdom took amiss,' reports the _First Crowland Continuation_. Henceforward the king favoured, pro-moted and endowed the queen's kin and 'banished from his presence his own brethren, and his kinsmen sprung from the royal blood, together with the Earl of Warwick, and the other nobles of realm who had always proved faithful to him'.[19] Pseudo-Worcester also records how objectionable to Warwick were some of the marriages that Edward arranged for his new in-laws.[20] Alone in denying this political impact to Edward's marriage was Crowland, who attributed the quarrel with Warwick to divisions over foreign policy,[21] in which, however, the queen's family's preference for Burgundy may have been decisive. There were indeed irreconcilable differences on foreign affairs, Warwick favouring the French and Edward Burgundy, which continued even after the conclusion of the Burgundian marriage alliance in 1468. Edward proved unable to attack France as intended and for which parliamentary taxation had been solicited. Such issues divided the Yorkist establishment and alienated from Edward a significant number of those who had made him king, to the point of repeated rebellions and even deposition.

Redesdale's rebellion was followed by the abortive reconciliation in 1469 and further conflicts the next year. _The Chronicle of the_

Rebellion in Lincolnshire is an official narrative of Edward's suppression of the uprising and hence favourable to him. Commencing from the presumption that it was a 'subtle and false conspiracy ... unnaturally and unkindly' fomented by Warwick and Clarence, to whom the king had shown only 'mercy and pity', it records the events in copious detail from the royal perspective. It does not explore the causes, except by implication, the objectives of the rebels or consider what justification, if any, they had. Never able to forecast what was to ensue, Edward was initially misled by treacherous deceit, and is revealed both as credulous and unduly trusting. However, he acted with decision, summarily executing Lord Welles, attacking the Lincolnshiremen at Empingham (Losecote Field) and relentlessly pursuing Warwick and Clarence into exile. The chronicler credited Edward's 'most noble and righteous courage' and attributed his victory to 'the help of almighty God', the king himself 'giving laud and praising almighty God' that evening at Stamford. The ringleaders once executed, for Edward's justice was rigorous, he used 'plenteously his mercy in saving of the lives of his poor and wretched commons'. He even allowed Warwick's retainers to renew their allegiance, always on his terms, not theirs. Even the duke and earl were offered opportunities to submit, although the king stood upon his dignity and refused to compromise his sovereignty by negotiation or guaranteeing them any specific terms. They wanted more. Though understandable, their refusal placed them even more irremediably in the wrong.[22]

There is no such narrative of the bloodless triumph of the Lancastrians later in 1470 or indeed, from their perspective, of the 1471 campaign, for which we are indebted principally to other official Yorkist narratives, the French 'Short Arrival' and the *Arrival* itself, and to Crowland, which took the same line. The *Arrival* commences thus:

> Hereafter followeth the manner how the most noble and right victorious prince Edward, by the grace of God, King of England and of France, and Lord of Ireland, in the year of grace 1471, in the month of March, departed out of Zeeland, took the sea, arrived in England, and, by his force and valour, reduced anew and reconquered the said realm, upon and against the Earl of Warwick, his traitor

and rebel, calling himself Lieutenant of England, by
pretended authority of the usurper Henry [VI] and his
accomplices.

Again, a detailed, circumstantial, and largely eyewitness account,
the *Arrival* explains Edward's decisions and actions. Full weight is
given to the difficulties – overcoming which, of course, contributed
to Edward's 'wisdom and policy' – and to 'his full noble and
knightly courage' that won him two battles and the most complete
of victories. Whilst prepared to temporize, as when claiming dis-
honestly only to be seeking the Duchy of York and when negotiating, from choice Edward preferred bold aggression, taunting
Warwick with challenges at Coventry, engaging him with a smaller
force at Barnet and Queen Margaret at Tewkesbury. Despite poor
visibility at Barnet, unfavourable terrain and tired troops, 'he
committed his cause and his quarrel to Almighty God, advanced
banners, did blow up trumpets, and set upon them'. However
much he wished to avoid the shedding of Christian blood, Edward
believed fervently in his cause, 'for to suppress the falsehood of all
them that so falsely and treacherously conspired against him', was
prepared to relinquish no iota of his honour and sovereignty, and
sincerely believed in God's favour – as evidenced, for instance, by a
miracle at Daventry. He prayed for aid before and gave thanks after
each battle. It was God who caused Warwick's cannons to over-
shoot. 'Blessed be God! – he won the field there'. 'And the victory
is given to him by God', concludes the *Arrival*, 'by the mediation of
the most blessed virgin and mother, our lady saint Mary the
glorious martyr St George, and all the saints of heaven, maintaining his quarrel to be true and righteous'.[23] The *Arrival*'s verdict is
also the message of the celebratory verses, which admit nevertheless, in further testimony of divine favour, that his victory was
against the odds. *Warkworth's Chronicle*, furthermore, asserts that
Londoners were generally sympathetic to the Bastard of
Fauconberg and that Oxford's forays from St Michael's Mount in
1473 were locally popular. Only miscalculations prevented
Edward's defeat.[24]

Nevertheless, stated Mancini, 'Edward's power in the kingdom
was reaffirmed'.[25] Unsullied by hindsight, the *Arrival* looked forward optimistically to the speedy pacification of the realm:

That peace and tranquillity shall grow and multiply in
the same, from day to day, to the honour and loving of
Almighty God, the increase of his [Edward's] singular
and famous renown, and to the great joy and consolation
of his friends, allies, and well-willers, and to all his
people, and to the great confusion of all his enemies and
evil willers.[26]

Again, heraldic treatises mark the visit of Lord Gruthuyse (1472),
the reinterment of the king's father and the marriage of his younger
son, but the nearest we have to a narrative, official or otherwise, is
Crowland. Though Lancastrianism was dead and though Edward's
crown was not to be challenged again, there were plenty of internal
divisions. That parliament confirmed the king's partition of the
Warwick inheritance did not make it right and its silent acquies-
cence in his destruction of his brother, Clarence, secured credence
for the charge and support for his action in none of the surviving
chronicles.[27] The years 1471–5, however, were dominated by
Edward's project to renew the Hundred Years War, invade and
conquer France. Much pressure was necessary to secure backing
from parliament for the war and the requisite finance. His precipitate peacemaking was controversial both in France, among the
invading army and council, and at home, where the king felt obliged
both to cow opponents by a judicial progress and to relinquish an
instalment of taxation that he feared would excite dissent.[28]

Edward's last years were dominated by foreign relations. The
Scottish campaigns of 1480–3 receive attention, although English
successes – the brief occupation of Edinburgh and the recovery of
Berwick, so highly praised by the 1483 parliament – look somewhat
different in the absence of opposition arising from domestic complications that are reported in Scottish sources. No English chronicler,
however, gives much weight to what, after the death of Charles the
Bold at Nancy in 1477, their continental counterparts recognized as
the key issue: Louis XI's war of conquest against Mary of Burgundy.
Albeit briefly interested in English candidates for her hand, no
English chronicler appreciated how Edward's neutrality had
alienated a political ally and left him friendless once the treaty of
Arras (1482) removed any need for Louis to pander to him or to
honour the betrothal of his son to Elizabeth of York. Edward

blamed the collapse of his foreign policy on Louis's deceit. Even as his Scottish entanglement dragged on expensively, Edward used his last months to persuade parliament of the need for revenge against the French, albeit when opportunity permitted. Crowland blamed the perfidious French and Scots for his problem.[29] Foreigners, in contrast, considered Edward to blame for his diplomatic predicament. He had allowed his modest pension (or tribute) from France to emasculate his foreign policy. Hence, observes Mancini, he had forfeited the allegiance of his 'ancient friends', the Flemings, and 'began to be regarded with scorn by the French'. Commynes and other continental commentators were just as critical.[30]

Contemporary assessments

Edward was a tall man and, to fifteenth-century tastes, extremely handsome. None of Edward's contemporaries disagree with More's description: 'he was a goodly personage, and very princely to behold, of visage lovely, of body mighty, strongly and clean made'. All agree also on the corpulence of his last years, the product of self-indulgence, which did not make him unattractive. Edward was lustful, drunk and so gluttonous that, Mancini reported, he even resorted to emetics. He looked every inch a king. Cheerful and affable, accessible and responsive to petitioners of every rank, if not to complaints against himself, he could remember the names and circumstances of all those he encountered. Courteous and merry, he made a point of entertaining (and hence flattering) the politically influential mayors and aldermen of London in his last years. Yet he could also 'assume an angry countenance, ... appear very terrible to beholders', and (according to Crowland) confronted his greatest noblemen with their faults even to their faces.[31]

Edward's death in 1483 not only ended his life and reign, but also, in retrospect, marked an era of relative tranquillity that his brother Richard III brusquely terminated. We have four strictly contemporary assessments in his surviving epitaphs, in prose or verse; all presumably date from around his death and funeral and none even hints at the upheavals that ensue. There follow, in approximate date order, those of Mancini (1483), Crowland (1486) and the two Henricians, More and Vergil, all four of whom were hostile to King Richard and hence contrasted him unfavourably with his elder brother. Mancini and Crowland, who lived during Edward's last years, remembered the international tensions and continuing popular dissent that never reached fruition and of which More and Vergil were ignorant. Edward's subjects respected him. Whether 'the substance of the people … heartily beloved him' is doubtful, since even More records the unpopularity of his taxes.[32] Even the *Lament of the Soul of Edward IV* concludes that he caused 'some men to pleasure and some men to no liking'.

Nobody doubted King Edward's tactical nous, his military prowess, or the 'great courage and hardiness' that his foes feared to confront. He had conquered (and reconquered) England, made Scotland yield and captured Berwick. He was the very model of a warrior king. 'Of heart courageous,' reports More, he was 'in war, sharp and fierce, in the field, bold and hardy'.

> In every field [he was] full ready for our right;
> It was no need to pray him for to fight;
> Ready he was, that was here yesterday.

According to his epitaph, Edward was the

> most dred prince that was under the sun,
> Through all this world renowned was his name;
> The doughtiest, the worthiest, without comparison.
> There was none such, but you reckon the same,
> Compassed the world, so spread his name [renown],
> And as in battle, the freshest I shall say.

More than that:

> In gestes [deeds], in romances, in chronicles nigh & far,
> Well known it is, as no men can deny,
> Peerless he was, and [he] was here yesterday.

Here, in their enthusiasm, his obituarists exaggerated somewhat. The case for Edward as a chivalric hero is harder to substantiate and his prowess was acknowledged principally in England. Where was the evidence that 'no earthly prince dared to make with him debate'? Even admitting that he had 'ruled England with great renown', as Mancini says, and was as glorious and illustrious as Crowland supposed, this was solely in an English context.[33]

Edward maintained an appropriately princely state. 'In his

household he kept the royal rout'. 'In these days', wrote Crowland, 'you might have seen a royal Court such as befitted a mighty kingdom, filled with riches and men of every nation'. Eulogists referred to his building at the Tower, Dover, London, Westminster and Eton; Nottingham which 'I made ... a palace royal'; and 'the new collegiate chapel of Windsor, which he had himself, in solemn style, raised from the foundations'. He was 'a very wealthy prince', concluded Crowland. That, of course, was what Edward wanted observers to believe. If court ceremonies were designed 'to mitigate or disguise this sorrow' at the collapse of his foreign policy, Mancini saw through the pretence and thought that 'he was never able altogether to hide it'.[34]

At home, however, the political advantages of such display were overlooked and the king's expenditure was criticized as extravagant and even pointless.

> And not being aware who should it occupy,
> I made the Tower strong, I know not why.
> I know not to whom I purchased Tattershall ...[35]

Succeeding to Henry VI's debts and inadequate income, and constantly faced by expensive challenges, Edward was always seeking money, which his subjects were consistently reluctant to provide. *Warkworth's Chronicle* meticulously documents (and often deplores) the king's levies of revenue. Parliament voted him in 1463 'as much money as the 15th part of a man's goods and an half more, whereof the people grudged sore', and his recoinage of the follow-ing year, 'by which he had great getting', was also 'to the great harm of the common people'. Another fifteenth was due in 1469–70, 'which annoyed the people, for they had paid a little afore a great tax, the 15th part of every man's goods, &c'. It was that tax that breached the king's promise to parliament. He heavily fined the Kentishmen in 1471, guilty and innocent alike, and pillaged the wealth of Archbishop Neville. The chronicler merely itemizes the revenues raised for Edward's war against France.[36] Taxpayers, Crowland reports, were understandably dissatisfied when Edward made peace almost at once. The king dared not levy the last instal-ment due and resorted to other financial expedients. Avarice was still perceived as the defect of Edward's last years by Mancini, Crowland and an obituarist. 'I had enough [but] I held me not content, without remembering that I should die'. Not only could he not take it with him, but he was liable for the sin of avarice. 'And more to increase was my intent'.

> I stored my coffers and also my chests
> With taxes taken of the communalty.[37]

What is alluded to here, the levy of taxes for a supposed war, is mentioned also by More and was portrayed by Mancini as a deliberate artifice. It did not make Edward any more prompt in paying his bills 'than when he was poor' or indeed any more generous. Rarely munificent and then only in moderation, remarks Mancini, it was his meanness that disastrously prevented him from helping the Flemings.[38]

Edward left his kingdom in good array. All was quiet and prosperous, declares More. There were no external threats, no war actual or potential, and peace and order prevailed at home.[39] If somewhat optimistic – More overlooks the collapse of Edward's foreign policy, chronic hostilities with Scotland and vengeance sought against France – his judgement conforms with that of the obituarists, Mancini and Crowland. The 'dissension between his friends', Lord Hastings versus the Wydevilles, had not worried the king when fit, 'because he thought whatsoever business should fall between them, himself should always be able to rule both parties'. He recognized the dangers when faced with death and sought to reconcile the rivals, notoriously without success.[40] Of course, Mancini, Crowland and More wished to blame all that went wrong afterwards on the deplorable Richard III, not on Edward's unfortunate legacy. Richard himself, Lord Chancellor Russell and *Titulus Regius* dissented.

Evidently Edward IV was a king about whom contemporaries were not agreed. How then can historians five centuries later choose between such conflicting judgements? Hence the importance that medievalists have always ascribed to authoritative contemporary interpreters, normally the best chroniclers of the day, but not necessarily the witnesses that ideally would have been selected. For the Yorkist era, there are two such figures: Crowland – an English civil servant – and the Burgundian statesman, Philippe de Commynes. Although an outsider primarily interested in events abroad and always a minor contributor to our fund of facts,

Commynes's assessment of Edward IV, so Professor Lander argued long ago, was imported to England in the late seventeenth century and has dominated all subsequent accounts, until Lander himself took up his pen.[41] Consequently, Commynes features much less in Ross's standard life and in publications since. Crowland, in contrast, was an Englishman, whose work was not available to Hall, Holinshed and Shakespeare. It is only relatively recently that he has come to be recognized as *the* interpreter of Yorkist England – Ross's most valued contemporary guide – and has perhaps even come to be, *faute de mieux*, over-appreciated. It is to these two authoritative contemporary commentators that this chapter now turns.

Against: Commynes

More and better history was being written among England's continental neighbours, where several significant chroniclers and many minor annalists were at work. They touched (or even dwelt) on English events whenever they interacted with the affairs of France, again the greatest European power, and the Duchy of Burgundy, which included in the modern Benelux countries the most urbanized and industrialized area of northern Europe. Scotland was a fourth participant in the north-west European diplomatic subsystem. If Edward IV did not abandon traditional English ambitions in France, it was more frequently the French and Burgundians who intervened in England, participating in every raid and invasion of the Wars of the Roses, and in particular in the four overthrows of reigning monarchs and dynasties between 1460 and 1485. Such issues were the preoccupation of Commynes, who composed his *Mémoires* about 1498.

Philippe de Commynes (1447–1506) belonged to a family of minor Flemish aristocrats with a long tradition of serving the rulers of Flanders. Having entered the service of Charles the Bold before his succession as Duke of Burgundy in 1467, he rose high in his intimate service, becoming both councillor and chamberlain, before in 1472 transferring – really, deserting – to the duke's rival King Louis XI, to whom he was an equally intimate and trusted servant. This may have been only briefly, however, since he seems to have faltered in Louis's esteem and never really recovered his former standing under Louis's son Charles VIII (1483–98), commencing his

Mémoires of 1496–8 whilst imprisoned. He posed as a wise elder statesman, who had experienced everything from within and from both sides, who understood both the intricacies and the general principles of international power politics and who explained events (and deduced lessons) in a proto-Machiavellian manner in terms of human actions and very human amoral motivation. His *Mémoires* have always been much appreciated for their wise insight into contemporary realpolitik and as a thoroughly modern work of secular history that anticipates Renaissance and later histories. Commynes knew Louis XI and Charles the Bold well. Louis was the model proto-Machiavellian – the spider at the centre of every machination – whom Commynes idolized to the point where all other princes suffered by comparison. But Commynes was not immune to – and indeed reproduced – the self-image and propaganda of a king who, as revealed by contemporary Italian diplomats, was a compulsive manipulator and meddler, confided completely in nobody and skilfully disseminated disinformation masquerading as sound intelligence. Commynes came to dislike, hate and despise Charles (as he thought Louis did) and disparaged him historically – somewhat unjustly, as modern research has shown. Commynes was writing, do not forget, as a disappointed man, whose treachery had not borne the fruits in rank, power or length of service that had been hoped. His overriding theme as a Fleming, the power struggle of France and Burgundy that was epitomized by his two masters, may not have so preoccupied them: certainly Charles was much concerned with his neighbours to the east and south, the Empire and the Swiss, who ultimately destroyed him; so too, perhaps, was Louis. Their domestic concerns, the bread-and-butter of everyday rule, interested Commynes not at all. Brilliant though his *Mémoires* are, they are partial in two senses – incomplete and biased – and they are not, on close inspection, as factually reliable as used to be supposed.[42] Nor indeed is his commentary as profound.[43]

Commynes did not visit England. There is much he cannot have known. Calais he did visit, frequently. He observed at close hand (or even participated in) relations with England from 1465 onwards. He is a valuable eyewitness to the Lancastrian readeption (1470) from Calais and the negotiation and conclusion of the Treaty of Picquigny. Commynes knew the Lancastrian refugees to Burgundy, Warwick, Wenlock and Warwick's other agents, Hastings and

Rivers, and had at least met Clarence, Gloucester, Howard and indeed the king himself. How sound a basis did such encounters provide for his psychological assessments? Commynes had much the same access (but perhaps more privileged access) as contemporary Italian ambassadors and continental chroniclers to the hard fact, rumour and error that flowed constantly across the Channel. Which category applies to information unique to himself? If hindsight winnowed out error, memory also erased and rationalized events and perhaps caused him to assume that results were always intended. He imparted to his readers the broad sweep of the Wars of the Roses rather than the details, showed little grasp of British geography and was quite uninterested in the domestic affairs that necessarily absorbed the king of England. It is his insights to personalities and his explanations that have most influenced later historians. Perhaps, however, it should be his broad overview and sense of proportion that English historians should value most, as he locates Edward's activities within a context wider than any English writer could do. Just as he was ignorant of and ignored Charles the Bold's activities to the east, always supposing (as a francophone and francophile) that Burgundy's relations with Louis XI took priority, so too he presumed that Anglo-French matters counted more than England's relations with Scotland (of which he knew little) to Edward himself, which may be incorrect. Almost all subsequent historians have followed his lead.

Amoral Commynes may have been, but he was always a Christian, who assigned roles in politics both to God and to Christian morality. He recounts the misfortunes of the Lancastrian dukes, exiled and reduced to begging in Burgundy, all of whom were afterwards slain in battle.

> Their fathers and their men had pillaged and destroyed
> the realm of France and possessed the most part for
> many years. All killed one-another. Those who survived
> in England and their children were fined, as you see. And
> yet people say [that] 'God does not punish any more as
> he was accustomed in the time of the children of Israel
> and tolerates bad princes and bad people'. I agree well
> that he does not speak any more to people as he used,
> because he has left enough examples in this world to be

believed, but you can see in reading these things, together with what you know of them besides, that none or few of these evil princes and others having authority in this world, who acted cruelly and tyrannically, escaped with impunity. However it was not always on the day nominated, nor at the hour which those who suffered desired.[44]

The cruel and wicked Richard III was a good instance! Note here also Commynes's belief that the Wars of the Roses were England's punishment for the Hundred Years War and his evident francophile approach to English affairs. It was God who caused Edward in 1470 to camp near the sea (at King's Lynn), so he could escape abroad.[45]

Edward was 'more handsome than any man who had lived in his time', Commynes twice declared. That was when Edward was young: 'for since he has become very fat'. Commynes had the greatest respect for the king's military prowess, again noting twice that 'he was a king very fortunate in his battles, for nine great battles at least were won'; moreover – even more impressive to Commynes! – 'all on foot'.[46] In other ways, however, he did not think him a man of high calibre:[47] a judgement substantiated by Edward's loss of his throne in 1470, which Commynes thought he should have avoided, and by the diplomatic rings run round him from 1475 on by Louis XI. Edward lived at his ease, 'thought only of women, too much for reason, and hunting and to indulge himself', which had serious political consequences on occasion – for example, his marriage and supposed pre-contract – and reduced in any case his concentration on and mastery of affairs. Louis, in contrast, was a professional. Commynes also thought that financial considerations, in particular Edward's French pension, were allowed to determine too much.

Commynes had been at Calais during the crucial summer months of 1470. He was critical both of Edward's defensive strategy and its implementation. The king certainly misread Wenlock's refusal to admit Warwick to Calais and was therefore wrong to appoint him captain. He also failed to take the threat of Warwick's invasion seriously enough: 'he had no fear, which to me seems a very great kind of folly, not to fear one's enemy is not to wish to understand anything'. Nor did Edward anticipate as he should the treason of

Warwick's brothers. In contrast, Charles the Bold was alarmed, bribed Wenlock to ensure his loyalty and forewarned Edward to which port Warwick was heading.[48] Commynes, of course, did not know what countermeasures Edward did have in train nor that the invasion was postponed; he was also unaware that the 1470 invasion was multi-pronged (and that Edward focused first on the first uprisings in the North and around London) and of the sheer difficulty of navigating through contrary winds to any particular English port.

Commynes took Edward's invasion of France very seriously and thought that it could have succeeded. 'Never before had any king of England crossed with such a powerful army at one time', he wrote twice,

> nor so disposed to fight. All the great lords of England
> were there without a single exception. There could have
> been 1500 men at arms, which was a great number for
> the English, all strongly equipped in everything and well
> accompanied, and 14,000 archers, carrying bows and
> arrows and all mounted, and enough others on foot
> servicing their host. And in all the army there was not
> one page. And, besides, the king of England was bound
> to despatch 3,000 men to Brittany to join the army of the
> duke.[49]

Had Edward arrived earlier in the campaigning season, delayed less and thus been less exposed and, above all, had Charles the Bold not lingered before Neuss, it could all have turned out very differently. 'But God, who always loves the kingdom, conducted these things as I will say afterwards'. Despite all their preparations, so 'marvellously miscontented' by Charles's tardiness were Edward and his lords that they were open to French overtures. They were understandably apprehensive for, wisely observed Commynes, 'it was not these English who had ruled in the time of his father and in the ancient wars in France, but these were all new and ignorant how things were in France'. The herald that Edward sent to defy Louis was suborned by the latter, who insinuated himself with the English chamberlain (Hastings) and steward (Stanley), and gladly accepted the terms needed to remove a dangerous threat and the English altogether from his realm – hence his refusal to accept vengeful

English offers of aid against Duke Charles. A delegation of English townsmen, who supposedly 'must have a battle whilst this side of sea', had to be persuaded of the risks and the desirability of peace. English pride was salved by mistitling the pension as tribute and Elizabeth as the dauphiness.[50]

Louis's concessions at Picquigny – reparations, an annual pension and the betrothal – mattered much more to Edward than to Louis, who cared little and was not to honour the engagement. Far from giving Edward the whip hand, Picquigny gave Louis leverage over Edward, who wanted to retain both pension – which he called tribute – and the marriage. Commynes, like Mancini and presumably their patron Archbishop Cato, perceived how such fragile advantages tied Edward's hands. They prevented him from supporting the proposal of his brother, Clarence, to marry Charles's daughter, Mary of Burgundy (who married Archduke Maximilian instead) or otherwise intervening on her side, which was what Louis most feared, until the French king had conquered the provinces that he wanted and had made peace at Arras (1482). Though Edward, in Commynes's view, 'was on top of his affairs and kingdom', possessed 50,000 ecus a year and was wallowing in wealth, yet

> suddenly he was dead and as though by melancholy, because of the marriage of our king, who reigns now [Charles VIII], to Madame Margaret, daughter of the duke of Austria [Maximilian]. And as soon as he had the news, he was taken ill. Thus he found himself deceived of the projected match of his daughter, that he caused to be called Madame the Dauphiness, and was broken the pension that he took of us, that he called tribute; but it was neither the one nor the other, as I have declared above.[51]

Edward ended without either alliance with a much weakened Burgundy or his pension and marriage alliance. Less politically adept than King Louis, he lacked the application to compete and squandered the opportunities he was offered. However formidable in battle, his pleasure-seeking amateurism detracted from his kingship.

For: Crowland

Crowland, in contrast, chose to write about English history between 1459 and 1485 – which he regarded as a distinct historical period, the Yorkist age – and to present its central figure, Edward IV, as an effective and successful ruler. Much ink has been spilt by the ablest twentieth-century late medievalists on who precisely he was, so far without success. Several clues to his identity written in the margins – that he was a doctor of canon law on a diplomatic mission to Burgundy in 1471, was called Richard or wrote the whole chronicle in the ten days up to 30 April 1486 – have not helped to date. Since the original chronicle in British Library Cotton MS Otho BXIII was largely destroyed in 1731 and is known principally through an extremely reliable 1684 edition,[52] we cannot tell today who wrote such comments, when or how authoritatively. The *Second Continuation* follows (and corrects) a *First Continuation* by the then prior of Crowland Abbey (Lincs.) to an earlier chronicle of the abbey's history since its legendary origins. Not by a monk, the *Second Continuation* is the political narrative of an outsider, who interpolated obituaries of three abbots written by Crowland monks and extended his own work beyond its original ending (before 9 November 1485) to some point in April 1486; a *Third Continuation* was added by another hand within a few weeks. Even without his name, 'from the internal evidence of the chronicle' we can be sure, as Ross said, 'that the author was a clerk, a royal servant with knowledge of chancery [and] a man of intelligence and high education who possessed a considerable inside knowledge of affairs'. He witnessed much that he recounted. 'Where his specific statements can be checked against other evidence', Ross continued, 'they are almost invariably correct. He must, therefore, be accepted as an authoritative witness in default of other evidence'.[53]

Ross was not alone in his praise, for twentieth-century historians have certainly not stinted on their appreciation of Crowland. His work has commonly been compared with that of Commynes, which was intended as high praise, first by Kingsford – for whom 'as a literary production it belongs to a new era' – and more recently by Hanham, Ross, Gransden, Pronay and Pollard. They have admired his long rational explanations of events.[54] 'Secular history', how Crowland describes his own history, has been taken up enthusiastically by modern historians, for whom secular equates with modern.

> The most astounding quality of this Canon lawyer [for Pronay] is that he has a more secular approach to politics than his lay compatriots who appear still-embued with the medieval Christian-ethical outlook ... He was 'a man of the world', a shrewd and secular-minded political observer, seeing the causes of events in the interplay of circumstances and personal qualities, in personal rivalries for power and influence inextricably intertwined with major policy disagreements, and not in any sense due to the hand of God moving in mysterious ways or to simple human pique or pride or ambition.

Crowland ridiculed those who saw God intervening in everyday events and applauds Edward's pragmatism in fighting on the holiest day of the Christian calendar.[55] His history has 'the unmistakable air of the new rationalism, secularism and amorality of the approach to politics of the later fifteenth century, which was as characteristic of Edward's England as Machiavelli's Italy'. He even favoured a new style of rule akin to that of Henry VII that was both calculating and suspicious of the people.[56] Such characteristics, Gransden considered, made Crowland into an open-minded chronicler of the reign of Edward IV.[57] Pollard was convinced, adding merely (but significantly) that 'from time to time he reveals a more traditional attitude', for example, in his opposition to taxation of the Church and his identification of Henry VII as the kingdom's saviour.[58] Actually traditional attitudes bulk much larger than this, as Crowland's assessment of Edward IV will show.

Crowland was certainly committed to the Yorkist dynasty: hence 'the characteristic "more in sorrow than in anger" tone of the Continuator, and his theme of the tragic waste of talent and resources as the characteristics of the age' that Pronay so perceptively identifies.[59] If Crowland wrote favourably of his master, he was not blind and his opinion 'is not that of a flatterer', thought Kingsford.[60] Edward's love of luxury and licentiousness did not pass uncriticized, but (in Crowland's view) it did not detract from his political effectiveness. Hence the appearance of a commanding monarch to which Pollard has most recently alluded.[61] What the

Continuator thought of his king during his second reign is revealed by his choice of adjectives: Edward was illustrious, 'foresighted' or 'prudent' (twice), spirited, bold and wealthy. It was the king himself who ran his own foreign policy, planned the invasion of France, arbitrated between his brothers, contracted the Treaty of Picquigny, reinterred his father and destroyed his brother, amassed treasure, defeated the Scots and captured Berwick.[62] Ever more secure on his throne, he passed it on to his son; what happened next was a fresh sequence of events.

If the *Second Continuation* is certainly not an official history of the House of York, as Williams suggested, it does indeed contain 'essentially the views of an old retainer or servant loyal to Edward IV himself and his children, described in intimate and loving detail during their last Christmas together in 1482'.[63] It apparently commenced with the rout of Ludford, as perceived from the losing side, accurately recorded the births and numbers of Edward's family, lamented the divisions of the royal brothers who would have been unbeatable if united and dwelt at length on King Edward's deathbed and his claims to salvation. Crowland identified himself with the king's faithful subjects and regarded the king's misfortunes as calamities.[64] Mortimer's Cross witnessed his 'famous victory ... over these same worthless enemies'. Fauconberg's men were also despised and Montagu was accused of fraud and treachery, but more of a semblance of even-handedness was generally preserved. We cannot tell in fact whether Crowland attributed the Wars of the Roses to a dynastic contest or to York's cause of reform, since he did not comment on the First Continuator's ill-informed and muddled explanation, but he certainly accepted the validity of both York's claim in 1460 and Edward's usurpation the following year. Edward was entitled Earl of March, not yet the future king. Edward IV's first decade was treated only in so far as the *First Continuation* required correction, so that far from emerging as prime mover, King Edward occurred only ten times before 1469, often laconically and *en passant*. Thereafter he came to the fore, as indeed he did in reality, at first in his titanic contest with Warwick and then free of such rivals. His glory, regrettably, was disturbed by his destruction of his brother Clarence, which Crowland thought both unjust and reprehensible, although he was comforted by his conviction that the king afterwards repented.

Crowland often leaves us in little doubt that he was an eyewitness. From 1469 he was always there – whether at London or Westminster – at councils, great councils, parliaments, Fauconberg's siege, in the abbey and the palace. Except when with Edward in France in 1475, he seldom appears anywhere else. He describes great events – the reconciliation of Edward and Warwick (1469), the contest between Clarence and Gloucester (1472) and Clarence's fall (1477–8) – and contributes to our understanding of both council and parliament. Several times he claims insight to Edward's private thoughts – his 'outraged majesty' in 1470, his posthumous repentance at Clarence's death and his regret at the cost of Berwick's recovery.[65] Crowland was in a position to know and writes with authority, correcting his predecessor and backing up his judgements both with argument and evidence. He was remarkably accurate, particularly on dates and people. His lapses, such as which princess Edward was courting in 1464 and in which years Clarence quarrelled and died, are unsurprising when recalled a decade or more later. Not only was he in a position to know, but likely to remember. The impression of knowing more than he reveals inspires confidence. He wrote authoritatively – his judgements have commonly been allowed by modern historians to prevail over alternative interpretations – and his accounts have also been credited where substantiation is lacking. Historians are rightly grateful for the facts he supplies.

Yet Crowland's interpretations are more suspect. His judgements, that Edward's military preparations in 1475, his taxes, his benevolences, the size of the northern army in 1483 and the 1484 attainder were unprecedented, unheard of and/or more than would ever be seen again,[66] show him to be no prophet, short on prescience and also oblivious to quite recent past precedents. Even if he were an ecclesiastical dignitary and a doctor of laws, which is not established, he was clearly a junior figure in government: present in councils and parliaments, but no politician. He was neither privy to the innermost councils nor did he carry much political weight himself. However much he disapproved, the royal dukes would have their way over the Warwick inheritance and parliament also at Clarence's trial. Several times he deferred to the experts. On occasion he also concealed facts inconvenient to the Yorkists or took the official Yorkist line in defiance of logic and common sense. The rout at Ludford (1459) is recounted without even a hint that the Yorkist commanders deserted the army of which he, apparently, was a member. Can he really have thought that 'since Henry VI is [involuntarily] associated with the killers of the earl's father [York], he is acting so as to break the whole force of the aforesaid decree of parliament, and it is broken so the earl no longer stands obliged to keep faith with him'?[67] Of course, not to believe would make Edward as guilty of breaking his allegiance as Henry IV was in 1399. King Henry IV had also supposedly perjured himself by claiming only his duchy, not the Crown. When Edward IV employed the same morally dubious *ruse de guerre*, Crowland excused it – it was not perjury, 'because it was necessary to disguise his intentions on account of his enemies there'. Fighting the battle of Barnet on Easter Sunday was foresighted of Edward, Crowland said, 'behaving rather in response to necessity than foolish propriety'; 'alas and for shame!' (*heu et pro dolor!*), in contrast, exclaims the *Brief Latin Chronicle*.[68] Somehow Crowland managed both to praise Charles the Bold for not producing his army in 1475 – his actions advanced the campaign and were those of a wise and confident prince, according to those of 'sounder mind' – and to approve Edward's desertion of Charles and his separate peace with Louis XI.[69] That it was so decided did not make the decision right. Here, as in 1460 and 1464, Crowland toed the official line, even backing Edward's judicial crushing of complaints that the chronicler himself recognized to be justified.[70] Similarly, in 1460, the acclamation of the populace and, in 1485, a petition of the three estates, each somewhat forced, justified King Edward's coronation and Henry VII's marriage.[71] Whilst admitting on these occasions to disagreement and debate, about which we might otherwise have been ignorant, is he not here promulgating the official view of the government? Sometimes he was the prisoner of official propaganda. Why, then, have so many historians accepted his view that it was differences in foreign policy *c.*1467–8 rather than the Wydeville marriage in 1464 that alienated Warwick, when so many other English chroniclers – indeed all the others – disagreed? It is because Warwick accepted the fait accompli at the Reading great council in 1464.[72] Of course he did, he had to, whether Crowland was right or not.

Crowland speaks with authority about parliament and council, and most probably served at the privy seal. Some items read as though they had crossed his desk, such as bishop's temporalities and the 1473 act of resumption, but not as though he had witnessed their implementation as he would have done in the exchequer or signet office. It is on the flimsiest of grounds that he has been credited with expertise in diplomacy and finance. Foreign affairs mattered. They do not bulk any larger in his story than they actually deserved. They were treated in detail only twice, in 1471 and 1484. The trips to Abbeville and Nottingham were exotic exceptions to a southerner who supposed that Olney (Bucks) was near Coventry (Warks).[73] His account of foreign affairs was nevertheless reliable, although he attributes the collapse of Edward's foreign policy, as did the king, wholly to the treachery of the French and Scots, rather than allotting any responsibility to Edward's conduct of it.

Crowland's account of royal finances is even less trustworthy. He reports the costs of the Scottish war of 1480–2 and the costs of holding Berwick, which he could have gleaned from the financial memoranda discussed by the young Edward V's council. He knew about Edward's French pension. He knew of the 1473 act of resumption, whereby 'he resumes possession of almost the whole of the royal patrimony, no matter to whom it had been granted, and applies it entirely to supporting the charges of the crown'. He reports Edward's benevolences and trading ventures, which we know about, his exploitation of episcopal vacancies, his search for concealments in records of chancery and fines for unlicensed liveries of inheritances, which we are ignorant of, but which Crowland, processing them, was well placed to observe. All this, Crowland adds,

> made him [Edward IV], within a few years, a very wealthy prince: so much so that in the collection of gold and silver vessels, tapestries and highly precious ornaments, both regal and religious, in the building of castles, colleges, and other notable places and in the acquisition of new lands and possessions not one of his ancestors could match his remarkable achievements.[74]

This reads exactly like Edward's official epitaph – which Crowland had surely read: the king's projection of himself as a wealthy prince in possession of treasure. Crowland continued to believe in Edward's hoard and blamed Richard III for squandering it, even though Edward actually left insufficient to pay for his funeral.

Crowland certainly thought that Edward left enough to pay for his bequests,[75] but his executors refused the administration. Crowland may have been an executor, but he did not understand. Clarence apart, we know that almost everybody was exempted from the 1473 act of resumption; Edward's other expedients, on the evidence, can have made only minor contributions to his finances. So much for Crowland's insights into Edward's finances.

As a Christian, a cleric and indeed a moralist, Crowland could not approve of Edward's worldliness and self-indulgence, his conviviality and his practice of four of the deadly sins (pride, gluttony, lechery and avarice), which would normally have deposited him directly in Hell. As a committed lifelong Yorkist and royal servant, he did want to believe his master eligible for salvation. To be set against such defects, and indeed highly praiseworthy and pleasing to God in Crowland's estimation, the king was the most faithful of Catholics, a most vigorous persecutor of Lollards, the kindliest patron of learned men and clerics, a devotee of the sacraments and most repentant of his sins. Crowland took comfort from the manner of Edward's death, for the king ordered the repayment of all debts and the righting of any wrongs he had committed. Edward's exemplary intentions should be credited, so Crowland argued, not their non-fulfilment, citing in support Christ's approval of Zachaeus's intention to leave half his wealth to the poor. Fully realizing how the imminence of death and damnation had prompted the king to change his will, he was grateful that Edward's time was too short 'before malice could intervene and change his mind'. Crowland surely was among 'all his faithful men [that] were given hope that he would not be cheated of his eternal reward'.[76] For Richard III, in contrast, his forecast was much less optimistic.

All Yorkist historians have to be grateful to Crowland for his *Second Continuation*. It is the best of a bad lot. Furthermore, here was a man at the heart of affairs, who witnessed key events, participated in them and interpreted them for us. He possessed a distinctive voice. On the face of it, however, there is much he did not know about or understand: no politician, no diplomat, no financier, he possessed little sense of precedent or proportion, decided nothing himself and seems to have influenced no decisions. He knew more about the patents that perhaps he helped to issue than about their enforcement and any consequences. He was the victim of official propaganda rather than its formulator. *Faute de mieux*, we have to use his history, which this book also quotes more than any other, but how many others of his colleagues and contemporaries could have made more reliable, more revealing and better sources had they so wished?

Rival assessments

Commynes and Crowland were writing about the same man. Both saw him as handsome and pleasure-loving, with a foreign policy that failed. Commynes blamed that on Edward, with considerable justice: the king's indolence and self-indulgence rendered him politically ineffective. Crowland stressed that such defects did not detract from his rule. Crowland was closer to Edward – perhaps too close – the prisoner of the king's own image and propaganda, whereas Commynes was perhaps too preoccupied with foreign policy and too great an admirer of Louis XI to see Edward in his English context. Our two best-informed contemporary interpreters offer us the same stark choice, which divides historians of Edward IV to this day.

4

The degeneration of Edward IV

Crowland and Commynes, the two most influential Yorkist historians, were too close to Edward IV, too involved on either side and too partisan to provide the balance and perspective that later generations require. Tudor and Stuart historians, distanced from events and able to recognize special pleading for what it was, did that: Edward emerges as a more effective king, but a worse man, in consequence. Most of the verdicts reached by the *Mirror of Magistrates* and by Habington went against Edward IV; to Hume and especially the Victorians, he was a bad king, a judgement sometimes tempered by condemnation of the era within which he had to live. Actually neither Crowland nor Commynes could contribute to what became the historical mainstream until Buck and Habington in the early seventeenth century used them and then only primarily for data supplementary to the accepted orthodoxy rather than as rival interpreters. Commynes was to influence interpretations more directly from Queen Anne's reign on,[1] but Crowland was not to achieve this distinction until the twentieth-century historians, Lander and Ross. When he did, as we shall see in Chapter 5, Edward's rehabilitation could commence.

Tudor and Stuart histories

Both Crowland and Commynes had known Edward IV in person, but both were writing after his death and the destruction of his dynasty, which affected their assessments directly and subconsciously too. It is notorious how willingly the historian John Rous completely changed the way he had originally presented Richard III.

Crowland and Commynes accepted Henry Tudor as a legitimate king. As early as 1486, Crowland reported that some greeted Henry as the saviour sent by God. He incorporated into his chronicle some of the stories, probably myths, surrounding Henry's victory at Bosworth.[2] The new king's title was weak and needed to be buttressed wherever possible. Much was made of Henry VII's supposed designation as his successor by Henry VI and his own Welsh ancestry and Arthurian antecedents. Within a year, Henry VII possessed a son and heir called Arthur. Poets, both Welsh bards and the blind Frenchman Bernard André, played important early roles. Obviously the Yorkist myth could not stand and had to be recast to culminate in the accession of the Tudors. Though a usurper, Henry VI had been nevertheless a king *de facto* and God's lieutenant, whom it had been a sin for Edward IV, even as God's instrument, to overthrow. Edward IV's sin of usurpation was visited on his son and Richard III's on himself. Richard was special: not merely a usurper, but a killer of innocent children and an aspirant to incest. Likened to Judas Iscariot and King Herod, it was no sin to depose or kill *him*. Instead, Tudor historians reconfigured the whole era from 1399 as a single providential cycle of sin and punishment in which Henry VII, who brought together the houses of Lancaster and York and united the red and white roses, was rightful heir to King Richard II – the last true Plantagenet. 'In the year 1485, on the 22nd day of August', already wrote (or quoted) Crowland, 'the tusks of the Boar [Richard III] were blunted and the red rose, the avenger of the white, shines upon us'.[3] The battle of Bosworth and the inauguration of the Tudor dynasty in 1485 was identified almost at once by Henry Tudor's propagandists as commencing a new era, just as the Yorkists had done in 1461. Both Yorkist and Lancastrian titles had to be accommodated. Henry VII's own title was Lancastrian – the son of a Beaufort, he was supposedly Henry VI's chosen heir. Most of his supporters, however, were Yorkists and loyal to his queen, Elizabeth, daughter of Edward IV, whom Henry had formally vowed to marry. Henry was therefore a Yorkist king and Tudor historians had to approve of Edward IV. Though this new vision involved distorting history and downplaying the gravity and justification of those who fought on after 1461, it was not in its turn superseded. Henry VII's grasp on the Crown endured. It was his message that was passed down from Polydore Vergil to Edward

Hall, William Shakespeare and hence to our own day. Other notions, such as the concept of order and the Church of England, were grafted on later. Though nobody today believes in the providential cycle, we still unwittingly subscribe to the Tudor myth.

Polydore Vergil's *English History* from the earliest times accepted the overriding providential scheme alluded to above and integrated Edward IV into it. 'Yet it may be peradventure,' he writes, that because of God's anger at the usurpation of 1399 'the grandfather's offence redounded unto the nephews'.[4] As an Italian, this official historiographer to Henry VII can have known nothing of Edward IV at first-hand, yet he contrived to assemble from oral and written sources the most detailed narrative to date, albeit one that sometimes muddles, telescopes or otherwise distorts the order of events and that is fuller on Edward's earlier than his last years. Vergil accepts the Yorkist claim that Henry VI had breached the 1460 Accord and attributes to Edward '[sur]passing valour and ability ... liberality, clemency, integrity and fortitude [for which he was] praised generally of all men above the skies' and made himself 'like a triumphant emperor'. Vergil approved of his common touch, 'which trade of life he never changed', and repeatedly substantiates both his liberality, especially with Lancastrian forfeitures, and his willingness to forgive which won him so many friends and made him so formidable.

Against these credits, he had not a good word to say about Edward's marriage, which he thought unworthy. He blamed this marriage and the king's own jealousy (and ingratitude) for his dissension with Warwick. 'So we find by experience', wrote Vergil, 'that friends do very seldom answer like for like, yea rather unthankful minds do requite much good with much evil'. Possibly Edward also tried to seduce one of Warwick's household damsels. If Vergil had read Crowland, as Dr Alison Hanham has suggested,[5] he did not regard him as his prime source or indeed respect his judgements. Vergil had come across two of Crowland's claims, that it was Margaret of York's Burgundian marriage that caused the breach with Warwick and that the victorious earl released the king in 1469, but he rejected them both, the former as 'a fable of the people' and the latter as defying common sense. Vergil confessed the popularity of the rebels in 1470, without explaining Edward's unpopularity. Whilst admitting how expedient it was for Edward to claim merely

to be pursuing his duchy next year, Vergil was nevertheless shocked
– the italics are his own:

> so that the next day very early in the morning, *while a
> priest said mass* at the gate whereby he was to enter the
> town, he among *the holy mysteries* promised by oath,
> devoutly and reverently, to observe both two, and so he
> was received into the town. Who, notwithstanding, was
> so far from having any mind to observe the one
> (according as forthwith after appeared evident) that he
> resolved to regard even nothing more than to persecute
> King Henry, and to thrust him from the possession of his
> kingdom. Thus oftentimes as well men of high as of low
> calling blinded with covetousness, and forgetting all
> religion and honesty, are wont to make promise in
> swearing by the immortal God, which promise
> nevertheless they are already determined to break before
> they make it.

Edward's children, he ominously suggested, were to pay the penalty.
Louis XI's backing for Warwick and Edward's obligation to Duke
Charles gave the king no choice in 1475 but to invade France,
though he had no serious intention of conquest; Vergil easily
explained Edward's disengagement by divisions at home, shortage
of funds, Charles's inadequacies and the marriage and pension that
Louis offered. Although unable satisfactorily to explain Clarence's
death, he condemned it as 'the worst example that ever man could
remember'. Much space was devoted to Edward's efforts to
repatriate Henry Tudor – actually a very minor aspect of the Second
Reign – and to the successful war with Scotland. Vergil thought that
Edward nominated his brother, Gloucester, to rule for his son. Quite
apart from his prowess, Vergil thought Edward IV a good king, 'of
sharp wit', retentive memory and hardworking ('diligent in doing
his affairs'), who singled out for service and reward those with
merit. It was regrettable, admittedly, that 'a little before his death'
(and therefore not before) 'he began to slide little by little into
avarice'. Given that he succeeded by force to a bankrupt realm, 'he
left a most wealthy realm abounding in all things'. Vergil's main
complaint about Edward's 'bodily lust' was that, combined with his
geniality, it sometimes caused him to forget the respect due to his

majesty. Vergil did not believe the pre-contract story. Edward's passing was much lamented.[6]

Sir Thomas More can have had few personal memories of the king who died before his sixth birthday, but obviously he grew up among people who had and was well placed to find out more from those acquainted with the king if he had wished. Edward IV was not the monarch about whom More chose to write *c*.1516, but rather his brother, Richard III. More's *History*, whilst acknowledging Richard's merits, reinforced the existing portrait of a wrongful king, a usurper and a regicidal and thoroughly evil man. Stripped of his precision and the careful qualification of his judgements, More's *Richard III* became standard for four centuries until crudely rejected by Ricardians as Tudor propaganda. For More, therefore, his brief references to Edward IV and his reign functioned principally as backcloth and contrast, as evidence of the satisfactory state of England before Richard's usurpation and what a good king should be. Not that More was uncritical or 'sanitized' Edward to contrast with his wicked brother.[7] More registers Edward's self-indulgence, his gluttony and lasciviousness ('fleshly wantonness'), which he adjudged had no public dimension, because it affected very few, 'for neither could any one man's pleasure stretch and extend to the displeasure of very many', and because his energies waned with age, 'lessened and well left'. He went to considerable lengths to refute the pre-contract story, which he wrongly supposed involved Elizabeth Lucy, not Eleanor Butler. More deplored the death of Clarence, which he could not satisfactorily explain, and confessed the unpopularity of Edward's financial exactions, which diminished in his last years because of the French pension. Edward, he declared, was

> of heart courageous, politic in counsel, in adversity
> nothing abashed, in prosperity rather joyful than proud
> [exultant], in peace just and merciful, in war sharp and
> fierce, in the field bold and hardy, and nevertheless – no
> farther than wisdom would – adventurous. Whose wars
> who so well consider, he shall no less commend his
> wisdom where he avoided than his manhood where he
> vanquished.

It is a considered verdict, but not a eulogy. Tone and language alike are measured and paper over any cracks. At the end it appears to commend Edward's decision to make peace at Picquigny in 1475. Although 'attaining the crown by battle', Edward had outlived Lancastrianism and indeed advanced some individual ex-Lancastrians. He ruled so well 'that there was never any prince of this land so heartily beloved with the substance of his people', particularly 'at the time of his death', which was widely lamented. Berwick had just been recaptured. He left his kingdom 'quiet and prosperous'. There was no danger 'of outward enemies, no war in hand, nor none toward, but such as no man looked for; the people toward the prince not in constrained fear, but in a willing and loving obedience, among themselves, the commons in good peace'. Those divisions amongst the court nobility which he could control, though irksome, were reconciled on his deathbed. Edward had the common touch and valued to the end the friendship of the City corporation and the 'hearty favour' of the populace secured by affable interaction and gifts of royal venison.[8]

It is the kind of review of which any king could be proud! It is not, however, everything that More had to say, for Edward occurs elsewhere also, in verbatim speeches, which More cannot have heard himself and must therefore have reconstructed. Yet the information may be authentic. Edward's queen, for instance, is made to record how in 1471, 'went I hence to welcome him home; and from hence [Westminster Abbey] I brought my babe, the prince, unto his father, when he first took him in his arms',[9] which we know, from the *Arrival* and celebratory poetry, to have been precisely true. Whatever use he made of his material, More was very well informed about what actually happened and about stories circulating in his own day. More than any other source, he tells us about Edward's sexual liaisons, whilst appreciating that some of his information may be apocryphal. His initial character sketch of the king may have been intended to refute some of the allegations attributed to Gloucester and Buckingham, which subsequent historians have usually overlooked, understandably but unwisely.

More's Gloucester, for instance, makes much of the self-interested factionalism of Edward's court that More had earlier declared to be under control.

> You remember, I trust, King Edward himself, albeit he
> was a man of age and of discretion, yet was he in many

things ruled by the bend [faction], more than stood either with his honour or our profit, or with the commodity [convenience] of any man else, except only the immoderate advancement of themselves. Which whether they sorer thirsted after their own weal or our woe, it were hard, I know, to guess.[10]

More's Buckingham stressed the financial exactions that More had earlier belittled, 'of which there was never end and often no need, or if there were, it rather grew of riot and unreasonable waste than any necessary or honourable charges'. Taxes were insufficient, so he resorted to

benevolence[s] and good will, … as though the name of benevolence had signified that every man should pay, not what himself of his good will let to grant, but what the king of his good will choose to take; which never asked little, but everything was enhanced above the measure: amercements turned into fines, fines into ransom, small trespass to misprision, misprision into treason.

More, as we have seen, had earlier claimed that such problems had stopped – an admission, of course, that they had once applied – but the abolition of benevolences by Richard III's parliament indicates that that grievance was still current. The final transformation, from misprision to treason alluded obviously to Sir Thomas Cook, 'your own worshipful neighbour, alderman and mayor of this worshipful city', who was fined 8,000 marks. 'Who is of you either so negligent that he knoweth not', Buckingham demanded, 'or so forgetful that he remembereth not, or so hardhearted that he pitieth not that worshipful man's loss?' Chief Justice Markham, who was wrongly dismissed in consequence, and Clarence's client, Thomas Burdet, 'cruelly beheaded by the misconstruing of the law of this realm for the prince's pleasure', are mere examples of so many others 'as well [in] their goods as their persons greatly endangered, either by feigned quarrels or small matters aggrieved with heinous names'. Are there echoes here (and deliberate comparisons) with the notorious closing years of Henry VII? They signal the arrival of both the Cook and Burdet legends in mainstream history. More also doubted Clarence's guilt. Buckingham supposedly dwelt further on the costs in manpower and materials of the Wars of the Roses and declared that there *was* a public dimension to the Edward's lust.

> the king's greedy appetite was insatiable and everywhere over all the realm intolerable. For no woman was there anywhere, young or old, rich or poor, whom he set his eye upon, in whom he anything liked, either person or appearance, speech, pace, or countenance, but without any fear of God or respect of his honour, murmur or grudge of the world, he would importunely pursue his appetite and have her, to the great destruction of many a good woman and great dolour to her husband and their other friends.[11]

Though More openly disagreed, Richard certainly found plenty of political mileage in denouncing the sexual immorality of his foes and the exemplary humiliation of Elizabeth Shore. Evidently much more damning assessments of Edward IV than More's official line were current in the early years of King Henry VIII for More to pick up and transmit to us.

The working-out of God's providence from Richard II on is the overriding theme that determines the structure of *Hall's Chronicle*, in which 'the Prosperous Reigne of King Edward the Fourth' occupies no less than eighty pages. It melded Vergil, More and the London chronicles with other limited data from sources no longer extant, such as the king's interview on the field of Tewkesbury with Edward of Lancaster, so fatal to the latter. Edward rightly replaced Henry VI: even those unfortunate Lancastrians who escaped perished at Hexham, he recorded, receiving 'death for their reward and guerdon'. Although Hall had good reason to be favourable to the grandfather of the current monarch (and indeed thought well of his reign), he was far from uncritical. He attributed the disasters of 1469–71 to Edward's ill-considered marriage, blamed him additionally for the betrayal of Lord Welles (1470) and the men of York (following Vergil) in 1471, and concluded that 'the progeny of King Edward escaped not ... from this open perjury'.[12]

Somewhat abridged by the committee that was Raphael Holinshed and afforded by documents in Stow's *Annales*, Hall's narrative sets a critical tone to subsequent histories. It underpins all the Elizabethan representations in drama of Edward IV. First in time, but slighter in content, Thomas Heywood's two plays on Edward IV say little about chronological events or his rule but make much of his vices. King Edward is a jovial Falstaffian seducer, often disguised and hobnobbing with low company. Mistress Shore features prominently. More seriously, his mother condemns his choice of marriage, he extracts benevolences from citizens and is outwitted by the cunning French and Burgundians. He is oblivious to Clarence's innocence.[13]

Edward IV features in three of Shakespeare's fifteenth-century history plays. In *Henry VI Part II*, he stands bail for his father, York, at Dartford and utters a single line, much less than his brother, Richard (the future Richard III), not yet born in reality.[14] In *Part III*, it is again Richard, at Sandal in Yorkshire, who persuades the duke to take the throne, which Edward enthusiastically supports:

> But for a kingdom, any oath may be broken:
> I would break a thousand oaths to reign one year.

Such perjury he was indeed later to commit. Once York is killed, it is again Richard who urges him onwards to the throne, but it is Edward who bandies challenges with Henry VI and fights the decisive battle at Towton. There is scope here in plenty to play Edward as a hero. Strangely Shakespeare chose to call a play that happened almost entirely in Edward's reign, 1460–71, *Henry VI Part III*. Edward is a major figure – not more so, however, than Warwick, who is presented favourably, or even Margaret of Anjou or King Henry. Remembering the Tudor providential cycle and anticipating plays of his own as yet unwritten, Shakespeare already has Richard looking forward to the throne and planning to 'set the murderous Machiavel to school'. Thereafter Shakespeare reports Edward's wooing of Elizabeth Grey (née Wydeville) and the collapse of his First Reign, discussed in Chapter 6. Following his defeat and exile, Edward secures admission to York by claiming only his duchy – a deliberately dishonest ruse – and subsequently wins Sir John Montgomery and others by claiming his Crown. He commands at Barnet and Tewkesbury and also brangles with Edward of Lancaster, as in *Hall's Chronicle*, and first knifes him. Gloucester, the second stabber, eliminates King Henry in the Tower off his own bat and soliloquizes about disposing of Clarence 'and then the rest'. The play ends with the royal dukes' acknowledgement of Edward's

own son, Edward, as his heir, Gloucester, of course, insincerely, and
a paean of triumph from Edward IV himself:

> And now what rests but that we spend the time
> With stately triumphs, mirthful comic shows,
> Such as befit the pleasure of the court?
> Sound drums and trumpets! Farewell, sour annoy!
> For here, I hope, begins our lasting joy![15]

Edward is still king at the start of Shakespeare's *Richard III*.
Although Richard III immediately follows these victories, Edward of
Lancaster being yet to be interred, the king's sons – for now there
are two – are children and King Edward is in decay, unwell and
dying. He represents authority, but is unseeing and ineffective. All
actions are shaped by the cunning Gloucester, who marries the
widowed Anne Neville and orchestrates the murder of Clarence in
spite of Edward's real wishes. Before his death Edward seeks to
reconcile the warring factions – the Queen, Dorset and Rivers,
Hastings – but unavailingly, and leaves them exposed to
Gloucester's wickedness.[16] The tragedy duly follows. Aspersions
later made against Edward, such as his bastardy and the invalidity
of his marriage, were groundless slanders uttered in pursuit of
Richard's heinous ends.

Shakespeare left Edward IV looking ineffective and irrelevant.
That only *Richard III* was of the highest quality and was therefore
regularly performed and that Edward IV fails to dominate any of
Shakespeare's plays also helps explain why he was insufficiently
memorable to feature significantly in *1066 And All That*. He
certainly does not escape criticism. A much stronger image, perhaps
much more influential at the time, was presented by the *Mirror for
Magistrates* of 1559, and after, a series of verse tragedies that
imparted morals from history, many from fifteenth-century history.
Cumulatively it damns Edward IV. His brief tragedy or playlet
reproduces one of Edward's deathbed laments. Its caption – 'How
King Edward through his surfeiting and intemperate life suddenly
died amidst his prosperity' – is much less sympathetic and makes
him into an ominous warning of the mutability of fate and
inevitability of death and final accountability. Much more to
Edward's discredit emerges in the other tragedies relating to his
subjects. Edward it was who 'to a widow rashly wedded was' and

who was inclined to dispense with his faith. It was Edward's butcherly commandments that Tiptoft implemented and for which he was justly executed in 1470. Once Edward was king,

> The pride whereof so deep his stomach pierced,
> That he forgot his friends, despised his kin,
> Of oath or office passing not a pin.

The poet robustly backed 'faithful' Warwick, who was 'no hippocrite' and whose regrettable death 'decayed the keys of chivalry'. Warwick's 'chiefest care' was the 'commonweal', which he placed ahead of his own advantage, which was recognized at the time, and which the poet recommends to his reader. Warwick was as consistent in opposing 'King Edward's sinful pranks' as he had been against the abuses of King Henry VI. Clarence had real grievances too and suffered both from Edward's jealousy and his ridiculous reliance on false prophecies. Edward 'wrongfully imprisoned his brother Clarence' and suffered him to be 'by his brother Richard miserably murdered'. Edward's desire to promote his children

> Provoked him against both law and right
> To murder me, his brother, and his knight.

A whole tragedy was devoted to Shore's wife.[17]

At least all writers so far had agreed on the villainy of Richard III, beside whom Edward IV always looked good, but Sir George Buck (d. 1622) favoured Richard. It was for Richard that an ancestor had suffered in 1485 and whom he had allegedly served. His *History of King Richard III* (1619) is the best documented and by far the most critical and best referenced history to date. Master of the Revels and classically educated, he knew the classics and freely applies parallels, arguments and lessons from the classical past to Yorkist England. Buck was biased towards those of rank, such as the nobility, gentry and former historians. Proud of his own gentility and scholarship, he treated Commynes, More and Bishop Stillington with great respect and condemned the Wydevilles, mere parvenus who opposed the great lords of the blood. He accepted the Yorkist title to the Crown and (as a patriotic Englishman) refuted Commynes on the French pension, which he thought was properly a tribute for English possessions in France wrongly seized by the French king. He recognized Edward's good qualities. 'And indeed the name of

Edward and of the Earl of March was counted terrible, and he esteemed the thunder and lightning of arms where his keen and victorious sword was drawn'. He was 'very wise and provident', ultimately popular with all except those diehard Lancastrians, who wanted all Yorkists dead. Buck's very different perspective caused him to look at Edward's reign in different ways, approving, for instance, his war with the Scots, acquitting Richard but leaving Edward 'accused of the murder and death of the king, St Harry, and of the Prince of Wales', and, most significantly, prompting him to project back and reintegrate the pre-contract story into the reign. Protesting that he was merely relaying opinions of the time, he declared that the fate of the princes

> cannot be well known without the true report made of
> the sundry loves, wooings, especially contracts and
> marriages of the king their father. Therefore, I must crave
> leave to unfold and to relate these. I shall not need to
> intimate how amorous he was, and wanton, for that is
> well known. Yet it shall not be amiss to say something
> here, and how that he had many mistresses, or amasias,
> and who were kept in several houses and very
> honourably entertained, after the manner of the seraglios
> of the great Turks.

Buck was convinced that Edward had married Eleanor Butler before Queen Elizabeth and that his sexual adventures mattered politically. He rather more than implies that Edward was responsible for his sons' illegitimacy and their supercession by Richard III. Never having served the king, like Crowland, he thought him damned for his adulteries, fornications, bloodshed and the oath-breaking of which Vergil accused him.

> But it may be thought that the judgement of God,
> hanging over the king for his many and great offences,
> captivated and took his understanding and provident care
> from him ... And these indeed are the just causes of
> God's punishments against men. And many times He is
> pleased to leave them so blinded and secure in their
> sensualities and sins that they have no sense or power to
> see or prevent the mischiefs that stand at their doors.

That Edward was damned, the verdict also of Vergil and the *Mirror*, is the only aspect wholly omitted in the abridgement published by Buck's nephew and namesake in 1647.[18]

Well over two hundred pages long, *The History of Edward the Fourth King of England* (1640) of William Habington, the Worcestershire esquire, is an impressive work for its time and much the fullest and most judicious life of the king before Scofield, almost three centuries later. Although correct chronological sequences had to await Rapin's analysis of Rymer's *Foedera,* Habington evidently used a range of sources, including Commynes (whom he deprecated), Crowland and perhaps also pseudo-Worcester, and interlarded his detailed narrative with aphorisms, shrewd comments and general lessons. His Edward was in charge and indeed his own principal asset. Edward is praised for his military skill, his self-confidence, his wisdom and interpersonal skills, and for 'the destruction (since no gentler way had authority) of mighty opposers'. Habington pulled no punches. Edward's marriage caused the disasters of 1469–71 and divisions at court, by implication, underwrote that of 1483. 'This was the outward face of the Court full of the hearts of dignity and Majesty', he wrote, 'while the inward was all rotten with discord and envy'. Edward was blamed for his lust, the expensive pleasures which forced him into avarice, additional exactions and his injustice to Sir Thomas Cook. The executions of Oxford and Tuddenham in 1462, supposedly 'without answer', were 'a rough proceeding which favoured something too much of the Conqueror'; those of Welles and Dymmock (and indeed the bastard of Fauconberg) 'violated his word'; Edward of Lancaster was 'barbarously murdered'; and for the elimination of his brother, Clarence, there were only *Turkish* precedents. Ironically, Edward's attribution to Clarence of the charge that he himself was a bastard (again) misfired, since it was recycled by Gloucester against Edward's son, Edward V, in 1483: 'whereby God's severe judgement manifests, how unsafe it is in a Prince, by false accusations to condemn the innocent'. It is a damning picture.

In view of all these strictures, which collectively anticipate those of modern critics such as Richmond, it must come as a shock that Habington's splendidly judicious assessment finds Edward 'worthy to be ranked among the best' by comparision 'with the lives of Princes in general' and that he judged the reign on balance to be a success. 'His life presents your eye with rugged times, yet smooth'd by his prevailing Fortune, and a just cause. Faction begat many tempests: but Sovereignty found a happier calm'. Acknowledging Edward's physique and martial qualities, he extols his wit – not cunning or deceit but judgement – and declares that he made no mistakes, since his worsting by Louis XI and Warwick was achieved by fraud, not straight dealing. He laments that Edward's 'frequent' oath-breaking was commonplace amongst princes, excuses his severity to Cook as 'short tempests' rather than habitual and to Clarence because he was not the prime mover. Genuinely committed to law and order, Edward passed wholesome laws for the common good, was diligent and lived in appropriate splendour. Edward inherited rather than created the sea of blood through which he swam and to which he could only add. Inevitably, some blame for the sins of others sticks to the king. All his good fortune, Habington observes, did not make Edward tyrannical. He was rather compla-cent than proud or disdainful to the vanquished, and admirably temperate. Perhaps it was because Habington had a low opinion of princes – though his book was dedicated to Charles I! – and because he was realistic in what he expected that he rated Edward relatively highly.[19] It is the relativity that makes this the faintest of praise. Yet Habington's account is balanced, perceptive and still worth reading.

Hanoverian and Victorian histories

Subsequent historians were more secular in outlook: Edward's chances of salvation do not recur. Habington and the abridged Buck, initially as separates and then reprinted in White Kennett's *History of England*, were the standard histories of Edward IV until they were superseded by Rapin de Thoyras in 1723. Rapin added to the stock of data with the first infusion of record sources derived from Rymer's *Foedera* and was thus able to construct the detailed chronology on which we rely today. Being a Frenchman, however, he also accepted the interpretation as well as the factual data of Commynes and presented a picture of a pleasure-loving and extrav-agant king who had to raise money by extortion. This is the 'Modern Legend' that Lander argues has unfavourably distorted interpretations of Edward ever since and that he strove to correct.[20] Whilst Commynes's historiographical influence did affect Rapin,

Lander did not appreciate how unfavourable existing orthodoxies about Edward IV already were and seriously exaggerates his importance to later writers. There were to be other changes in historical perception. Like every other historical topic, the Wars of the Roses and the Yorkist Age were to be exposed to the different and successive perspectives of the Enlightenment, Romanticism and the critical scientific and constitutional historians of the Victorian age. Edward IV's reputation was to suffer henceforth from disdain towards the violent animosities, bastard feudalism and (by their standards) constitutional impropriety of the Wars of the Roses. All the Scottish Enlightenment historian David Hume (1711–76) 'could distinguish with certainty', for instance, 'is a scene of horror and bloodshed, savage matters, arbitrary executions, and treacherous, dishonourable conduct on all parties', for which 'there is no possibility … of accounting'. Commynes's influence on him and indeed subsequent writers is not extensive.

Hume's *History of England* (1761) is a well-written and blow-by-blow political narrative of the reign, well founded in the sources, but profoundly unsympathetic to the Yorkist era. He accepted Edward's title to the throne and martial prowess, and even found his pursuit of pleasure, which he otherwise deplored, both inoffensive and popular, but he disapproved of much else. 'Young Edward', he begins,

> was of a temper well fitted to make his way through such a scene of war, havoc, and devastation, as must conduct him to the full possession of that crown, which he claimed from hereditary right, but which he had assumed from the tumultuary election of his own party. He was bold, active, enterprising; and his hardness of heart and severity of character rendered him impregnable to all those movements of compassion, which might relax his vigour in the prosecution of the most bloody revenge upon his enemies. The very commencement of his reign gave symptoms of his sanguinary disposition.

Horace Walpole similarly ascribes to Edward IV 'singular bravery and address', but 'with all the arts of a politician and the cruelty of a conqueror'.[21] Once secure, continues Hume, 'so libertine a prince' succumbed to 'the dissipation of amusement, or the allurements of passion'. The 'amorous temper of Edward led him into a snare', his marriage, 'which [was] fatal to his repose, and to the stability of his throne'. Edward was at fault and his motives unaccountable. It was, however, Hume who initiated the more critical assessments of Warwick that have prevailed ever since. If Edward's prowess brought him victory, there his glories ceased. Hume surmises, 'his spirit seems afterwards to have sunk in indolence and pleasure, or his measures were frustrated by imprudence and the want of fore-sight'; for instance, his invasion of France and subsequent peace, which 'did very little honour to either of the monarchs', and the failed diplomatic marriages of his children. When Louis XI attacked Burgundy, 'Edward was no less defective in policy, and was no less actuated by private passions, unworthy of a sovereign and a statesman'. To Hume, Clarence's destruction was one of 'the most flagrant acts of injustice or tyranny' committed by king and parlia-ment. Edward's last years were peaceful and prosperous, marred only by the court intrigues that he himself could manage and which he tried to reconcile. He was, concludes Hume shrewdly and succinctly,

> a prince more splendid and showy, than either prudent or
> virtuous; brave, though cruel; addicted to pleasure,
> though capable of activity in great emergencies; and less
> fitted to prevent ills by wise precautions, than to remedy
> them, after they took place, by vigour and enterprize.

Bigger changes in interpretation came late in the nineteenth century. It was then that history first became a university subject in England, the critical scientific history associated with Leopold von Ranke arrived and detailed research on Yorkist records effectively began. Important sources were discovered. The publication of the confession of Sir Robert Welles in 1831 and the *Chronicle of the Lincolnshire Rebellion* in 1836 did render (or should have rendered) untenable one charge of oath-breaking against the king, regarding the execution of Richard Lord Welles, which disappeared quietly from subsequent histories. At Oxford, Reverends William Denton, John Richard Green and Charles Plummer, Bishop William Stubbs and, at the Public Record Office, Dr James Gairdner researched and wrote on the Yorkists from the 1870s. Ramsay, Oman and Stratford followed. As befitted such clerical callings, the Oxford fellows took a moral stance on history and were concerned to trace the evolution of the perfections (as they saw them) of the British constitution, its parliamentary democracy, liberty of the subject and rule of law, down to their own day. They were appalled by late medieval society, with its violence and perversion of justice perpetrated by the great, which they dubbed alternately 'livery and maintenance' and 'bastard feudalism', and especially by its lowest pit – the Wars of the Roses. 'There are few periods in our annals from which we turn with such weariness and disgust as from the Wars of the Roses', wrote Green.[22] Kings whom they perceived as contributing to constitutional progress, like Henry IV, or who attacked bastard feudalism, like Henry VII, were approved; Edward IV, who reigned during the worst excesses of the Wars of the Roses, indeed emerged from them and contributed to them, was not.

To such historians, Edward was without doubt a bad king. His reign was 'an epoch of constitutional retrogression in which the slow work of the age that went before it was thoroughly undone': parliament was manipulated or supplanted by the royal council, arbitrary taxation and arbitrary imprisonment multiplied, and 'justice was degraded'. 'So vast and sweeping was the change [from Edward IV on] that to careless observers of a later day the constitutional monarchy of the Edwards and the Henries deemed suddenly to have transformed itself under the Tudors into a despotism as complete as the despotism of the Turk'. Edward was not merely tarnished by association, but was primarily responsible for it. He was a king 'of iron will and great fixity of purpose'. Under a cloak of 'indolence and gaiety', King Edward shrouded 'a profound political ability [and] was silently laying the foundations of an absolute rule'. Parliament almost ceased, reforming laws actually did, and taxes were misappropriated or extracted by force. 'It was to Edward that his Tudor successors owed the introduction of an elaborate Spy-system, the use of the rack, and the practice of interference with the purity of justice'. 'A consummate general', a libertine and 'the most pitiless of the warriors of the civil war', Edward came to outdo even his mentor, Warwick, in his subtle treachery.[23]

Stubbs, the first and greatest of the constitutional historians, set the tone for three-quarters of a century of historical writing. Stubbs was a critical scientific historian and a *Rolls Series* editor, whose primary research lay somewhat earlier, but he made extensive use of the printed chronicles and rolls of parliament for the Yorkist age. Stubbs's verdict on Edward IV could not be more damning. He bracketed him with his successor, Richard III. 'The most ardent champion of the divine right of hereditary succession must allow', he wrote, 'that the rule of Edward IV and Richard III was unconstitutional, arbitrary, and sanguinary'. Whilst recognizing Edward's youthful promise, courage and pretensions to justice, he found nothing else in his favour and labels him a voluptuary and a tyrant. Stubbs was really more sympathetic to Warwick, admittedly 'in some respects only an exaggeration of the common baronial type', but also 'a far-seeing politician' in whom he found 'some elements of greatness'. Edward was at fault in his marriage and by 1469 'the more apathetic mass of the nation discovered that the peace and security of life and property were no better cared for under the new dynasty than they had been under the old'. If he was more successful and even popular in his Second Reign, his benevolences were worse than Richard II's blank charters, the Treaty of Picquigny was shameful, his destruction of Clarence was a judicial cruelty and the usurpation of Richard III exposed his lack of foresight. His government was no better than Henry VI's. Stubbs quoted Hallam that there was 'no single enactment ... for increasing the liberty of the subject'. 'Edward IV was not perhaps quite as bad a man or so bad a king as his enemies have represented', concluded Stubbs,

> but even those writers who have laboured hardest to rehabilitate him have failed to discover any conspicuous merit. He was a man vicious far beyond any king that England had seen since the days of John; and more cruel and bloodthirsty than any king she had ever known; he had too a conspicuous talent for extortion. There had been fierce deeds of bloodshed under [earlier kings] ... But Edward IV far outdid all that his forefathers and his enemies had done.[24]

Richard III was no monster, declared Gairdner, rather 'the natural outgrowth of monstrous and horrible times' and 'the fitting termination of the rule of the house of York'. Under Edward IV indeed violence became the norm. 'The House of York abused their triumph, became intolerant of rivals, and imbrued their hands in the blood of princes. Hardened by degrees in acts of cruelty and perfidy, they grew faithless to one another'. Edward's benevolences were 'a very evil precedent'. He had proved by 1469 no improvement on 'the rival he had deposed'. Yet Gairdner commits himself to few judgements in his short account of Edward's reign, which focuses on Richard III and relies principally on Crowland and the Paston Letters as his sources.[25] Although it was Gairdner who was regarded as the historian of the Yorkists and the expert on their records, the fullest account to date, especially strong on financial matters, was supplied by Sir James Ramsay. Whilst seldom indulging in interpretation, Ramsay reports how Edward moved from being the most trusting to the most suspicious of kings, praises his prowess and tactical skill, deplores his benevolences and notes his geniality and sex life. Whilst generally allowing his facts to speak for themselves, Ramsay somewhat tempers current verdicts by measuring Edward against contemporary standards.

> Edward IV was not a bad King for the times in which he
> lived: he was a man of much the same type as the
> Fastolfs, the Pastons, and the Plumptons, who have left
> us their portraits in their private correspondence: hard
> narrow, unscrupulous; and endowed with the iron will
> and relentless purpose necessary to keep the men he had
> to rule in order.[26]

Two early twentieth-century lives

This survey culminates with two very different early twentieth-century lives, by Laurence Stratford and Cora Scofield. Stratford's volume in the Makers of National History series briefly, succinctly and remarkably effectively codified and summarized his generation's view. Yet it had a short shelf-life, being largely ignored by subsequent writers, both because it belongs to a particular era, now lost, and because it was eclipsed by Scofield's more comprehensive treatment.

Although wholly reliant on printed sources, especially narratives, and not uncritical of them, Stratford appreciated, as perhaps we cannot, contemporary shock at Edward's destruction of the de Veres in 1462 and some of the king's other actions. Edward had potential.

Already popular, 'the finest soldier in the country at his accession', a good judge of men and an inspiration for them, he was also hard-working – 'his system required it' – and an able administrator and director of others. If his private life came to be scandalous, at least it did not detract from his popularity. Stratford sympathized with Edward – his father's fate was hideous and influences on him, such as his queen, malign – and he appreciated how difficult was rule for a teenaged king. It was not Edward's fault that neither rigour nor leniency worked with erstwhile Lancastrians, nor that Warwick, 'the idol of the democracy', initially overshadowed him. 'It may be said, with no great exaggeration of the facts, that Edward IV reigned, and the Earl of Warwick ruled in England', he quoted from Oman, shrewdly adding that 'the activity of Warwick does not necessarily imply the inactivity of Edward'. Edward did his best: Warwick should have submitted and had no answers to the constitutional imperatives of the time. Regrettably, however, Edward himself went to the bad. If illustrative of the declining standards of honour and right over the past fifty years, Edward's 'unblushing perjury', sacrilege and treacheries, cruelty, cold-hearted killings and his murder of Henry VI recur as crimes that 'nothing can remove, nothing extenuate'. The promising adolescent became 'the ruthless, perfidious man of twenty-nine. But if he had lost his character, he had plainly gained in ability'. From 1471 Edward was definitely in charge. A masterful absolutist, he was a ruthless eliminator of foes, intolerant of opponents like Clarence, and impatient of legal or con-stitutional forms. 'He attempted no alteration of the constitutional enactments – he merely ignored them' and 'was content to have power rather than to claim it'. Royal power was advanced at the expense of his subjects' liberty and property and justice too. Yet Edward had his limits. His very control let in Richard III. 'If a man grasped that [the crown] he grasped all'. He could not conquer France – his invasion in 1475 was an act of the most cynical self-interest – and Louis XI completely outwitted him. He was 'easily deceived, no diplomatist, no politician in the sense it is now under-stood'. If nevertheless 'his mind was of the coming rather than the departing age' and 'he left a country at peace, and with signs of increasing prosperity', Edward IV also left behind a strong and popular monarchy and prepared the way for the reforms and revival of learning of the Tudors.[27]

What a contrast to Stratford's *Edward the Fourth* is presented by the two massive volumes of Cora L. Scofield, who had devoted her whole life to him. That she was an American gave her some distance from English constitutionalists, who influenced her nevertheless, but her contribution was to be the substantial research and sober discussion so useful to all subsequent interpreters, for and against. Scofield added scarcely anything to the constitutional and administrative history fashionable in her day, whose ideals she shared but to which she offered merely lip-service near the end of her great book, but she made the fullest and most effective use of the Yorkists' public records to date. She read all the available published sources, in English, French, German and Latin, all the secondary material – much scarcely known to us today – and, with extraordinary thoroughness, all the chancery rolls, warrants for the great and privy seals, warrants and rolls of the treasury of receipt and much else from the British Museum, Bodleian Library and other repositories. She was the mistress of all that the Public Record Office then offered. A handful of notes and documents preceded the two volumes and 1,121 pages of her *Life and Reign of Edward the Fourth* in 1923. It is as comprehensive a study as was possible at the time. Little that is new has or can be gleaned from the sources that she consulted. What Miss Scofield purveyed was grand narrative, an account of Edward's life and reign that judiciously integrates the political and diplomatic affairs of his reign and scrupulously footnotes them. She wrote what the sources permitted and what the topic demanded, supplying us for instance with remarkably full royal itineraries and details of the recoinage of 1464, but also pursuing as assiduously and exhaustingly red herrings, like the death of Owen Tudor and complaints of Richard Heron, as she did the key events. Amazingly for such a pioneer, her chronologies and explanations have stood the test of time. Only rarely, as in Warwick's whereabouts in 1464, has she been shown to have misunderstood her source. Occasionally her work has been and will be supplemented in detail. More frequently it is adjusted in perspective. Generally however, her chronologies and explanations demand our confidence and are the first port of call – and often, infallibly, the last also – for almost any topic or event. Scofield wrote well, often with vitality and humour, but is valued most today as a source of precise reference: what a pity, therefore, that the precise years are so seldom stated and that the index is so poor! Scofield wrote within the prevailing tradition of constitutional history, which, however, scarcely features in her blow-by-blow accounts of events, in which material motives – such as personal gain and security – crowd out almost completely both principles and idealism. Her explanations seldom move beyond sequences of events to their wider significance: what she wrote was 'magisterial narrative', in the words of Dockray, and in those of Ross 'an exhaustive (and sometimes exhausting) but indispensable narrative of the reign which is unlikely ever to be superseded'.[28] Three final chapters of miscellanea treat themes that she could not otherwise fit in, such as relations with the Church and Lollards, Edward's patronage of learning, the coming of the Renaissance and printing, the quality of Edward's administration of the law and his finances, his trading ventures and relations with parliament. Sadly, it is just such side issues that have most interested more recent scholars. All modern historians must start, nevertheless, with Scofield's *Edward the Fourth*.

Whilst conscious sometimes of gaps or conflicts in evidence, Scofield belonged to that school of historians who believed that the facts speak for themselves. It is not through high rhetoric, persuasive argument or elaborate explanations that she presented her view, but through her arrangement of material, so that only one interpretation was usually possible. She was convinced by York's charges, really propaganda, against the governments of Henry VI, but thought like the duke that the king himself fell short. He was 'a proud and ambitious man rather than a great one' and lacked most of the qualities required of a great leader.[29]

The press of events of Edward's early reign is followed in 1463–4 by a succinct assessment of the new king's performance to date. Since his victories,

> which have made him for ever famous as a warrior king
> … he had been energetic and, on the whole, successful in
> defending the kingdom; and he had shown a highly
> commendable interest in the administration of justice –
> even going to the length of sitting in person for three
> days in the court of King's Bench – and a firm
> determination that the laws of the land should be
> enforced with thoroughness and impartiality. He had also

shown skill in his dealings with friends and foes abroad;
he had even succeeded in outwitting Louis XI, past
master in craft though Louis already was.

Against such favourable reports she cited his taking of money from
his subjects ahead of parliamentary authority, his over-generous
patronage to the undeserving and his extravagance, but allows for
mitigating factors. If 'the favours ... heaped on Somerset' were 'the
most flagrant example of Edward's lack of discretion and taste',
nevertheless 'forgiveness was necessary if the wounds of civil war
were to be healed', whilst display had political value and engendered
pride and popularity in his subjects. She was critical of Edward's
marriage, 'very likely' the product of his 'thoughtlessness and youthful passion', 'both very strange and very unwise', and especially of
its concealment. 'Like all easy-going people', she observed, Edward
'detested a quarrel, and he put off the evil day of confession as long
as he could'. Moreover, 'what was far worse, he let Warwick go on
laying matrimonial plans for him ... What could possibly be more
galling to the man who felt that he had made Edward king?' Here
Edward was clearly at fault and Scofield found it 'impossible not to
sympathise with Warwick at this moment, however much one may
condemn his subsequent acts'. She gave high priority also to the
rival allurements of King Louis and mistakenly follows confused
contemporaries who wrongly connected Warwick's dissatisfaction
with renewed Lancastrian insurgency in 1465–9. Whilst condemn-
ing Edward's cruel manner of revealing to Archbishop Neville his
failure to secure a cardinal's hat and subscribing to the worst interpretations of Wydeville greed and Cook's case, Scofield did not
appear to appreciate what justice there was in the strictures against
Edward's government by the rebels of 1469. Edward's discomfitures
in 1469 and 1470 were attributed in part to himself, not always
justifiably, but his victories in 1471 were fully acknowledged.

Like Stratford, who evidently influenced her more than she
realised, Scofield perceived an early deterioration in the king.

But if out of the troubles of the last ten years Edward the
king had emerged triumphant, Edward the man, sad to
say, had gone down in defeat. Very different from the
brave, frank, generous, well-intentioned youth who had
taken the crown from Henry VI with Warwick's aid in

1461 was the man who came back to England in 1471 to
slay Warwick on the battlefield and Henry in a dungeon
in the Tower. Edward of York was still a young man in
1471 … He was also a brave man still. But ten years of
kingship had taught him many bitter truths and adversity,
instead of making him wiser and better, had coarsened
and brutalised him.

Neither by instinct a despot or a tyrant, Scofield considered that
Edward degenerated from a 'keen sense of the responsibilities of his
high office' and a determination to do well. Sometimes he was
bound to 'offend against the rights and liberties of his subjects' and
a combination of 'experiences of bitter reality … evil and selfish
influences … seemed to cause his nature to undergo a sad alteration', best exemplified in the administration of justice which he
perverted and subverted. There were no constitutional innovations,
'not a single law of lasting value', and indeed he tried to rule
without parliament. 'The most remarkable financial feat Edward
ever accomplished was the waging of war on Scotland for nearly
two years without a grant from parliament for the purpose', which
he managed by decidedly 'high-handed measures'. Apart from his
dealings with Clarence, of which she generally approves, Scofield
concentrates in Edward's Second Reign (1471–83) on his foreign
policy. She documents in pitiless detail the laborious build-up to his
invasion of France, the Treaty of Picquigny, which on the whole she
excuses, and Edward's abject manipulation thereafter by Louis XI,
whose pension was allowed to take priority. 'Edward was blind
indeed', she writes at one point, 'if he could not see that Maximilian
could not possibly hold out much longer. Yet he made no move'.
'No matter how frantically he tried', she writes again, 'Edward
could not prevent the inevitable results of his own folly and wrong-
doing'. Learning of the treaty of Arras between Louis and
Maximilian, she continues,

> The scales dropped from Edward's eyes for ever. Now at
> last he saw how blind and heedless he had been and how
> completely he had allowed Louis to trick him. With what
> eagerness would he now have snatched at a proposal
> from Maximilian for a joint invasion of France! How
> gladly would he have whetted his sword and plunged it

to the hilt in Louis's breast! But the day when he might have done these things had passed never to return, and as he stood viewing the ruins of his impossible foreign policy – impossible because it was conceived, as he well knew, in opposition to his people's wishes and best interests – he must have blushed with shame. Nor was there anything he could do to rectify his blunder or redeem his fame. He had made his bed and he, and England too, must lie in it.

It was an abject ending, followed almost immediately by Edward's death, and marked perhaps the lowest point in the king's historical reputation.

Whilst recognizing the political dangers ensuing from this premature demise, 'when his restraining hand was removed and the sceptre passed to his young and inexperienced son', Edward's legacy was not pursued beyond his death and funeral, and no responsibility is attributed to Edward in what follows. Scofield did not believe the pre-contract story and did not take a moral line. Whilst fully crediting Edward for winning his throne, she awarded him few marks for remaining or for quality of government and damned certain aspects of his rule, some albeit by anachronistic expectations of constitutional progress and judicial independence.[30]

5

The rehabilitation of Edward IV

Edward IV since the Second World War

1923 marked another nadir in Edward IV's degeneration. Henceforth the trend had to be upwards, to at least partial rehabilitation. By the standards of her age, Scofield was a great historian. Her huge book is the foundation for all current and future histories of Edward IV. It contains most of the information that the narrative sources and the government archives have to offer, and presents them methodically and judicially to future historians. As a collection of data it remains indispensable. Scofield was, however, a historian of a particular type and of her time. Since 1923, chronicles and records alike are better understood, as biases are identified, administrative procedures elucidated and legal fictions exposed, and much evidence has ceased to be passive and inert. Other chronicles and classes of record have become available and such categories as records of the central courts, estate accounts and genealogies have been revealed to be relevant. For some historians and some perspectives, as we shall see, such records are supreme: deductions based upon them override all the writers of the past and become almost everything. Moreover, modern historians are much more aware than their predecessors of historiographical processes: that interpretations change. History from below and pacifism have entered the picture. Seldom indeed is only one interpretation possible. Historians today integrate a much wider range of factors and perspectives in the history that they wish to recount. There was no regional dimension to Scofield. She and her predecessors concerned themselves with the provinces and such local disorders as the battle of Nibley Green only where these impinged directly on national events or where such standard sources as the Paston Letters had contributions to make. Much new history has been written on the Yorkists and their age. Although relatively little focuses on Edward IV in person, his brother, Richard, now being much more popular, interpretations of Edward IV have nevertheless changed radically. His reputation is much enhanced.

Scofield wrote within the critical scientific tradition of such constitutional historians as Bishop Stubbs and administrative historians like T.F. Tout. Also a product of both was the Oxford historian, K.B. McFarlane, a remarkable revolutionary who profoundly changed how twentieth-century historians viewed the politics of the whole of late medieval England and not just the Yorkist age.[1] McFarlane refused to see English politics purely through the eyes of the king and to regard the nobility alternatively as obediently loyal or as subversive opponents. English kings normally lacked the inclination to dictate and the power to ride roughshod over their magnates. Politics was a means of reconciling the differing perspectives of plural participants, who socialized, interacted and cooperated. Personal relationships, so Galbraith long ago argued, really mattered;[2] so did the personal compatibility and connections borne of a common aristocratic upbringing, kinship and intermarriage. The greater and lesser aristocracy, in England titled respectively the magnates, nobility and gentry, possessed by their own hereditary right the landed estates that conferred wealth, command over men (bastard feudalism) and local standing, that made them the natural rulers of their home localities and enabled them to wield power and influence in national affairs both in peace and war. They were the king's natural counsellors, those whom the king naturally consulted in parliament, his council and, more informally, who were the obvious agents to fill his offices and implement his commands. It was also they in the last resort, rarely and unwillingly, who challenged him in civil war. If none of them possessed equivalent resources to the king or his claim on his subjects' allegiance, on occasion a few individuals were able to play the overmighty subject.[3] Collectively, there was strength in numbers that no king could disregard. Recognizing how such men mattered, McFarlane appreciated the need to understand their resources, interests, aspirations and points of view, and their ties with those beneath them who supplied the manpower that really counted. His insight occurred, ironically, just as the landed aristocracy faced their greatest challenge and embarked on their final defeat. It is applied today by historians who scarcely have a chance to encounter any English aristocrat or observe them at first hand and has to be transmitted, in an uphill struggle, to undergraduates and readers for whom aristocratic power and privilege is entirely alien, incomprehensible and wrong. Since McFarlane's death in 1966, his approach has continued and has been applied lower down the social scale, to the country gentry and their county communities. McFarlane himself was not really a historian of the Yorkist period, but he inspired those who were – his friend, John Armstrong, his pupils, Charles Ross, David Morgan and Colin Richmond, pupils of his pupils, such as Christine Carpenter, Keith Dockray, Michael Hicks, Rosemary Horrox, and Anthony Pollard – and many others more indirectly. Ross, as we shall see, was to write a full-scale biography of the king in 1974 that has yet to be superseded; it was hailed at the time – and was indeed – 'a political biography in the best tradition of K.B. McFarlane'.[4] Carpenter, Hicks, Horrox and Pollard have approached the reign from the perspectives of his contemporaries or from the standpoints of particular English provinces. The study of particular individuals like Warwick the Kingmaker, particular families like the Hungerfords, particular counties or regions like Warwickshire and the North, and particular disputes like the Great Berkeley Lawsuit have inevitably impacted on the reign and its ruler.

McFarlane's research students did not confine themselves to the study of noble families and individuals. Like the master himself, who explored Lancastrian government in depth, they and others applied themselves to the operations of the government machine. Central to any such study is the royal household: Alec Myers edited the *Black Book* of Edward IV's household and the 1478 household ordinance, whilst David Morgan addressed the role of the household within the royal affinity and in politics.[5] The most influential work on the Yorkist council was by Jack Lander, who demonstrated both its existence and effectiveness, and on Yorkist estate management by Bertram Wolffe, who claimed that Edward had improved the exploitation of the royal estates, enlarged the royal demesne and enhanced substantially its contribution to royal revenues in anticipation of the better-known achievements of Henry VII.[6] Much else has been written. Whilst the Yorkist parliament awaits its historian, although the new edition of the rolls of parliament and ongoing research of the History of Parliament Trust may change that, both Myers and A.L. Brown have surveyed its operation; Lander, Hicks and others have investigated particular acts, types of acts and occasions.[7] Since Scofield's day, major advances have been made in our understanding of the legal system, with full-length studies of the central courts and the justices of the peace. Historians now appreciate how important was mediation and settlement out of court for the peaceful resolution of disputes. The records of the royal courts have become so readily available that historians now routinely use the ancient indictments of the king's bench (KB 9), early chancery proceedings (C 1) and arbitration awards. Professor John Bellamy broke new ground when he assessed the state of law and order and Edward's judicial policy through surviving records;[8] many others have followed, examining particular cases, feuds and actions in detail. The case for Yorkist innovation was judiciously assessed by Charles Ross. It is discussed fully in Chapter 8. Never has so much research been in progress, either specifically on or touching on Edward IV. We now know much more about him and his reign; indeed some accounts scarcely touch on what went before.

Our knowledge of Edward IV and our understanding of him have been profoundly shaped by studies of Richard III. The twentieth century witnessed first resistance to the hostile interpretation of Richard III promulgated by Shakespeare, and then its overthrow. Shakespeare's orthodoxy is now commonly discounted as Tudor propaganda and public debates invariably exonerate King Richard of all blame. The greatest credit here belongs to the Richard III Society, from its first inception, but it is based also on serious historical works by Alec Myers, Paul Murray Kendall and their successors. Assessments of Richard III have always brought in Edward IV. They were brothers. Richard was Edward's successor and dethroned his son Edward V. Richard's youth and early career were passed during Edward's reign and in his service. Richard's earliest crimes, so More and Shakespeare claim, were committed during Edward's reign. Reassessment of Richard, therefore, implies some revision to the reign and contribution of Edward IV. As long ago as 1954, Myers demonstrated how the crimes supposedly committed by Richard III before his accession grew in the telling, particularly after he had been revealed as a wicked king, and were generally absent from the earliest, contemporary sources. Shortly afterwards, Kendall's apology for Richard III dealt at length with his career as Duke of Gloucester under Edward IV. He was consistently loyal, unlike his brother Clarence, a critic of the French treaty in 1475 and a successful commander against Scotland in 1482–3. Heir by marriage of Warwick, he was the greatest of the northern magnates and the king's viceroy in the North, where he was popular, kept good order and whence he drew the forces that made him king. It was Kendall who renewed attention to Edward's devolution of the regions on his most trusted magnates. Richard was revealed as Edward's right-hand man.[9]

The popularity of Richard III has brought funding to the Yorkist era and has thus financed new editions of source material. Whilst certain chronicles remain accessible only in Victorian or earlier editions, such as the *Annales Rerum Anglicarum* (*Annals of English Matters*), attributed to William Worcester and Gregory's Chronicle, the Crowland Chronicle, the short version of *The Arrival of Edward IV*, *Warkworth's Chronicle*, the histories of Richard III of Dominic Mancini and Thomas More and shorter heraldic pieces have been published in modern editions. Some older works have also been reissued. New editions – and critical re-examinations of these sources – have contributed greatly to our understanding of these texts. Many historians have followed Myers' exemplary exculpation of Richard III from crimes committed before his accession. The anthologies of Dockray, Hammond and Sutton, and Myers have made the crucial sources much better known.

Post-war historians made most of the published calendars of the chancery rolls to study royal grants, appointments and commissions. Patronage was the central theme. Not only did this represent concrete evidence of royal intentions and of who was actually in charge in the localities, but it also indicated the relative standing of beneficiaries in royal favour. Since almost all royal grants were in response to petitions from the recipients, it is reasonable to regard them as evidence of the recipients' aspirations and self-interested attitude to royal service. Much valuable work is built on such premises. The problem, however, was that politics was reduced to self-interest and material motivation, often perhaps correctly, little or no allowance being made for ideological issues or principle.

Contemporary appeals to principle were cynically rejected as self-
seeking propaganda. Some preliminary studies of instances demand-
ing such explanations were undertaken by Hicks ahead of the
reassertion of constitutional history by Powell and Carpenter,[10] and
Hughes' exploration of the role of alchemy and myth in the
development of Edward IV's personality and rule.

Yesterday's Edward IV

Jack Lander and Charles Ross were the most influential historians
of the post-war generation and remain so in spite of the amount that
has been written since. Their role is very different. As befitted a
McFarlane pupil, Ross started out as a historian of the nobility and
their records, and was commissioned to write *Edward IV* for the
English Monarchs series. Published in 1974 and recently reissued, it
is the best modern life. Lander, in contrast, started off with the
Yorkists' public archive. His prime contribution is a mere handful of
seminal articles that determine especially how the era is to be interpreted. Both additionally wrote more wide-ranging textbooks. Both
became masters of the surviving narratives, sceptical and critical in
searching for inconsistencies and bias, authoritative in their application of first principles and sure-footed in their judgements. Lander
has influenced those who read his work; Ross taught directly most
subsequent historians of Edward IV. Whilst recognizing the king's
temperamental weaknesses, both ranked him more highly as a king
than Scofield or Stratford.

Lander depicted an England that was neither riven with war nor
particularly with disorder in which the lightning campaigns of the
Wars of the Roses took place. Mortality there certainly was among
the elite and massive loss of property too, but even the latter was
exaggerated, as the long rolls of victims in acts of attainder were
mitigated by clemency, good service and plea bargains, and modified
by the king's brothers and other key figures, who preferred the
permanent security of inheritance to the uncertainty of royal grants
of contested property. Two articles demonstrated the importance
and ubiquity of the Yorkist council in the operation of government.
Another set the two great family networks of the Nevilles and
Wydevilles on solid ground and explored their significance. 'Edward
IV was made king by a faction' dominated by Warwick the

Kingmaker. It was also Warwick who was most offended by the Wydevilles, a worthy and not ineligible family whose rewards were not excessive, if at Warwick's expense, and who have been misrepresented in the historical record by their foes. One focuses on Edward's invasion of France, for which the minimum funding was extracted with difficulty from a reluctant parliament, and another on the state trial of Edward's brother, Clarence, where Lander undermined one of the central charges. Lander's key publication, however, was the earliest, in which he reassessed Edward as a whole, repudiating the 'Modern Legend' deriving from Commynes, whom he thought ill informed, too pro-Louis XI and perversely hostile to Edward IV. He reverted in preference to what Crowland and the public records tell us. Although the historiographical section is insubstantial and actually only a few pages long, it has convinced historians for nearly fifty years: it was the backcloth – and indeed often the foreground – of Dockray's valuable survey in 1999. Whilst admitting that 'by 1469 Yorkist government was so unsuccessful that it was as discredited as Lancastrian government had been ten years earlier', Lander not only showed that the situation was remedied, but also demonstrated how in certain areas – notably law and order – reforms had been attempted from the start. Edward, he demonstrated, kept a close eye on provincial affairs, paid off royal debts and reconstructed royal finances along the lines so praised for Henry VII, and almost certainly anticipated the latter's improvements in public order too. He was not to be blamed for what followed. 'The margin between order and disorder was still small, as it remained for a long time to come, and it depended on the action of a strong king'. His subjects were impressed. Hence Lander felt justified in asserting that Edward was 'a strong man who began to "break the teeth of the sinners", to restore order and even possibly financial stability, and who made easier the work of Henry VII'.[11]

Lander's reassessment needs to be taken with the simultaneous work of A.R. Myers and B.P. Wolffe. If the former re-examined the sources, repudiating Tudor accretions and hence moderating the excesses of Edward's brother, Richard, he contributed also to a more favourable assessment of the household and government of both.[12] It was Wolffe, as we shall see, who made the case for the enlargement of the royal demesne, its more efficient exploitation and its direct control by the king through his chamber, to which he very largely attributed the reconstruction of royal finances (and hence royal power) achieved by King Edward IV.[13] Between them they have given us 'a far more informed understanding of the practical problems of government in late medieval England, and of Edward's considerable success in finding solutions, albeit highly personal solutions, to the more pressing difficulties confronting him'.

The standard view of this generation of historians was represented by the briefly influential textbook of Professor Stanley Chrimes, an administrative and constitutional historian contemporary to McFarlane. Like Lander, Chrimes appreciated just how few backed Edward's usurpation and duly deplored his marriage, but he recognized from the start that 'his aim was untrammelled power for himself as king' and that 'the principal aim of his domestic policy' must be 'the better endowment of the Crown'. 'If the government of England was to continue along its historic path,' declared Chrimes as constitutional historian, it was 'very necessary ... that the monarchy should be restored, re-invigorated, and set along lines which would ensure a far more efficient and vigorous government than Lancaster had ever been able to provide'. All this was made feasible by Edward's 'masterly' recovery of his throne in 1471, which displayed 'his striking abilities ... as never before nor after; his tremendous resilience, energy, and courage; his brilliant military capacity, [and] ... a good measure of guile and cunning'. Not only victory was achieved, but also

> a state of tranquillity and stability for the rest of his life
> such as it has not known for many decades ... Edward IV
> had now attained a position of strength such as no king
> of England had secured for more than a hundred years,
> perhaps indeed not since the days of Edward I in his
> zenith. For the remaining twelve years of his life and
> reign he was without a rival; he was undisputed master
> of his realm ... There was no great magnate left to over-
> shadow the king.

Regrettably, Edward came to suffer 'a certain lassitude and lack of purpose' and 'a decline in his powers of judgement'. It may be that adversity rather than success brought out his best qualities, Chrimes perceptively observed, and that his successes left him 'with no clear objectives. Very likely his tendency to over-indulgence in sensual pleasures of one kind or another induced a loss of grip on matters of state'. If the Picquigny settlement was both common sense and realistic in the manner of Machiavelli, yet nevertheless 'Louis XI had got the better of him'.[14]

> He was to show himself a realist who sought after solid gains rather than vainglory. He did much to consolidate the monarchy, to rehabilitate its finances and to restore its prestige. He stopped the process of decay in monarchy and government. He went far to remedy the 'lack of politique reule and governance' which had brought Henry VI to disaster; he was not to be led astray by Henry V's martial dreams; he grasped firmly the financial nettles which Henry IV had either evaded or sown. He achieved much that Richard II had tried but failed to do … Edward IV's achievements as man and king were not small … The foundations of what has commonly been called the 'New Monarchy' were laid not by Henry VII, but by Edward IV.[15]

Twice quoted by Professor Charles Ross, Chrimes's confident judgement was the starting point for his own work, and it was of Chrimes especially that Ross was thinking when he warned against crediting a consistency of policy that Edward had neither sought nor fulfilled. 'Edward IV', Ross wrote in 1974, 'is the only fifteenth-century king whose reputation stands substantially higher today than it did half a century ago'. 'Of the seven kings who ruled England in the fifteenth century', he had written more fully in 1972, 'only Edward IV stands today in substantially higher repute amongst historians than he did a century, a half-century or even twenty-five years ago'.[16] Advocates of Richard III, then and now, must disagree.

Edward IV did indeed deserve a more favourable press, he concurred, but reassessment could be carried too far, 'investing his policies with a degree of consistency which they did not possess'. Attention should not be deflected from his defects, personal and political, and from his mistakes, some of them big ones. His over-promotion of the Nevilles, his choice of marriage partner and his harassment of Sir Thomas Cook were obvious examples. Apart from 'a sensual disposition which could afterwards be used to blacken his reputation, he was at various times to show traits of impulsiveness, inconsistency, irresolution, and over-confidence'. 'It may also be argued that he was more self interested and lacking in principle'. Edward was guilty of 'extremes of political management'. Much of the blame for the loss of his throne in 1470 was his own fault, 'especially his failure to do much to remedy the abuses which had proliferated under Henry VI'. The deposition of his son in 1483 again depended much on the legacy of political division that Edward IV left behind and had actually largely created. Moreover 'he did not shun Henry V's martial dreams', although he ended up with nothing to show for them, and his reign culminated in his deception by Louis XI and the collapse of his foreign policy. Here Ross's documented and measured verdict aligns closely with those of Commynes and Scofield. 'In recent years', wrote Ross, 'Edward's failings as a politician have tended to be overlooked amidst the general chorus of praise for his achievement in domestic govern-ment'. He then proceeded to downgrade that too. 'Edward's modern reputation rests squarely on his work as a renovator of the royal authority, as a king who brought wealth to the Crown and to his people, as a strong man who kept the peace of the realm'. Whilst all these occurred, they happened in his Second Reign, and were a good deal less thoroughgoing and complete than Wolffe, for instance, had argued. 'Too often there was a gap between theory and practice'; the biggest gap of all, perhaps, and the most fatal, was the making of Richard Duke of Gloucester into the overmightiest of overmighty subjects.

Yet Ross certainly did not take the hatchet to Edward IV. His book is a full account of the reign, up to date and critical, narrative and descriptive where it needed to be, but conceived thematically, proceeding analytically and everywhere judicious in its assessments. Full credit is given to Edward's achievements, which greatly out-weigh any of his deficiencies: his victories; his success in retaining his throne; the reconstruction of royal authority at home and abroad; and the solvency that distinguished him from almost all his predecessors. Neither saint nor scholar, Edward 'possessed many of the assets which go to make a successful king'. Endowed with intelligence and a good memory, he was able and willing to charm anyone, outgoing and liberal, good-natured and even-tempered. A splendid physique was accompanied by all the personal courage and prowess, the self-confidence and inspirational drive to be desired in a military leader of the aristocratic caste to which he himself belonged. Whatever his financial straits, he reinforced his regal image and hence authority by maximizing the magnificent panoply of kingship in a dazzling display of dress, ceremonial, buildings, books, ordnance and the open-handed patronage that successful kings were supposed to practise. He was a hard-working king, active in the office, council and parliament, always with his personal finger upon the pulse and the trigger. 'If he made mistakes, they sprang from the errors of judgement to which he was prone, not from inattention to the kingly business of government'.

Always able to make up his mind and nobody's creature, Edward dealt with the realities of politics rather than abstractions, with real men rather than institutions. 'In his eyes no subject could be over-mighty as long as he enjoyed the royal confidence'. At his accession Edward 'enjoyed exceptional advantages' in the enormous forfeitures of the Lancastrians, which he chose to dispense politically, to build up and buy noble support, rather than to enhance the royal finances – a judgement much criticized by modern historians and which could have been handled better. He never commanded 'anything comparable with the great "Lancastrian connection"'. He advanced those whom he trusted and ruled through them, allowing them considerable freedom in retaining and bastard feudal abuse. Initially Edward relied on the faction that made him king, but a progressively larger group, amongst them the queen's Wydeville relatives, became increasingly prominent. Whatever error this involved, it did not cost Edward much financially, and his new nobility served him well enough, if unsuccessfully, at Edgecote. Following the upheavals of 1469–71, Edward had to 'devise new political settlements for the most rebellious and lawless regions of his realm', albeit with 'very different consequences', and once again relying on those whom he trusted most, henceforth the potentially overmighty subjects who fought out events in 1483. 'The real answer [then] lies in the continued dependence of the Yorkist regime at the highest political level on a small group of over-mighty or mighty subjects'. Only some of the nobility participated in and benefited from Edward's rule and had a stake in that of his son. He read the divisions of 1483 far back into the Second Reign. In his *Richard III* (1981), Ross made even more of this theme, stressing the over-advancement of Gloucester and the unpopular Wydevilles alike and adding a yet graver charge: 'What he had not counted on, or provided for, was his own premature death while his heir was still a minor'. 'In fact it can reasonably be argued that if Edward did not actually increase aristocratic power, he did nothing to diminish it ... He had done nothing to cure the problem of the over-mighty – or even the mighty – subject'. Edward, in short, was a conventional medieval king, who accepted Bishop Russell's later dictum that 'the politic rule of every country rests with the nobility', and who was content to make a success of traditional patterns of rule rather than to change them to something new and progressive. That was the achievement of Henry VII.

Edward was certainly concerned about law and order, and responded vigorously to complaints about its lack. The territorial dispositions of his Second Reign did restore order and perhaps justice too, though Ross was always sceptical about that and Edward may not have cared particularly. Edward was able to achieve the solvency of his last years. The £65,000 to £70,000 annual revenues that he accrued fell far short of those of Henry VII and could have been improved by more systematic exploitation of Wolffe's estate strategy, but political considerations always took priority over financial ones. Thus it was only 'a relative affluence [that] was part of Edward's strength'. Once Edward had survived the foreign-inspired plots of his early years and had at last the leisure to choose without risk his own foreign policy, the king seems to have wished to resume the Hundred Years War and had serious aspirations to be crowned King of France at Rheims when invading France in 1475. Nothing came of it. This aim was not achieved nor seriously attempted. Defeat was avoided on terms that Edward was able to present as victory and some other Englishmen accepted. As Commynes said, Edward's avarice, represented by his French pension and dowry-less marriages for his daughters, came unfortunately to shape policy more than it should have. That war with Scotland resumed in 1480 was very much Edward's choice. It was, Ross thought, a mistake, not only because of its cost and limited success, but because it sidelined him during the struggle between France and Burgundy in which England's real interests were engaged and left him frustrated and impotently raging when he died.

Today's Edward IV

'Almost a quarter of a century on', writes Griffiths, 'Ross's Edward IV remains authoritative ... It is likely to remain the most reliable port of call for anyone seeking to understand Edward IV and his impact on England ... [His] Ross's judgement has not been seriously undermined'.[17] Some of Ross's interpretation 'has certainly not gone unchallenged' even at the time, writes Dockray, citing the reviews *inter alia* by Lander and Wolffe, who generally thought Ross hypercritical, notably on the collapse of Edward's foreign policy and the usurpation of 1483. Yet when Lander next wrote, he tempered his praise of Edward IV.[18] Other historians have started from and written within Ross's new orthodoxy, at least until the last decade, which has produced a surprising outburst of conflicting interpetations. Regrettably, Lander, Myers, Ross and Wolffe have all passed away. It is therefore a new generation of mature scholars that has risen to take their place. All belong to the McFarlane school: Professor Colin Richmond and Mr David Morgan were indeed amongst the last of McFarlane's pupils. Ross himself spawned another four: Dockray, Griffiths, Hicks and Pollard. The academic descent of Carpenter and Horrox is via Dr Gerald Harriss, another eminent McFarlane pupil. As they wrote simultaneously and indeed continue to write, taking each other's works into account rather than actively debating, the following discussion could in fact have treated them in any order.

Since 1974, the most prolific writer on the Yorkist age has been the present author, Michael Hicks. A pupil of Ross, Armstrong and Pugh, he therefore falls within the McFarlane tradition. Hicks's first study of Clarence sought to place Edward's brother on a solid footing, to make sense of and to explain (but not excuse) the duke's turbulent career and to establish the domestic chronology that was lacking for the king's Second Reign, especially the Warwick inheritance dispute and the duke's fall. A series of articles have focused on Edward's contemporaries (Cook, Hastings, the Hungerfords, Northumberland, Gloucester, the Countess of Oxford, Somerset, the Wydevilles), sometimes through episodes crucial to Edward's historiographical reputation, on particular regions and on specific events and acts of parliament. Inheritance, attainder, resumption and their manipulation by king and subjects underpin much of his work. Several papers examine the reality of Gloucester's career as duke and regime in the North in 1471–83; they present a rougher, more thrusting and self-interested duke than the idealization beloved of the Ricardians. These led into a book on Richard himself, since much enlarged, and the most thorough biography of Warwick the Kingmaker to date. Hicks's *Warwick* again attempts to explain rather than to justify the unjustifiable. It documents the earl's dominance in 1461–7 and his neglected popularity – and hence Edward IV's unpopularity – in 1469–71. Not only had Edward lost much of his original appeal, but his recovery of his throne, the fruit of his own prowess, was much against the odds. Hicks has argued forcefully that a combination of foreign intervention by France and Burgundy, popular engagement in politics and financial weaknesses exposed English governments during the Wars of the Roses and made them exceptionally easy to unseat – from which Edward both benefited, in 1460–1 and 1471, and suffered, in 1470. Most recently he has substantiated the immorality that endangered Edward's throne in 1469 and facilitated the deposition of his son, further documented the Wydeville-dominated 'rule' of Wales and revealed more fully the land settlements of his last years that so aggrieved particular magnates. Here and elsewhere, like Horrox, he depicts the Second Reign as essentially peaceful and ordered, in which any fundamental differences between the great were latent rather than active and were far from certain to explode in 1483. Hicks has reassessed a series of modern orthodoxies about Edward and, in the words of Dobson, has become something of a re-revisionist; neither has he been afraid to amend his own work when another approach proves his own interpretation no longer fits. Hicks's work has rather revolved around Edward IV, viewing him from the vantage of a succession of contemporaries, than focused on him, but has offered glimpses of many aspects of him. Edward emerges through Hicks's works both as a sovereign who insisted on his dignity and respect, an effective ruler prepared to engage in endless detail and interviews and a good delegator, but also as a man emotional in his relationships, unwilling to correct his most powerful subjects, unduly trusting and lacking in perception, inclined to let things run and easily managed by those about him who knew what they wanted and planned ahead. Latterly Hicks has become more sceptical of the certainties of the McFarlane school and, like others, has stressed the ideological component of fifteenth-century political culture.[19]

The two Cambridge 'grandpupils' of McFarlane who have written on Edward IV and his reign are Dr Rosemary Horrox and Dr Christine Carpenter. Horrox's principal work is the most detailed study of Richard III's service to Edward IV and of his own servants. It impacts substantially on the Second Reign.[20] It is discussed in Chapter 11. Carpenter is very definitely the principal protagonist for Edward IV writing today. She outshines even Lander's reassessment and is perhaps Edward's strongest partisan since Crowland himself. Few hints of this enthusiasm were included in the Yorkist political narrative contained in the vast study of fifteenth-century Warwickshire (1992) that underpins her *Wars of the Roses* and which at several moments is her model for what was happening nationally. Edward IV was a nobleman first, she reminds us, the natural ally of the nobility, and indicates where this really mattered. Political management is her focus: how Edward managed his realm and how effectively he did so. The challenges faced at his accession are rightly stressed and great weight is attached to the continuing threat posed by Lancastrianism: Henry VI, she argues, should have been put down when captured (in 1465). Having overcome Lancastrian resistance with credit and resurrected respect for the Crown, Edward was confronted by Warwick, who repeatedly refused to 'see reason and accept a position as greatest magnate under the crown rather than persist with his grandiose view of himself as arbiter of England's destinies at home and abroad'. Perhaps the king should have been less casual about rebellions, but 'Edward did not lose his throne in 1470–1 because he had misgoverned … not from bad kingship but from one great noble's personal ambition and the conditions that, most unusually, allowed its free rein'. Back in 1471, Edward made a great success of his Second Reign, except possibly 'in his handling of foreign policy and taxation'. Recovering Berwick was 'militarily and psychologically greatly significant'. Edward was concerned above all with the rule of the provinces. He planned and implemented the devolution of regional power to those he most trusted, who acted thereafter on his behalf, constructed an enormous royal affinity and exercised interventionist control everywhere through agents owing obedience primarily to him. 'Royal governance was operating at a deeper level than in the hey-day of direct rule in the twelfth and thirteenth centuries' – successfully. 'If there is every sign that Edward exercised authority in his second reign on a scale that had never before been seen in England', Carpenter declares, 'there is good evidence that he used it with remarkable wisdom ... What little we know about the effects of all this reordering of the crown's personal power suggests that it served its purpose'. Carpenter, in short, approves Edward's family policy and praises his management of the nobility. She rejects ill-informed critiques from all directions, that Edward was too weak, too easygoing, too strong, too soft on bastard feudalism or indeed responsible for the disaster that followed. Having secured his dynasty, Edward did not plan to die 'at the worst possible moment' (undefined); how could he have expected Gloucester to react 'with an ineptitude that beggars belief'? His rule was almost perfect and 'he should be acknowledged as one of the greatest of English kings'. Nobody has ever written so favourably of Edward IV![21]

Colin Richmond, another pupil of McFarlane, approved Ross's depiction of the fifteenth century, yet his review questioned whether Ross had overstressed Edward's weaknesses[22] – an uncertainty that he has since discarded. Richmond now stands out as the principal prosecutor of Edward IV – our current protagonist of the case against. Richmond's principal work on Edward IV, shared with Margaret Kekewich, is his characteristically trenchant commentary on the state papers in *John Vale's Book* dealing with the crises of his reign. As Edward did not deal well with these crises, nor with the underlying grievances that he failed to remedy, Richmond's assessment was bound to be critical. 'While he was not Henry VI, he was not Henry V either'. 'This chapter traces his failure at critical junctures of his reign to safeguard the long term interests of his dynasty ... The king's governance was less than competent'. Whilst disapproving of Edward's marriage, it was differences in foreign policy, sealed by Margaret of York's Burgundian marriage in 1468, that caused the rift with Warwick: 'The stage was set for the drama of 1469'. By then Edward had failed to fulfil the expectations of his people, manage relations with the Hanse, accommodate the ambitions of Clarence and 'grasp the extent to which he had alienated' Warwick. He handled badly the crisis of 1469, when he was too dilatory and failed 'to gauge both the temper of the political elite and the nation at large', and that of 1470, when he was complacent (as Commynes thought). Edward's opponents, however, 'were shown to be factious rather than offering a genuine initiative for reform', especially Warwick, whose

> confusing, apparently unstructured and unconstructive career has not found favour in our sight. In this post-modernist age the time has perhaps come for revision. Yet what stands in its way is Warwick's amorality: he seems to have been the first of the serial killers of the Wars of the Roses and his bad habits rubbed off on his ward, Richard of Gloucester.

Anachronistic prejudice wars here with penetrating insights. Though the subject matter of the Second Reign differs, mainly in foreign policy, the adverse judgement on Edward IV is repeated. 'To bring the civil wars to what seemed their end was a creditable achievement', but it proved temporary, for his life only, because he created what became the rival powers of Gloucester and the Wydevilles. Richmond doubts that Edward seriously intended the conquest of France in 1475, but is clear about the failure of his foreign policy towards France, Burgundy and Scotland. The Scottish war may have been foisted on him by Gloucester, who also destroyed his domestic settlement. Ultimately it was Edward, the touchstone of government and politics, who was defective.[23]

Between the extremes of Carpenter and Richmond, there fall the moderate updating of Ross undertaken by Griffiths[24] and Dockray, and the major work of Pollard. Professor Anthony (Tony) Pollard, yet another pupil of Ross, has written extensively on the North, particularly of Richard III. A series of exemplary studies of society in Richmondshire and County Durham under the Nevilles and Gloucester culminated in his massive regional study of the north-east, a life of Richard III himself, a textbook on the Wars of the Roses and a judicious and lucid political narrative that treads deftly between the extremes of Richmond and Carpenter. At his accession, Edward was indeed weak and deserves much credit for consolidating his rule, but he failed to satisfy expectations and prevent general disillusion by 1468. Whilst he relied heavily on the Nevilles, he was never their puppet, but over-rewarded them. He offended Warwick unnecessarily with his marriage, made friction into a rift by his foreign policy and generally handled him badly, but Warwick, also

and indeed especially, expected too much and ultimately precipitated the civil wars of 1469–71. Edward won his kingdom back and
kept it. Pollard credits Edward with his victory and with his financial achievements. He is critical of Edward's French policy both in
1475 and after. The devolution of regional power so stressed by
Carpenter was significant, but not original, and appears to have
kept the peace, but Pollard questions whether it operated to the
king's advantage. It was mistaken to advance the royal family over
royal servants, to devolve power locally to mutually antagonistic
factions and especially to advance Gloucester in the North so excessively that he came to shape the king's other policies. It was
Gloucester who wanted war with Scotland and made support for
Burgundy impossible. Far from securing his regime, as Carpenter
supposed, Pollard argues, like Richmond, that Edward left his realm
riven with internal contradictions and hence easy to destroy.

> He was no Henry V or Henry VIII: he did not command
> the same dread as other monarchs whose dynasties
> survived minorities. His interest in the affairs of state and
> the act of governing was neither intense nor sustained.
> His vision did not stretch beyond his origins. His rule
> stayed as it had begun, that of a faction victorious in two
> civil wars ... Unlike Henry V, [he was] unable to
> transcend in the wider interests of the kingdom the
> partisan character of his dynasty's origins and the family's
> self-interest. Yet the house of York, unlike the house of
> Lancaster, shows little sense of family solidarity. It should
> thus not occasion surprise that Edward V's sons were
> quickly removed not from without by his family's
> enemies, but from within by one of its own members, the
> dead king's brother, Richard of Gloucester.[25]

Keith Dockray, a fourth pupil of Ross, did not incorporate new
research in his sourcebook on Edward IV, but he did bring to it a
first-hand familiarity with the period over many years, an exhaustive reading of the secondary literature, including authors not
reviewed here, and a capacity for trenchant criticism, perceptive
insights and, on occasion, shrewd discrimination between opposing
views. Often he offers the most rapid and sure-footed access to
current issues for and against. Dockray starts with a survey of

historical writing on the king from his own day forth and moves on to a series of thematic chapters, each introducing a range of primary sources. Verdicts are offered on the controversies, mostly judicious, occasionally unduly tentative or perverse. Perhaps Dockray is at his best on the crises of 1469–71. 'Edward IV did not figure on the scene [in 1469] at all until it was over and it is difficult to avoid the conclusion that he had completely failed to appreciate the seriousness of the situation'. And 'even when all allowances are made for good fortune [in 1471], he was the prime architect of his own destiny'. On balance, Dockray is more favourable to the king than Ross, following most closely Pollard's lead and firmly rejecting Carpenter's eulogy. 'So very positive a judgement as Carpenter's ... is unlikely to win general acceptance by most fifteenth-century historians: it *is*, however, very much in the tradition of so many outspoken verdicts on this fascinating and controversial king'.[26]

Tomorrow's Edward IV?

Dockray, of course, was writing the final word when writing in 1999, but others have written since. The school of McFarlane rules the Yorkist roost and debates about Edward IV. McFarlane taught his followers to stress practical considerations and material motives, which they accessed most often through the chancery rolls and the patronage that was a dominant theme of the fifteenth-century conferences in the 1970s. McFarlane explicitly rejected the anachronistic constitutionalism of Bishop Stubbs and his other immediate predecessors. Ideas and principles were not to be ignored, when explicitly recorded and asserted, but it was in self-conscious reaction to this materialism and patronage-led history that Carpenter, Hicks, Horrox and Powell have argued for their resurrection and indeed primacy. Here they meant not our values and expectations – not the political correctness of either Stubbs's Victorian or their own third-millennium Britain – but those that were current in what they recognized was a significantly different culture from our own. Obviously such ideas mattered, influenced the political actors, including the kings, and even determined their actions. Contemporary concerns about Edward IV's perjuries and his skilful deflection of them are obvious instances. To establish such ideas, to analyse and to understand them better, though complex, is of course very different from the much more difficult task of charting their actual impact on particular individuals and specific events. Conceded that distinctive principles were commonly shared, how can we determine, five centuries afterwards, which ones must have prevailed in any given set of circumstances? Sometimes our actors have told us and sometimes deduction is feasible, as some limited case studies have shown, but in most cases we cannot know at present. Potentially this kind of history is so much more difficult that even its avowed protagonists, Carpenter and Hicks, have found it easier to write McFarlanesque histories of Edward IV and his contemporaries that do not differ in kind from those written by anyone else. The fullest survey to date (by Hicks) found too much to cover and deliberately excluded from its discussion as a step too far the 'symbolism, ceremony and ritual, folklore and literary culture, superstitions and the supernatural',[27] even though contemporaries took such matters seriously and surely sometimes allowed such considerations, we must suppose, to shape their actions. That list could well have been extended to include alchemy, astrology and myth, Arthurian and otherwise, which interested King Edward to at least some extent, which he apparently cultivated and thus ought somehow to have affected his actions and hence our assessment of him.

Jonathan Hughes's book, which explores such issues, therefore opens out a new way to approach and assess the king. He breaks with the McFarlane tradition, of which he sometimes reveals little awareness: if Hughes is not in command either of the standard primary sources or secondary literature, this need not necessarily discredit his approach when better executed. Hughes develops aspects of Edward's history that few historians understand. He focuses on the role of contemporary superstitions, which historians today discount, but which contemporaries – or at least some of them – took very seriously indeed. The Genesis story, Trojan and Arthurian myths were historically true, prophecies were authoritative predictions that needed to be applied correctly to events, and alchemy could indeed permit metals to be transmuted and ailments to be cured. Astrology and alchemy had determined temperaments, characters and talents, and were therefore harnessed through the medical regimes to which Henry VI and Edward IV were subjected. 'One key to Edward IV's sense of self and destiny was alchemy,' summarizes M.K. Jones.[28]

Alchemy and the stars shaped Edward's erratic and contradictory personality, alternately dynamic and inert. The most daring and aggressive warrior, assiduous administrator and ruthless politician could also be indolent, self-indulgent, forgiving to the point of folly and quite ineffective. Only his charm and geniality never left him. Emotional in foreign policy, Edward was decisively disadvantaged vis-à-vis the cool calculations of King Louis. Thus it is Edward, the real man behind the monarch, who is central to Hughes's book. Formative influences are explored. The vision of three suns at Mortimer's Cross, at a time of bereavement and supreme political crisis 'gave him an exalted sense of his own existence and power as a man of destiny chosen by God'.[29] Edward was a most charismatic youth, Hughes points out, who offered new hope and of whom everything was hoped, possessed a visionary sense of mission and asserted that astrology, alchemy, the lessons of history and myth were important guides. 'There is no gainsaying the achievement of Edward,' he writes, 'an essentially instinctive ruler, in assimilating, with the help of courtiers such as Anthony Woodville, pragmatic, scientific Roman values in government and education, and in creating out of the civil war thirteen years of relative peace and prosperity'. Even his recoinage, surely best explained as a money-raising expedient, was 'the most telling demonstration of the philosophical dimension to the pursuit of wealth'. Here Hughes exaggerates, as also in his belief that Edward's court was 'renowned throughout Europe for its wealth and glamour'.

Yet Hughes is not just *for* Edward IV. He has much to say *against* him also: Edward deteriorated, as indeed he did, and was already failing to fulfil his potential by 1470 when, not yet thirty, he was already 'a disempowered and enfeebled king [who] had lost his energy and vigour, dissipated in lust, eating, drinking and idleness' and could no longer rule by sheer force of personality. Avarice prevailed. The healing properties of alchemy demanded moderation to work. Here we hear echoes of Chrimes and even Stratford, who also thought that the king deteriorated. Yet Edward had another thirteen years of effective rule ahead of him. Clearly the physical deterioration that definitely did happen is antedated. Evidently also Hughes misunderstands Edward's need for money, not just for liberality and display but to survive, and is ignorant of the poverty in which he died.

Hughes builds on the genealogies used by Dr Alison Allan and Professor Glanmor Williams, supplements them with alchemical and other texts, exploits a wider range of allusions, both nominal and visual, and generally makes more of the data than anybody before him. More is also extracted from chronicles and other familiar texts, such as those of William Worcester. These essentially literary sources are multiplied, deeply analysed and cross-referenced most impressively. But what do they mean? They recycled the myths and traditions of Clare, Mortimer and York covered in Chapter 2, made out the case for the young king's accession and assisted his acceptance, celebrated his return in 1471 and prepared for his invasion of France, accompanied and decorated all the set-piece rites of passage of the new royal house. To show such ideas were current and self-consciously developed to the advantage of the Yorkists, to demonstrate that Edward himself encountered some of them and their specialist practitioners and that he would have liked some of the benefits does not, however, prove that the king understood them all, commissioned them, necessarily believed them or let them lead where he did not wish to go, nor indeed that they were widely known, understood, believed and acted on. How many people ever saw or could study in minute detail, even hanging up, genealogical rolls many feet long? How many appreciated all the other nuances of livery badges or picked up those esoteric allusions of which even Dr Hughes is unsure? Rhymes and manifestos could surely reach larger audiences, but with simpler messages. Convincing connections between the texts and symbols and political realities can be made as seldom as with ideas and principles, and Hughes too often leaps from the deductions of others to crude statements of fact. Whilst he has much to say that is new, original and valuable, as yet he is more successful in amplifying and developing what is already known than in substantially altering perceptions and assessments of King Edward IV. Perhaps others will follow where he has led. As yet it is too early to determine whether his book marks a change in direction and an enrichment of historians' study of the king – a preview of tomorrow's Edward IV – or whether it will prove a curious cul-de-sac. The book is not yet closed: Edward IV's turbulent posthumous career has not reached its full stop.

6

Edward's first reign

Success into failure

Edward IV acceded to the throne as the heir of Edward III through the female line via the second son, in preference to Lancaster's right through the third son. Justifiable under primogeniture, his succession nevertheless conflicted with much contemporary practice, for landholders frequently entailed their lands on males in preference to females, and his title was disputed vigorously. Sir John Fortescue, the Lancastrian's principal propagandist, produced yet other objections to the female succession. The Lancastrian cause was not refuted by argument, as rebellions persisted and a succession of plotters were uncovered, until in 1470 Henry VI was revealed to be overwhelmingly popular and generally acknowledged once again as the rightful king. The Yorkist title prevailed not in reasoned debate, but on the field of battle and by the extermination of the Lancastrian royal family, which their supporters had to accept. All subsequent dynasties have been descended from Edward IV and all subsequent historians have accepted Edward's case, even whilst admitting that had circumstances been different – had the sons of Henry IV produced legitimate sons and had there been a plethora of royal dukes in the 1450s – Lancastrian rule, backed by parliamentary and other male entails, would have continued.

It was a great achievement for Edward to retain the throne he won in battle. Historians of Edward's own day divided his First Reign into two parts. The opening years, up to his victory at Hexham (1464) and the capture of Henry VI (1465), were a series of campaigns against the Lancastrians in Northumberland. The second quinquennium, from then on, began with his marriage and recorded the frictions with Warwick that culminated in the latter's coups in 1469 and 1470 and Edward's deposition. An infusion of

records, from Rymer's *Foedera* to the *pièces justificatives* appended
to French chronicles and the chancery calendars, has facilitated a
much fuller picture. Historians now recognize Towton (1461) as
decisive. Thereafter Edward IV not only saw off remaining
Lancastrian resistance, but also in time secured foreign recognition,
winkled his rivals out of their foreign refuges and consolidated his
position at home through the exercise of patronage, devolution of
authority in the localities, his reforming policies and the promise to
attack France, which are discussed in subsequent chapters.
Resistance was confined to the peripheries, to Northumberland,
Harlech in North Wales and Jersey. Edward delegated their
reduction to others. The Lancastrians did not give up hope and did
not cease planning invasions and plottings, all of which were easily
quashed. How to decide whether the handful of Lancastrians
scattered countrywide exposed in Cook's case (1468) and on other
occasions were all there were, as many historians including the
present author suppose, or were symptomatic of deeper and more
dangerous unease, is difficult to decide.

The primary role of Warwick and the Nevilles in achieving the
first two results in the first four years of his reign has always been
universally admitted. Edward owed them much for their roles in
making him king, destroying the northern Lancastrians, conducting
much of his foreign policy and taking the lead both in council and
in court ceremonial. Warwick indeed was the public face of the
regime as seen abroad: of course, it suited the king that his representative should be thought able to deliver what he promised and it
enabled him to focus on other matters at home. On occasion it was
Warwick who was perceived by foreigners as the prime mover in
English affairs. The Nevilles were duly rewarded. It was Charles
Ross who first itemized the immense and almost monopolistic
grants that they accrued. They were known to have been well
rewarded. 'To list Warwick's dignities and rewards in detail', Ross
observed, 'would involve an excessively lengthy catalogue', which
he therefore located in an appendix. Even that can be augmented.
The king's 'debt to his political mentor and ally was clearly great',
yet it cannot 'dispel the impression that Edward was excessively
generous and Warwick excessively greedy'.[1] Evidently Ross felt that
the earl and the Nevilles were over-rewarded and that some cutback
was therefore to be expected. Naturally he was well aware of the rift

between king and earl that was to follow and could not altogether exclude it from the narrative that preceded it. Ross's line makes good twentieth-century sense and has been followed by almost all subsequent commentators.

Whether it made sense at the time is doubtful. The Nevilles' rewards came in stages – the captaincy of Calais, West March and keepership of the seas in the 1450s, the chancellorship and Cinque Ports in 1460 – all of which Edward was bound to confirm, and only parts (admittedly significant) thereafter. Inevitably the Nevilles expected further great services to bring additional rewards. Nor were the Nevilles monolithic. Warwick's uncle, Fauconberg, so recently lavishly endowed as Earl of Kent, died without male heirs in 1463, and a wedge was later to be driven between Warwick and his brother, Montagu. Their interests were bound to diverge. Nor was the Neville dominance lasting. The Fauconberg estates were partitioned among Kent's daughters and those of Warwick were scheduled to be splintered into three. Moreover, the Nevilles did deliver everything that Edward wanted of them. It was because it was Montagu who annihilated the northern Lancastrians that it was he who was created Earl of Northumberland in 1464. However immense were the rewards of the Nevilles, they posed no problem to the king, subject 'to the continuing identity of interest between the young king and his greatest subject'.[2] That of course was to be the point.

Chrimes stressed that Edward was always in charge even in his early years. 'However warily he may have had to walk' and however much Warwick may have been the public face of his regime abroad, the king 'was at no time a mere pawn' in Neville hands. 'He seems to have had no intention of allowing him [Warwick] to dominate the real course of diplomacy or to dictate the more conclusive negotiations. The vital decisions', Chrimes claimed somewhat less credibly, 'were taken behind his back or in spite of him'.[3] Ross was also anxious to establish that Edward was never the earl's puppet. Edward was certainly the front-runner in making himself monarch and in winning the requisite battles. Ross revealed that the Nevilles did not have everything their own way. Young and inexperienced though Edward was, suitably grateful and sometimes overawed by his cousin Warwick, he had to make use of and reward other supporters, to consult more widely during Warwick's frequent absences and proved capable, on occasion, of refusing the earl's requests, revoking grants already made and pursuing alternative policies. 'These actions, so early in the reign, are a very clear indication that Edward intended to be master where his own plans for government were at stake, and that his indulgence to his powerful cousin's ambition had definite limits'.[4] It was Herbert, formerly the officer of the earl as well as the king, not the insistent Warwick, who became the king's viceroy in South Wales. Edward deserves credit for holding the regime together from the centre, for maintaining and exploiting amicable relations with London and parliaments, and for reconciling many Lancastrians, albeit not all and not necessarily permanently. Whatever his avowed intentions, Edward did not in practice command any campaigns, but left them to the Nevilles in the North and to a succession of lieutenants in Wales, finally and successfully, William Herbert Earl of Pembroke. Edward was a good delegator. 'Together, in these years of crisis, the king and earl [of Warwick] formed a formidable partnership'.[5]

Thereafter things went wrong. There was much to commend Edward's decision to broaden his control and his selection of men to advance and trust. Their emergence, Ross declared, 'is the most important factor in the politics of Edward's first decade. As a group, the king's men showed considerable loyalty and political homeogenity'.[6] William Lord Herbert, from 1468 Earl of Pembroke, did for Edward in Wales what in the North was achieved by the Nevilles, with whom, however, his aspirations clashed. The king and the kingmaker quarrelled and from 1469 came to blows. There was nothing inevitable about this: a series of frictions and reconciliations intervened. Edward's men were defeated at Edgecote near Banbury and he himself was arrested. Released, he faced and quashed the Lincolnshire Rebellion in 1470 and expelled Warwick and Clarence from his realm, but was himself driven out the next year. Whilst Warwick's successful invasion enjoyed foreign support and the backing of the Lancastrians, the causes both of its occurrence and success lie in Edward's First Reign. This chapter considers three factors that have been cited by previous historians: the king's marriage and its consequences, in terms of the advancement of the Wydevilles and the realignment of his own foreign policy; the failures of Edward's own rule; and Warwick himself.

The king's marriage and its consequences

Unmarried at his succession, the new king needed to marry and produce the son who alone could secure the succession, continue the regime and ensure future stability. In the short run, an heir was not urgent, for Edward was young, had two brothers living and was not yet attractive to the continental powers into which kings of England customarily married. Once secure, his hand was sought by rulers anxious to provide for their female relatives and was indeed England's principal diplomatic asset. Whilst the king sought sexual gratification and may even have promised marriage elsewhere, all the king's councillors, his great council and parliament, and publicly the king himself, expected him to marry a foreign princess. Preliminary negotiations begun for several alternatives had by September 1464 reached the serious stage, when Warwick had reached an understanding with Louis XI for his sister-in-law Bona of Savoy. A decision now had to be made. At this point the king revealed that he was already married to Elizabeth Grey (née Wydeville), widow of Sir John Grey (d. 1460), heir presumptive to the modest Ferrers of Groby barony. She was daughter of Richard Wydeville, Lord Rivers, and Jacquetta of Luxemberg, Dowager-Duchess of Bedford. An English subject, with many English relatives which all continental princesses were without, she was not the customary virgin, but possessed two sons, Thomas and Richard Grey.

This match flouted the expectations of almost everyone: his mother, who supposedly denounced it; the great council, who apparently tried to annul it; Warwick and supposedly most of the nobility; and every historian up to Jack Lander in the mid-twentieth century. Elizabeth could offer none of the solid political advantages of a diplomatic marriage. Even her personal attributes were readily available to Edward in his mistresses. Love, passion and romance, Vergil observed, were irrational. They appealed nevertheless to the imagination. Hence the match was located, probably unhistorically, on May Day, the most romantic date in the calendar, and Elizabeth was presented as the model of virtue whom Edward could not seduce and had to marry instead. Both these stories date from the 1460s, in *Gregory's Chronicle* and Antonio Cornazzano's *Of Admirable Women* (1468); also to 1469, almost certainly, dates the tale of clandestine irregularity and even sorcery elaborated by Gloucester in 1483.[7] By casting doubt on all these versions, the fragmentary record evidence suggests that Edward regarded Elizabeth as his potential mistress rather than his consort. From 1483 it was claimed that Edward had promised marriage to another lady or ladies, Eleanor Butler and perhaps also Elizabeth Lucy, before Elizabeth Wydeville, and that such marriages took precedence over hers, which was therefore invalid. Since these pre-contract stories were publicized in support of Richard III, to justify his usurpation, most historians from Crowland and More have discounted or attempted to refute them.[8]

However that may be, the mainstream tradition was highly critical. With the exception of Crowland, *all* contemporary historians trace from this marriage the disasters of 1469–71. Everyone had perforce to accept the *fait accompli* and many of the highest nobility indeed hastened to marry their heirs to the new queen's sisters. They and their heirs, such as the second Henry Bourchier Earl of Essex (d. 1540), prided themselves on their consequent royal connections.[9] Prominent at court and with some say alongside such other Yorkist parvenus as Herbert, the Wydevilles made much of their links with continental royalty and were credited with encouraging Edward's decision to align his foreign policy with Burgundy rather than France. Hence the tournament of Anthony Wydeville, Lord Scales, with the Bastard of Burgundy (1467), the marriage of Margaret of York to Duke Charles of Burgundy (1468) and the aggressive alliance with Burgundy against France. Although Warwick swallowed any embarrassment with his diplomatic partners and also had to acknowledge his new queen, escort her into Reading Abbey in 1464 and preside over her churching, he was not altogether appeased and supposedly found many of the ensuing events offensive, some of which undoubtedly shut off his own legitimate aspirations for his heirs and rejected his own preference for a French alliance. Warwick's disaffection was connected by some contemporaries and subsequent historians with renewed Lancastrian subversion, although no connection was proven then or indeed has been since. The mainstream historical tradition from Edward's own day finds all these subsequent frictions and the eventual explosion to have been caused by the marriage. Crowland, in contrast and in isolation, stresses instead the differences in foreign policy, which Vergil and other successors who used his chronicle up until the late twentieth century rejected.

The mainstream tradition was codified under Henry VIII by Edward Hall, for whom the marriage was of prime significance. Hall devoted two whole folio pages of print to critically reassess the various candidates and the negotiations. Edward IV was in love. Moreover he deprecated Elizabeth's attractions: Edward 'phantasied' her, for she was a 'formal beauty' – soberly handsome – rather than a knockout. The nobility, he reports, were shocked. Hall dwells devastatingly on the disastrous consequences:

> what murder, what misery, and what trouble ensued by reason of this marriage; for it cannot be denied, but for this marriage King Edward was expelled [from] the realm, and durst not abide. For this marriage were the Earl of Warwick and his brother miserably slain. By this marriage were King Edward's two sons [the Princes in the Tower] declared bastards, and in conclusion deprived of their lives. And finally by this marriage, the queen's blood was utterly in manner destroyed. So that men did afterwards divine, that either God was not contented, nor yet pleased with this marriage, or else that he pursued King Edward in his posterity for the deep deceiving and covert cloaking with his faithful friend the Earl of Warwick.

Less convinced by this argument, perhaps more attributable to 'human conjecture' than to 'divine revelation', Hall nevertheless reported that 'all men', including himself, 'for the most part agree that this marriage was the only cause, why the Earl of Warwick bore grudge and made war on King Edward'.[10]

Hall's serious assessment was digested by Holinshed and Stow and recurs in Shakespeare's *Henry VI Part III*. Already a bachelor with sons, Edward's licentiousness is the essential backcloth to the courtship scene that Shakespeare borrows from More. Having lost her husband on the Yorkist side – simpler to explain than the truth – Elizabeth innocently sues for her dower, the king responding ambiguously but suggestively, against the running commentary of the king's two brothers, who anticipate what he wants in return.

Once this is made plain to her, 'He is the bluntest wooer in Christendom,' jokes Clarence. Elizabeth declines:

> Why, then, mine honesty shall be my dower;
> For by that loss [I] will not purchase them.

Impressed, Edward offers her marriage, at which she cavils.

> I know that I am too mean to be your queen,
> And yet too good to be your concubine.

When more sober considerations are raised, Edward sweeps them aside:

> Suppose they take offence without a cause,
> They are but Louis and Warwick; I am Edward,
> Your king and Warwick's, and must have my will.

A slave to his passions (and hence deplorable), the headstrong king has miscalculated badly.[11] Disasters inevitably ensue.

If not blaming everything on the marriage, nevertheless, Habington was highly critical and highly perceptive too. There were:

> Reasons of state ... against a marriage so unequal to
> Majesty, by alleging the peril of mutuality to so potent a
> neighbour as King Louis, and so dangerous a subject as
> Warwick, as likewise the inconvenience of raising a
> widow to his bed, who could bring nothing with her but
> poverty, and an unprovided issue. Who if not advanced
> by him, would be suitors to his children, if advanced a
> ruinous charge to his Exchequer and an envy both to the
> princes of his blood, and the nobility of his kingdom. But
> love like a cunning Sophister easily repelled all politic
> arguments ... The nobility in general looked
> discontented, or else forced a smile ... Hereafter his
> [Warwick's] thought grew dangerous, and only
> opportunity was wanting ...[12]

Because it was unpublished, Habington was quite unaware of the even worse picture presented by Buck, the first serious historian to credit the pre-contract story. To Buck, Eleanor Butler was respectable, the story derived from 'a grave and learned man and counsellor of state' in Bishop Stillington and reported 'by the honourable and veritable historian Philippe de Commynes'. After marrying Eleanor and fathering a child by her, Edward had married the unworthy Queen Elizabeth.

> And thus you see how this lustful [king] lost his honour
> and his reputation and very many and very great and best
> friends by this mean and base marriage, and he had much
> trouble afterwards ... Therefore, all circumstances
> considered, this marriage was a dishonourable and a rash
> contract and a perilous act.[13]

Almost all subsequent historians have agreed that Edward's Wydeville marriage was a gross personal and political error. 'The king had already committed a signal act of indiscretion, distasteful to the nation, and doubly so to the Nevilles,' declared Sir James Ramsay.[14] 'Dame Elizabeth' was succinctly dismissed by Chrimes as having 'indeed ... little to recommend her for the vacant post of Queen from anyone's point of view, least of all that of the Yorkist old guard'.[15] 'His singularly ill-advised marriage in 1464 to the penniless widow of a former Lancastrian [was] the first major blunder of his political career,' stated Ross yet more emphatically.

> The best explanation may also be the simplest – that it
> was the impulsive love match of an impetuous young
> man ... But on the most charitable view his marriage was
> an impulsive and unstatesmanlike act. He acted rashly
> and he acted alone ... Edward increased his difficulties by
> his refusal to face these issues squarely and without delay.
> If Edward's motives in making this remarkable
> misalliance remain a matter for awestruck speculation, its
> consequences were a matter of high political concern, and
> contributed ultimately to the downfall of the Yorkist
> dynasty.[16]

'The main motive behind what was in many ways a very unsuitable match for a king of England', Carpenter wrote twenty years later, 'was almost certainly youthful impetuosity, impelled principally by Elizabeth's desirability'. His marriage to Elizabeth Wydeville was a disastrous mistake, stated Dr Grant. Edward's 'unsuitable' marriage was also condemned by Professor Richmond: 'her large and impecunious family quickly became figures of hatred for the populace and occasions of discontent among the political elite'. 'The king's marriage to Elizabeth Woodville proved a major political blunder, as contemporary and near-contemporary sources make clear,' adjudged Dockray. 'Certainly critical comment far exceeded any compliments that came their way'.[17] As critical, but much more mildly so than another recent history, the almost avuncular Professor Pollard thinks Elizabeth not

> entirely the appropriate choice for a king. It can only be the case that he married Elizabeth, in the face of convention and in preference to the expected diplomatic match, because he was in love ... Matters were made worse by the king's deception. ... It was the manner of the marriage, as much as the fact, which shows Edward's lack of confidence and judgement.[18]

Even if 'the shock/horror reaction to the new queen proved to be no more than a nine days' wonder', as Dockray sensible opines, what was 'more politically significant ... was the advancement of the Woodville clan which almost inevitably followed'. The queen's kin were both numerous and predatory.[19] The traditional orthodoxy had been thoroughly reassessed for the first time in 1963 by Lander, who found it wanting. Elizabeth's lineage was not as humble as hitherto supposed, nor were her family unduly advanced. Their main rewards arose from voluntary marriages with the nobility at no cost to the Crown, which were somewhat misrepresented by the pro-Warwick chronicler pseudo-Worcester, who stressed the objections, themselves sometimes unreasonable, of Warwick himself.[20] Actually Lander miscalculated somewhat. The Wydevilles were less landed than he supposed, their rewards – such as the Lord Treasurership – were not to be belittled, and it is anyway contemporary perceptions, almost universally derogatory, that should guide us today. Furthermore, T.B. Pugh showed from one contract between the queen's father, Earl Rivers, and Lord Herbert, that the costs of the marriage of their children were met by lands from the Crown. 'This document reflects Lord Rivers's confidence that he could induce Edward IV to do exactly what suited the Wydevills'.[21] In response, Ross broadly accepted Lander's refutation of the 'inordinate promotion of the queens relatives', which 'has shown these criticisms to be excessive in many respects'. Edward had not endowed them himself, matrimony was achieved voluntarily and, above all, provision 'largely achieved without impoverishing the crown'. The financial cost 'had not, after all, proved high'.[22] That has been contested, since several others of the Wydeville marriages were sweetened with hereditary estates from the Crown;[23] in another instance the queen herself advanced the necessary money to betroth her own son, Thomas Grey, to the Exeter heiress, Anne Holland. Evidently Edward decided not merely to support and advance the queen's family, but to raise all her sisters to at least comital status: a remarkably inflated assessment of their standing in the light of their origins, the paucity of contemporary earls and from almost any other angle. Carpenter comments unfavourably on the number of beneficiaries. To compound the situation, Anne Holland was actually already plighted to George Neville, the young nephew and male heir of Warwick himself, to whom this was a direct insult.[24] Other potential spouses for Warwick's own daughters were denied to them. The political costs of the Wydeville marriages therefore remained substantial. Letting the Wydevilles scoop the marriage market gave Warwick a genuine grievance. Since the king's brothers were also barred to Warwick's daughters, Clarence was also aggrieved: for him, Warwick's daughter was the most attractive spouse to hand.

Obviously the rise of the Wydevilles and any consequent frictions originated in the marriage of the queen, but Elizabeth herself may not have been involved, so Pollard has cogently argued,[25] and certainly not so actively as her father, brother and sons. Some personal interest can definitely be attributed to her, for example in funding her sons' successive marriages and endowments,[26] but no blame from such conduct necessarily accrues. Providing for her sons was the sort of patronage to her family that was to be expected of any queen, most of whom, however, were foreigners with few domestic connections. Any other behaviour would have been frowned upon. The willingness of other noble houses owed much to the endowments and comital titles that they secured by marrying into the queen's kindred. That such extensive provision for the Wydevilles was made was the decision of the king in the light of his own somewhat inflated notion of what was appropriate. That Warwick's reaction was so extreme was also not to be expected.

About the same time that Lander exposed pseudo-Worcester and Commynes, the accounts of Sir Thomas More and Polydore Vergil were being impugned by Ricardians as Tudor propagandists, leaving only Crowland as a front-rank source to explain the collapse into further civil wars in 1469–71. Admittedly strictly contemporary and well informed, Crowland was now the prime source, whom both Lander and Ross rated very highly. Faced by the *First Continuation*'s claim that Edward IV's Wydeville marriage was the root cause of his breach with Warwick, Crowland had deliberately and firmly disagreed. It was foreign policy, he said, that was the key.[27] Led first by Chrimes and Ross, subsequent historians such as Hicks (1978, 1998 and 2003), Dockray (1999) and Pollard (2003) have accepted Crowland's judgement. 'The second Crowland continuator, indeed, specifically identified disagreement over foreign policy as the truly authentic key to Warwick's behaviour in the later 1460s'.[28] We all appear to have been wrong. It has long been realized that the story that Edward IV was a bastard was circulated in 1469, almost certainly with Warwick's approval, to undermine Edward's title to the Crown. It now also appears much more likely that the sorcery charge that Warwick orchestrated against the queen's mother aimed to discredit the king's Wydeville marriage and hence to bastardize his legitimate offspring.[29] On the strength of Crowland's account, modern historians have implied that these charges were tactics pursued in the quarrel rather than the real causes of it, which lay in differences over foreign policy. Now that it is fully apparent that Crowland stands on his own, in contradiction of almost all contemporary and other primary testimonies,[30] this looks less likely. On other occasions, Crowland took what appears a perverse but official line in his verdicts on Charles the Bold's conduct and the honourable treaty of the Picquigny expedition and the draconian justice of the king immediately afterwards.[31] Edward IV and the Wydevilles, we may imagine, were anxious to deflect blame for what followed from the king's marriage. Perhaps Crowland toed this line. He certainly appears to be incorrect. Differences on foreign policy both symptomized the discord between king and earl and exacerbated it. Moreover, Warwick seems to have had the last laugh. As we shall see, Edward's aggressive coalition against France was scuppered almost at once by the Treaty of Péronne.[32]

Edward IV's unpopularity

Richard Duke of York made reform into a popular cause in the 1450s and in 1460, when the Yorkists seized power in his Third Protectorate, but the Yorkist bid for the Crown, which involved deposing Henry VI, seems to have given the Lancastrians a cause and supporters to fight for them. Just how popular the young Edward was at his succession – when, as we have seen, his propagandists did their best for him – is not at all clear. Certainly he posed as the heir of reform, committed to peace, better governance, solvency and justice. Apparently he was accepted as such by the London mercantile élite who funded him, and it was as such that he chose to pose on occasion, most notably when telling the 1467 parliament that he intended to finance his own regime from his ordinary revenues except 'in great and urgent causes'. These promises were difficult to keep. Edward conspicuously failed to bring peace. Rather than extending support for the regime, his distribution of titles and lands and territorial reordering fomented division, setting Lords Herbert and Stafford of Southwick fatally at odds at Edgecote in 1469. Carpenter rates highly among his difficulties the existence of an alternative monarch in Henry VI,[33] but except for the most conscientious Lancastrian it was not a real alternative with any likelihood of coming to pass. Plotters had to take the greatest of risks on the off-chance of success, which few, surely, were prepared to do. Even though Lancastrian rebels and plotters may never seriously have threatened the regime, suppressing them – not once but repeatedly – strained Edward's military and financial resources to the limit. The letter begging for money that he directed to Alderman Sir Thomas Cook, which appears to originate in Cook's personal archive,[34] surely had counterparts sent to the other twenty-five aldermen of London and many other local authorities besides. It seemed to be one thing after another. And if the claims that Cook himself was unjustly treated when tried for treason in 1468 were contemporary and were disbelieved, they may also have alienated Londoners from Edward the following year.

It was during Edward's Second Reign, historians are agreed, from 1471, that any improvements in government must be located and should be sought. Edward had achieved remarkably little of his reforming agenda by 1469. In part this was doubtless because it was too difficult, perhaps because of the contemporary economic slump, commercial rivalries, and the time it took to consolidate the regime, but Edward's own policies, such as his rapid dispersal of Lancastrian forfeitures, may indeed have been contributory. Perhaps it was not his fault, although reform does seem to have fallen down his agenda. What is certain is that he was exposed to the charges laid against him during Robin of Redesdale's rebellion in 1469.[35] However doubtful the underlying motives and however slanted the presentation, these articles were intended to appeal to the populace of south-eastern England and appear, from Warwick's success in recruitment, to have struck the right chord. Undoubtedly King Edward had engaged in recoinage to his own financial advantage, he had levied taxes that had not been spent on 'great and urgent causes', and his favourites had taken the opportunity to advance themselves financially and to bend the law. All medieval favourites did. It was the Wydevilles and Edward's other 'new nobility' now who appeared immune from punishment.

Warwick raised an army in the south-east in 1469 that reached Edgecote too late to fight. His invasion next year was too powerful for King Edward to withstand. 'The various errors and omissions of Edward's government,' wrote Ross, 'especially his failure to do much to remedy the abuses which had proliferated under Henry VI, were to cost him his throne in 1470. His people were disillusioned with him'.[36] In 1471 Edward was the underdog who achieved his victories against the odds. He had no popular mandate. Yorkist England, of course, was no democracy. Even without popular backing, had the Yorkist regime been united there is no reason to suppose that he could not have maintained his hold on his Crown. But it was divided and it was Warwick who posed as the populist during the crises of the reign. We have considered the contribution of Edward's unfortunate marriage and his foreign policy in this disaster. Warwick himself remains a factor to be considered.

Edward vs Warwick

Richard Earl of Warwick had supported Richard Duke of York in politics from 1454 to 1460, both as a critic of the ruling regime and as lord protector. Only with the 1460 Accord did he commit himself to the eventual succession of the House of York to the Crown of

England. Only from 4 March 1461 did this entail recognizing York's son, Edward, as his monarch. Henceforth Edward IV was the king and Warwick the Kingmaker was his subject. There has never been any doubt that this relationship imposed on Warwick all the duties of allegiance of any other subject and that the earl was wrong to deny this obligation. Obviously he did come to feel himself (as York felt before him) incapable of treason and unwilling to bow to authority with which he disagreed. It is apparent, however, that the Wars of the Roses did change contemporary perspectives to such constitutional norms. In 1459 the *Somnium Vigilantis* faithfully presents York himself as taking the stance that his son the king was vigorously to rebut in 1470. Standards changed. Warwick had good grounds to fear Edward's malevolent intent, especially as frictions, rebellions and reconciliations multiplied. Edward was a vengeful man, as Warwick knew better than ourselves, but he never made it impossible for Warwick to keep his allegiance. 'But it would be false to suppose', Ross stressed, 'that by a series of calculated insults Edward deliberately drove Warwick into a position from which rebellion was the only honourable escape'.[37] He was not wholly out of favour until after he rebelled. What Warwick did was never unforgivable: in 1469 Edward pardoned him and in 1471, albeit against his better judgement and over-persuaded by his brother Clarence, he was prepared to do so again.

Warwick made many enemies of his own. He did come to be seen by the king's favourites as enjoying rewards that they wanted for themselves. He and his brother, John, were inevitably the principal losers designated by the restoration of the Percy and Tudor heirs that Herbert planned and which the king appeared likely to allow and did indeed eventually authorize. As Hicks has shown, both Warwick and Clarence as principal beneficiaries appeared predestined to lose out.[38] Warwick was the bogeyman for most foreign observers, especially Burgundians, who gave him a bad press in his own day,[39] but patriotic Englishmen did not think that to his discredit. Most English historians of his own and the next few generations approved the ancestral lineage and hereditary rights that bestowed wealth and standing on themselves as well as Warwick, and had no objection to the offices and estates accrued by him, which they accepted he had earned and did not think excessive. To the *Mirror for Magistrates*, Warwick was faithful, chivalric, principled and public-spirited. Many indeed of those historians discussed in earlier chapters thought that Warwick was badly treated by the king – they swallowed his propaganda, one might ungraciously say – and took his side in the rift that followed.[40] They also identified him with principles and remedies that even Scofield long ago revealed to have some validity. In 1469–70, sincere or not, it was Warwick not King Edward who was the champion of reform. *For* Warwick, chroniclers and early modern historians were often *against* Edward IV himself, whom they held at fault. They thought these other considerations outweighed Warwick's breaches of allegiance. It is a point of view that deserves serious consideration and should not be overruled by modern historians who were not involved.

The political culture that tolerated and even applauded great men like Warwick has passed away. Since the eighteenth century, historians have been first divided and then opposed to Warwick. Most modern writers have been hostile to him, have considered Edward too generous to him and felt that he needed to be cut down to size. 'The heady wine of making and unmaking kings was too much for him ... We may indeed well believe', Chrimes tentatively surmised, that Edward was 'not reluctant to see the support for his throne spread more widely than it was in 1461, and to reduce the heavy weight of Neville influence on the government'. If Edward was bound therefore to curb the Nevilles and create his own new nobility, 'the final rupture between the two does not bear the look of malice-aforethought, but sprang rather from the inevitable force of circumstances, the consequences of which as they accumulated bit by bit could not be evaded'.[41] Modern academics have generally doubted that Warwick's populist principles were more than lip-service. Carpenter is very much *for* Edward IV *against* this 'single very-ambitious nobleman'.[42] Warwick could not be left so much power – to Pollard, 'it was folly' ever to have been allowed – and it was inevitable that Edward jettisoned Warwick and that a clash occurred. Warwick should not have overreacted. However much he was acting to preserve himself, writes Pollard, and however badly Edward had handled him, the kingmaker ended up as a rogue elephant.[43] Dockray is prepared to concede the earl some 'good qualities (such as they were)', but argues that all these 'pale into insignificance besides his ruthless arrogance and immense ambition'. Motivated by ambition for himself and his family, 'above all, he proved congenitally incapable of accepting a subordinate position (even to the king)'.[44]

Should the cause that Warwick was held to stand for, the disillusion of the majority that Ross identified and their search for something preferable now count for nothing? Warwick was never so powerful that he could make or unmake kings on his own. Ironically in a democratic age, historians are inclined to reject the popular vote. More seriously, current interpretations befit our modern exaltation of the state over even the greatest subjects, our egalitarian distaste for hereditary grandees, our constant search for short-term evidence of progress and our enthusiasm for progressive Tudoresque restructurings of power. We expect conflict, rather than coexistence and submission, to have resulted from the overruling of past subjects by their kings, even though we now know cooperation to have been the norm. We think that past magnates should have been cut down to size even when they were working *with* the government. Warwick's contemporaries, historians and historical dramatists of the next two centuries thought otherwise. Our critiques of Warwick would not have been comprehensible to his contemporaries. They insert present-day standards into the past, presenting Warwick as he appears to us today rather than as he appeared at the time, which is anachronistic and disqualified as history.

Of course, conflict did occur. It was regrettable and should have been avoided. Warwick certainly did overstep some contemporary conventions, the conventions that were to win the Wars of the Roses and that came to be enshrined in the Tudor myth and the Tudor concept of order, but that were not yet firmly established. We cannot disregard either the contrary assessments of so many contemporaries or several centuries of successors in favour of Warwick and against the king. Neither, surely, should we forget the popularity of the cause that Warwick espoused, that (however deceitfully) he was seen to stand for popular principles and the remedy of popular grievances, nor how bereft Edward found himself in 1470 and the Yorkist admission, both in prose and verse, that he won in defiance of the odds.

Stratford, Scofield, Ross and Richmond all accepted that by 1469 Edward had lost his popular support. Was there anything he could

have done to have retained his throne in 1470? He could have dis-
armed popular criticisms. Evidently he could have retained more of
the Lancastrian forfeitures in his own hands – his generosity was
extravagant by any previous standard – and he could have made
more progress thereby in achieving solvency. He could have devoted the attention to law and order in his First Reign that he did in his
Second. It was not necessary to pursue an aggressive foreign policy
that divided his supporters and that he could not yet deliver. If he
had to marry his Wydeville queen, he could have avoided so self-
consciously advancing his Wydeville sisters-in-law and in the
process flouting Warwick's legitimate aspirations. Warwick was
wrong to react by rebelling, but Edward miscalculated his reactions.
Moreover, Edward's deposition in 1470 was far from inevitable. He
could have handled Warwick better before 1469 and he could have
reconciled properly with Warwick in 1469 rather than excluding
him with a new royalist faction that could not deliver the goods.
Had Herbert and Stafford cooperated, they might have won the
battle of Edgecote. In retrospect it was another error by Edward not
to treat with Warwick and Clarence after the Lincolnshire
Rebellion. The king gambled on a complete victory and lost. All
these are imponderable might-have-beens, whereas history must be
about what was and what did happen. Yet none of these factors
need have led to disaster. It was because Edward was perceived (and
presented) as having failed, because of the unpopularity of his 'new
nobility' and the popularity of Warwick, because of his alienation of
Warwick and Clarence, because he never eradicated underlying
loyalties to Henry VI, and for a whole series of contingencies, that
Edward lost his throne. Edward bears some share of the responsibility. It was exceptionally easy for kings to be overthrown during
the Wars of the Roses. That Edward shared this fate may well mean
that he lacked foresight, but it does not mean that he ruled badly in
the 1460s or that he was a bad late-medieval king. Here Carpenter
is surely right.

The break-up of the faction that had made Edward king undid a
decade of consolidation during which Edward had come to be
routinely accepted as the rightful king. His enemies were defeated,
foreign recognition was achieved, his finances were stabilized and a
male heir was eagerly anticipated. He had been a very young and
inexperienced king. To be visible, active and authoritative at the

centre was an unaccustomed strength for the new regime. Whatever Edward's shadowy actions, on judicial progress, in council and as judge, it was nevertheless the Nevilles, especially Warwick and Montagu, who were most visible because they undertook the most signal services. That Edward occasionally withstood Warwick's blandishments indicates that he had to be managed rather than that he was in independent control. His apprehension about revealing his marriage was shaped primarily by what Warwick would think! Edward was fortunate indeed to possess such competent and energetic agents as the Nevilles. If his arrival on the borders was not actually necessary nor particularly desired and was once prevented by illness, it remained that it was expected, repeatedly promised and yet never actually occurred. Routine fulfilment of the duties of kingship was apparently already accompanied by pleasure-seeking and sexual adventures with mistresses and his queen, which left legacies he could not predict.

Edward was very young and inexperienced and had to learn how to manage his subjects. With his Lancastrian enemies, he tried both excessive rigour with the de Veres, arousing widespread disapproval and lasting enmity, and unconditional leniency, which was equally criticized. He had to devise an appropriate strategy where none was written down as Stratford shrewdly appreciated. Grateful to his own supporters and faced with an apparently unlimited pool of forfeitures, he gave to them (not just the Nevilles) with open hands – according to his assessment of their merits, admittedly, but lavishly and without restraint – until he had nothing more to give. Reaching that point as early as 1464, by when the Lancastrians were defeated and had no more to lose, the king was obliged to change his tack. To endow his queen and brothers, which he had to do, and his sisters-in-law, which he needed not, and to do so on the scale that he thought appropriate but that extended far beyond traditional measures, he had only three expedients to adopt: he could alienate parts of the Duchy of Lancaster, the permanent royal demesne; he could redistribute patronage through acts of resumption, downgrading some trusted servants in favour of others; and he could reward at no financial cost to himself by intervening in the marriage market, as he did. If such rewards were insufficient for his new favourites, as ambitious, as aggrandizing as Warwick and much more hasty, then perhaps the gap could be bridged by the informal speculation on restoration of forfeitures undertaken by Herbert and the engineering of further forfeitures suspected of Stafford, which Edward did not plan but appeared ready to condone. Such activity undercut the Nevilles and other loyal Yorkists, and fomented tensions and enmities in the ruling faction which Edward did not plan or apparently foresee and which he did not prevent. To plan a continental war in the late 1460s was premature indeed.

7

The king's wars

Multinational themes

Edward IV required foreign help to make himself king, to reinforce and to regain his throne; his opponents were the stronger because they could shelter abroad and invade in foreign ships or across the northern borders, backed by foreign money and foreign troops. Never before was England so often invaded. Never before or since has England seemed less of an island. At one level, the Wars of the Roses were purely domestic conflicts with purely English causes – dynastic, principled, self-interested, personal – but followed, stimulated and exploited by adjoining powers. At another level, they were that part of the struggle between France and Burgundy which was fought on English soil. Which great power to back was a significant element, occasionally crucial in domestic as well as foreign politics, sometimes shaping and sometimes shaped by internal political alliances and divisions. There was interaction also with the aftermath of the Hundred Years War – or its continuation, depending on interpretation. Underlying such major themes were the continuous commercial, dynastic and everyday relations of neighbouring states. There were traditional alignments between England, France and Scotland: the 'Auld Alliance' of France and Scotland mattered. For Edward IV, such issues coexisted, alternated in importance and had to be reviewed constantly in the light of other priorities, notably security and finance. If the greatest achievement of Edward's foreign policy was to keep him on his throne, his deposition in 1470, however temporary, was its most disastrous failure.

Warwick brought the Calais garrison to Ludford (Salop) in 1459 and retired thereafter into exile at Calais with his father. The Yorkist earls landed in Kent in 1460, en route to victory at Northampton and the great battles that brought Edward to his throne. There were

Lancastrian-inspired invasions across the borders and from the sea into Northumberland until 1464 and repeatedly via Harlech in Wales until 1468. When Warwick broke with Edward in 1469, he brought across the Calais garrison. The next year he fled to France, re-embarking from the Côtentin to place Henry VI on the throne. It was from the Low Countries that King Edward invaded Yorkshire in 1471. Significant numbers of foreign troops accompanied De Brézé to Northumberland in 1461 and participated after Edward's death in 1485 and 1487, yet normally foreign involvement was small in scale. The manpower that mattered was Englishmen responding to English leaders in what were essentially English quarrels. They were the foundation and launch pads for such enterprises.

The Treaty of Arras of 1435 had realigned the warring states of north-western Europe by transferring Burgundy from the English camp to the French. Charles VII of France was the victor: not only did he recover English conquests in northern France, but also Gascony to the south-west. Not yet as extensive as modern France, his kingdom contained within it important feudatories who ruled their own provinces, notably Brittany on the north-west and Burgundy on the east. Apart from Burgundy itself, the Valois Dukes of Burgundy ruled, under various titles and in a fairly continuous bloc, Picardy and Artois in north-eastern France and the provinces that now constitute the Low Countries of Belgium, Luxembourg and the Netherlands, most of them within the Holy Roman Empire. Not only did the sheer number of such provinces justify Burgundy's description as 'the great duchy of the west', but so too did its resources. Flanders and Brabant were the most commercialized, industrialized, urbanized and wealthy region of northern Europe, and Antwerp was the centre of international trade. Perhaps Burgundy wielded more resources and counted for more internationally during Edward IV's reign than England itself. Despite the *rapprochement* in 1435 and Louis XI's sojourn there in exile during his father's lifetime, Louis XI's foreign policy was unsympathetic to Burgundy and can be interpreted as consistently anti-Burgundian, designed to cut Burgundy down to size. That was how Commynes retrospectively read it. Louis's foe was not so much the ageing Philip the Good (d. 1467), but his son, Charles the Bold – or Rash, the French being *Téméraire* – Count of Charolais and Duke of

Burgundy, who was slain at Nancy in 1477, and Charles's daughter, Mary of Burgundy (d. 1482). French and Burgundians engaged in the Wars of the Roses by invitation of the warring parties from 1461 and both sought to lure the English into their own wars on the continent, twice – in 1471 and 1475 – successfully. Charles was aware of his descent from John of Gaunt and of a potential claim to the English Crown, but fortunately for Edward neither he nor Louis seriously aspired to conquer England. Both contented themselves with maintaining or unseating English contenders with a view to negating their intervention on the continent against them or securing their active support against the other side. Edward's own claims to the Crown of Castile were never seriously raised.

Charters, letters patent and close, and writs of all kinds addressed recipients in the name of 'Edward by the grace of God King of England *and of France*'. Edward succeeded in 1461 to the fact of the English throne and to a claim to that of France. It was a title rather than a reality, for only Calais remained of all the English inheritances and conquests in France last lost in 1453. Edward's claim required the invalidation of the Salic law which bestowed France on the direct male heir from Charles IV (1322–8) to the Valois King Louis XI (1461–83). Given that considerable proviso, Edward was indeed the next heir of Charles IV's sister, Isabella, consort of Edward II; he also claimed as successor to the Lancastrians under Henry V's Treaty of Troyes (1420). Royal letters, proclamations and supplications constantly reminded Edward of his claim to France. It had moreover been Henry VI's critics in the 1450s, headed by Edward's father, York, and including York himself, who had expressed outrage at the English defeat, blamed it on the corruption, treachery and pusillanimity of Somerset, constantly seeking retribution, and indicated thereby that the Hundred Years War was not yet resolved and might yet be reversed. Veterans saw in Richard the man to overturn the disasters. Certainly Calais could never be conceded to the French. Edward inherited this uncompromising and aggressive stance, even if he could do nothing about it initially. The expulsion of the English had not resulted in a peace treaty or the renunciation of the English claim, which repeatedly justified invasions of France by Edward IV and his successors. Such claims did not expire with time. The Hundred Years War was not yet finally lost.

England shared a border with Scotland, which armies traversed during the wars at the start and end of Edward's reign, and across which raids and other violent infringements of trace were frequent and perhaps continuous. England engaged with foreign trade with the rest of northern Europe and with galleys from Italy. The most important commercial connections were with Burgundy, which took the bulk of England's principal export of woollen cloths, and via the Hanseatic League with Germany and the Baltic. An important source of customs, Edward's principal revenue and the major imperative of Edward's financial backers of the City of London, peaceful commerce with Burgundy ought to have been and perhaps was a significant factor in Edward's foreign policy. Nevertheless, trade was apparently suspended and/or depressed for several years in the 1460s.[1]

What historians have not assessed (and cannot readily discern) is what Edward brought from his own experience to foreign policy. Edward may have been conceived abroad (just possibly to a French father!) and was certainly born abroad, at Rouen, when his father was lieutenant of France, and apparently stayed long enough, until 1446, not to remember anything, but to have internalized some French culture, especially via his nurse, Anne, who hailed from Caux in Normandy. York made his French lieutenancy one of his talking points. After a flying visit to the Channel Isles, Edward was next abroad for almost eight months at Calais, an enclave in French-speaking Burgundy. He certainly learnt much of its strategic value, the importance of the wool trade and hence of the merchants of the staple of Calais, and of international commerce in the Channel on which the Yorkists preyed. There he observed defences and artillery in use, during constant border infractions, there he experienced both a siege and countermeasures against isolated besiegers, there he learnt how to fight at sea and how to undertake combined operations. Probably he encountered continental troops, armaments and tactics and almost certainly met the Burgundian envoys with whom Warwick negotiated. It was De La Barde's Burgundian handgunners that served with him at Towton. Surely Edward appreciated how very different were the wars of movement and manoeuvre, the half-trained amateurs and logistical simplicity, the pitched battles and absence of sieges of the English Wars of the Roses from the time-consuming, laborious and professional campaigns of France and

Burgundy? Whatever his sources of information, Edward certainly did not underrate the military potential of his continental counterparts.

The 1460s

Foreign relations during the 1460s fell into two halves: the search for security up to 1465 and a more ambitious and aggressive taking of sides thereafter. Claims to the kingdom of France had to be sidelined in 1461–4, when Edward's primary objective was to hold on to the kingdom that he did occupy. He tried to stop foreign interventions on behalf of the Lancastrian royal family, who were still at large and to secure their extradition, confinement and presumably also their elimination. Universal recognition of his dynasty, the ending of official foreign intervention and the isolation of the Lancastrian queen and prince were indeed achieved. Lancastrian plots and incursions, however, were merely restricted and persisted throughout Edward's First Reign.

It had been the Lancastrian dynasty that was universally recognized and that had enjoyed amicable relations with most European powers. These were advantages which Edward had to secure for himself. He had to show Europeans that he had come to stay. Initially prospects were unfavourable, both France and Scotland backing Henry VI. Charles sent De Brézé to seize Jersey and was planning a French invasion before 22 July 1461, when he died and the imminent threat receded. Unfounded rumours of an international coalition were also generating alarm in England the following year. If Burgundy was much more sympathetic, had supplied Edward with some troops and lent him diplomatic support in his dealings with Scotland, Lancastrian refugees were neither expelled nor extradited.

With Scotland, Queen Margaret had contracted some arrangement early in 1461 at Lincluden College.[2] She later surrendered Berwick to the Scottish dowager, Mary of Guelders, receiving in return safe haven and some intermittent military support. On 5 January 1463 the Earl of Angus evacuated the Alnwick garrison with an army powerful enough to have defeated Warwick's blockading force had he so wished.[3] The Scots were divided, however, and Edward sought to divert their attentions from his borders by allying with the dissident Earl of Ross from 1462. The decisive defeat of the northern Lancastrians was followed on 1 June 1464 by a short truce that was much extended the next year: an action which recognized that within Edward's lifetime 'retrieving Roxburgh and Berwick was unattainable'.[4] This was unfinished business which Edward was to take up again in 1480.

If Louis XI failed initially to continue his father's policies, he sought nevertheless to maximize French advantage from the English mess, certainly postponing any resumption of English claims to France, but seeking additional benefits also. Following the Berwick precedent, Queen Margaret in 1462 bargained away future rights to Calais – the recovery of which would have been the final seal to French victory in the Hundred Years War – in return for Louis's support in secret treaties at Chinon and Tours. Unfortunately for her case and very fortunately for Edward IV, Louis was disinclined to commit very much and allowed himself to be deterred by reminders of English potential for trouble through the Earl of Kent's naval raids on the French coast. By 1464 the Yorkists were so secure that Louis sought to seal his amity by marrying his sister-in-law, Bona of Savoy, to King Edward. Diplomatically isolated, Queen Margaret and Prince Edward took shelter in her father's lands in Bar, beyond the borders of both France and Burgundy, whilst King Henry sheltered with sympathizers in England until apprehended in 1465. Domestic consolidation and foreign recognition still had to take precedence in 1465 when Edward declined to join Charles the Bold and other feudatories in the rebellion against King Louis known as the War of the Public Weal.

Crowland blamed differences in foreign policy for Edward's rift with Warwick, the Wydevilles backing Burgundy and Warwick favouring France. Most recent historians have followed his lead.[5] Although perhaps mistaken in originating their quarrel in foreign policy and perhaps antedating the moment of decision for each side, there can be no doubt of the importance of the issue. In spite of discarding his principal card, his own hand in marriage, Edward possessed others in the hands of his unmarried siblings and he found himself courted by both France and Burgundy. Obviously Louis XI and Duke Charles were pursuing their own agendas, particularly in their Franco-Burgundian rivalry, specifically practical military support against the other or at least neutrality. From such negotiations,

Edward could have emerged secure. He had no pressing need to commit himself to intervention on either side – to make an enemy and a threat of one of his neighbours as well as a friend of the other. Instead he contracted aggressive alliances that committed him to war and might have had serious consequences had they been implemented.

Bar commercial differences, England's relations with Burgundy were fairly friendly throughout Edward's First Reign and were encouraged by the Wydevilles, who had connections via the Duchess Jacquetta with the Count of St Pol and other Burgundian nobles. An international chivalric event was made of the tournament of Anthony, Grand Bastard of Burgundy, with the queen's brother (and Edward's brother-in-law) Anthony Wydeville, Lord Scales. Those celebrations were cut short by the death of the sympathetic Duke Philip and his replacement by the more sceptical Duke Charles, whose stance, however, changed on his succession. The following year, in 1468, Edward's remaining unmarried sister, Margaret of York, became the third consort to Charles the Bold himself. To achieve this, Edward had to promise a dowry of 200,000 crowns (£41,666 13s. 4d.) and have it independently guaranteed, supply an expensive trousseau and make important commercial concessions against the wishes of English merchants without reciprocation. 'With the new Duke Charles the bargaining was hard', wrote Ross, 'and the English got the worst of it'.[6] Evidently Edward wanted agreement more than Charles. To counter an aggressive Anglo-Burgundian alliance, Louis was ready to cap whatever Burgundy offered: alternative marriage alliances for Margaret, Clarence and Gloucester, a substantial pension and shares in conquered Burgundian territory, perhaps including appanages for the king's brothers. Edward's renunciation of his claim to France was probably desirable rather than essential and can never have been seriously attainable.[7] It is interesting that Edward disregarded the pension promise that was so attractive a decade later. It all proved academic, however, for although negotiations with both parties continued – and indeed Warwick's diplomacy influenced Burgundy's terms – Edward appears to have preferred a Burgundian alliance throughout.

On 17 May 1468, Lord Chancellor Stillington informed parliament of the king's intention to invade France. Taxes were duly voted. By then the king had contracted alliances (or was about to contract them) not only with Burgundy, but with Brittany, Aragon, Castile, Denmark, the emperor, Naples and Scotland. Brittany had agreed to a military and commercial alliance and was to receive 3,000 English archers in support.[8] Perhaps Edward also hoped for further insurrections by the French feudatories. Clearly he did intend to invade France in person, in 1469 or later, and to wage war against King Louis. Obviously he was not acting as Charles's agent, but on his own behalf. In reopening the Hundred Years War, it is unclear how far Edward hoped or expected to proceed. Did he think the Crown attainable? Was he seeking Gascony and Henry V's conquests? What was he willing to settle for? We cannot tell, because nothing came of the project.

It is difficult to tell how realistic or serious this proposal was since it failed early on. Although military support was indeed despatched to Brittany, no recruitment, or collection of armaments or supplies for war were undertaken. Realistically, Edward was in no financial position to engage in a protracted war. He was pressed to raise merely the downpayment of a quarter of his sister's dowry, and much of the tax voted in 1468 went towards the costs of her marriage.[9] Edward never supposed that he could fight France on his own. Evidently he thought allies were essential. Few of those contracted, in southern Europe for instance, were of much value against France; perhaps Edward realized this and cited them only to impress the Commons. He was let down by Burgundy and Brittany. In retrospect, but predictably, too much weight was attached to them. Diplomacy was an exercise in self-advantage, the priorities of one's allies not coinciding with one's own. Edward, the inexperienced diplomat, expected his allies to keep faith even against their better interests.

Moreover he does not appear to have been prepared for the countermeasures that Louis deployed to disperse Edward's coalition against him. How uncertain Edward's hold was upon England was quickly made apparent. In June King Louis despatched Jasper Tudor once again to Harlech. Elsewhere, in the West Country, East Anglia and Yorkshire, a whole series of Lancastrian plotters, even including three London aldermen, were uncovered in the summer and autumn of 1468 and the following winter. The rumours were even more disturbing. Certainly Edward was alarmed. The treatment of

Sir Thomas Cook is evidence. Was England secure enough for the king to leave? It was a choice that Edward did not need to make, since he was quickly stripped of allies. Striking quickly at Brittany, before the English archers had arrived and even before Edward had ratified the treaty, Louis forced Duke Francis to abandon his English alliance on 10 September. Louis's agreement with Duke Charles was more involuntary: their Treaty of Péronne conceded to the duke his war aims and removed him from Edward's military allies. That was on 14 October.[10] Within five months of Stillington's speech, Edward's encircling coalition had dissolved and his project was defunct unless he was willing to go it alone, which there is no evidence he ever was. Louis had outfoxed the king. At the end of his First Reign the king's foreign policy was in collapse. As the rebel manifesto pointed out, he had taken taxes without fighting the war that justified them.[11] If he was no nearer to conquering France, King Louis recognized him as a potential foe and was therefore open to the proposals to dethrone him when circumstances in 1470 proved propitious. Once Warwick had escaped to France, it is not obvious what Edward could have done to prevent the invasion that ensued.

Edward was secure from 1464. Alignment and active engagement in the Franco-Burgundian feud, even ostensibly the resumption of the Hundred Years War, was potentially destabilizing and threatened that achievement. Edward's proposed French war came to nought because of a combination of over-ambition, naïve over-confidence in the strength of his alliances, and a lack of foresight: for Edward had not yet learnt the measure of Louis XI. He was fortunate not to have tested his resources in money and manpower. As yet he did not appreciate the costs of continental war, the minimalism of English parliamentary support, nor the limits to his credit. Warwick was certainly right that Edward could not wage effective war against the French in the 1460s. Nor however could England have afforded to join France against Burgundy. When this did happen, in 1471, Burgundian intervention helped unseat the readeption government. An aggressive foreign policy was too perilous. Louis was unlikely to keep fighting until the most distant provinces were delivered into English hands: but Warwick, the experienced diplomat, may not seriously have expected this. Renunciation of the English title to the French Crown was politically impossible and the French were less popular outside mercantile circles, yet amity and even peaceful alignment with the most powerful neighbouring state of France was the safest if most pusillanimous option as Warwick may have recognized. The earl might have proved as impracticably aggressive *for* the French as Edward was *against* them. Sitting on the fence was a real option not dissimilar in results to the fruitless manoeuvres that did ensue. Moreover it was much less risky.

1471–5

From an English perspective, what happened in 1471–5 repeated Edward's manoeuvres of 1467–8, but this time France was actually invaded. Parliament again voted taxes, a coalition with Brittany and Burgundy was assembled, Scotland was neutralized and an army comparable in numbers and equipment to any of its predecessors was prepared and successfully disembarked in Calais. A brief and bloodless parade in northern France was followed, within three months, by a treaty (Picquigny) and evacuation. Hence historians have questioned how serious were Edward's intentions. Did Edward actually eschew continental adventures, as Chrimes suggested? Was the Picquigny campaign merely a bargaining counter designed to secure more French concessions?[12]

There is no doubt that after recovering his throne in 1471 Edward wanted revenge on Louis XI as the only architect of his deposition as yet unpunished. A personal and chivalric note implying that war was a game appears both in Louis's insulting gift of animals to Edward and Edward's bantering challenge in 1474.[13] Edward's response was not precipitate, but unhurried, cautious and delayed until his domestic dispositions had been completed. Edward did not minimize the scale of the challenge. His prowess under English conditions did not appear particularly relevant to France. He did not plan a rapid campaign of *chevauchée* and pitched battles, investing instead in the ordnance employed on the continent in anticipation, most probably, of continental strategies and tactics. Once abroad, the dashing Edward IV ironically resembled the hyper-cautious Warwick whom he had already vanquished. By seeking supply for a year's service,[14] Edward showed that he expected campaigning to continue through the winter. The high proportion of archers in his army may not indicate a lack of commitment amongst potential men-at-arms, as Lander argued,[15] but the high estimation for this one element of English armies shown by Burgundians and Bretons alike. Was service alongside the Burgundians required to produce a properly balanced fighting force? Even survivors of Edward's English campaigns were comparative novices at war by continental standards, though capable, Commynes reminds us, of being brought up to scratch.[16] All that England could raise could not equal the power of France in Edward's eyes. Edward never considered invading France without support from both Burgundy and Brittany. First he moved his landing from relative exposure in Normandy to relative security at Calais. He took no effective action when Burgundian support was not forthcoming. He was remarkably quick to seize on the exit proffered by Louis once it was apparent that Burgundian backing would be delayed indefinitely. 'It is also clear from his later actions', wrote Ross, 'that he regarded the active and committed co-operation of the duke of Burgundy, whose army was regarded as unquestionably the best in Europe, as an essential prerequisite for a major attack on France'.[17] Edward was acutely aware in 1475 of risks that he did not need to take. Unlike 1461 and 1471, neither his Crown nor his life was at stake. However bitter his wrath and thirst for revenge in 1471, it was overtaken in time by calculation and careful planning, designed to minimize the dangers.

When Louis reconciled Warwick and Queen Margaret in 1470, he breached the Treaty of Péronne. Next he required Warwick to attack Burgundy, a fatal error that precipitated Burgundy's backing for Edward's successful recovery of England. Louis had dismantled the diplomatic agreements that had saved him from invasion in 1468. Crowland reports that it was the Burgundians using highfalutin language – Edward was 'Your Serenity' and France became Gaul[18] – who first proposed an alliance which an English envoy (whom we now know to be Bishop Russell) travelled to Abbeville to elucidate.[19] In 1472 Edward agreed with Brittany for an invasion of Gascony or Normandy the next year, with England to retain any conquests. Similarly, the terms he initially offered Burgundy 'were specific and practical and clearly indicate Edward's serious intent to make war'.[20] Agreement followed. In 1474, to secure the northern borders against Scottish intervention, Edward prolonged the existing truce to 1519 and reinforced it with a marriage alliance, between his third daughter, Cecily and the future James IV. The potential threat that the Hansards posed in the Channel was also bought off with the Treaty of Utrecht (1474).

What Charles the Bold wanted most from the English alliance was to end or reduce the threat posed by Louis XI. Replacing Louis with Edward was an obvious (if drastic) route to this end. So, more practically, were the territorial concessions that Charles sought from his alliance with Edward, to be held in full sovereignty, independent of any future king the counties of Champagne, Nevers, Rethel, Eu, Guise and the Duchy of Bar, the lands of the count of St Pol and the Somme towns. Much enlarged, Charles's disparate territories in the Low Countries and Burgundy would have been united into a coherent bloc.[21] Perhaps Louis might have surrendered even these to Charles to break the alliance? There was the precedent of the Somme towns that Louis had conceded at Péronne. What territory might Louis have conceded in return for Edward's renunciation of his claim to the throne of France? Not that Edward seems to have considered that. In 1472 he did reassert ancestral claims to Normandy and Gascony, but Louis would not give them up without a fight. Would he do so then? 'Exactly what Edward hoped to achieve by his invasion of France in 1475 would be difficult to say with certainty,' wrote Ross, but it was certainly not what actually resulted.[22] In negotiations with Charles, only concluded in 1474, Edward insisted on access through Champagne to Rheims for one day only for his coronation.[23] Louis did not attempt to negotiate away the English claim at Picquigny. It was with the Crown of France that Burgundian envoys tempted Edward and also appear to have offered parliament.[24]

Although somewhat belated, in November 1472, the first session of Edward's multi-session parliament of 1472–75 celebrated both the king's victorious resumption of his throne and the birth to him of his heir, Edward Prince of Wales, Duke of Cornwall and Earl of Chester. Interspersed with parliamentary business, some of it indeed staged in parliament, were the ceremonial thanks, honouring and creation as Earl of Winchester of Edward's Burgundian host-in-exile, Louis of Bruges, Lord Gruthuyse.[25] The guest was also a diplomatic emissary and it may have been at this time that he (or another in his entourage) added weight to Edward's proposal of war with France which, Crowland tells us, was Edward's principal objective. 'Many eloquent speeches were addressed to Parliament by speakers from home and abroad and especially on behalf of the duke of Burgundy', and a written declaration was also circulated.[26] Edward assured parliament of the support of both Burgundy and Brittany before negotiations were complete; he did not report a year-long truce in 1473–4. Such arguments appear not to have made much impact, perhaps because France was a different kingdom and Englishmen did not include its conquest, however desirable, within the 'great and urgent causes' that they were obliged to finance. Instead a long list of other advantages were cited (as in 1468) that might appeal to parliament, but were obviously not Edward's prime objectives: the diversion of unruly elements from English crime to war abroad; the support of essential but potential disorderly soldiers in garrisons; the endowment with French lands of younger sons; the control of the southern coast of the Channel and hence the securing of free passage without need for a navy. One such anonymous oration that survives at great length touches on Edward's French Crown only as part of its argument that attack was the best form of defence, the surest way to peace and hence to riches.[27] Hence Lander's rather negative interpretation, which applies more convincingly to parliament than to the king.

> We should therefore see the campaign of 1475 not as a
> revival of the genuinely aggressive policies of Henry V,
> but as a reaction to this background of deep, intense
> suspicions and fears, and as a somewhat defensive
> reaction to the development of Anglo-Burgundian
> French-relationships over the past two decades.[28]

The defensive tone that Lander noted may also have been for the very good reason that financial support could reasonably be invoked only for defensive measures.[29] Such speeches were for public consumption. Even if Edward had rated the spin-offs, was he prepared to pay the price in money and risk for so little? Edward got what he wanted – parliamentary permission – but perhaps not the degree of support that he desired.

Crowland, who was present, also records that 'all applauded' Edward's plans and voted numerous taxes, but large though these were, they did not suffice.[30] Factually correct, Crowland drew the wrong inferences. A supreme effort was needed to persuade parliament to provide support, Lander has pointed out. 'It looks as if

Edward IV realised that he must use all the arts of propaganda at his disposal to whip up an aggressive spirit in a blasé and indifferent people'.[31] What was voted was inadequate and was trammelled with conditions. Understandably reluctant to trust a king who had twice used war taxes for other purposes, the Commons revived the use of special treasurers and special treasuries outside royal control and specified that taxation be refunded if the terms were not observed. What parliament agreed, £118,000 to support 13,000 archers for a year or the equivalent of four complete fifteenths and tenths,[32] was actually an enormous sum. Both Lords and Commons, however, sought to minimize the burdens by experimenting with untried taxes of uncertain yield to be paid by less burdened or hitherto untaxed but prosperous sections of the populace, who perhaps did not exist. That only £2,461 was raised in income tax from all the peers suggests that they seriously under-assessed themselves;[33] other taxpayers resisted or delayed payment. It took several returns to parliament for enough money to be raised, the final instalment even so falling due a year later, in 1476. Had the full sums been raised, which they were not, they would have been spread over four years at £29,000 per annum, a far less impressive tax-loading. No wonder Edward resorted to forced gifts or benevolences, which caused a great fuss, but apparently raised only £282.[34] Although funded sufficiently for his first campaign, Edward could have had no confidence about parliamentary finance for subsequent seasons. He could afford one campaign and no more.

Lander was also critical of Edward's army. If the force that was raised of at least 11,451 combatants, or 20,000 including support staff, was indeed 'the largest army which had so far crossed the English Channel during the fifteenth century' as Ross calculated, it was not particularly impressive by continental standards and its composition, so Lander reported, was unsatisfactory. By the standards of Henry V, the proportion of archers to men-at-arms was excessive – 7:1 rather than 3:1 – and men-at-arms indeed amounted to 'a miserable total which seems to indicate that most people were indifferent, if not hostile to the war policy'.[35] It is possible however that Lander was wrong to presume that the standards of 1415 were still applicable and/or that the English force was meant to stand alone. The one element of English manpower that foreigners respected, repeatedly sought to recruit and negotiated as subsidies were archers; it was

13,000 archers that parliament voted and that Edward had presumably requested. The 1,500 men-at-arms were impressive by English standards and every major nobleman without exception enlisted, so Commynes reports.[36] Lander's derogatory observations about the absence of provincial aristocrats of substance are based on those who indented or were paid as captains with the Crown, most of them 'court noblemen' or other courtiers. Such captains, however, subcontracted with provincials to make up the numbers. Thus Clarence subcontracted with James Hyde of Caversham (Oxon) and William Floyer of Floiers Hays (Dorset) for eight of his thousand-strong company: Sir Reginald Stourton and Sir John St Lo, both West Countrymen, and the West Midlander William Berkeley of Weoley (Worcs) served with him too. Just possibly Lander was confusing a change in recruitment, with more responsibility being taken by courtiers, with an actual change in composition and participation. What matters is that Edward did indeed raise the numbers he wished. A very large army was arrayed. What is known about other aspects of Edward's preparations, such as his expenditure on ordnance, suggests that nothing was left to chance.

If Commynes doubted that Edward intended a serious invasion and thought him temperamentally unsuited for systematic sieges, Crowland and most of his contemporaries in a better position to know thought that Edward was quite serious in his intention to renew the Hundred Years War. So, too, it seems did Louis XI, who tried once again to destabilize Edward's regime by exciting the Scots, encouraging Jasper Tudor in Wales and despatching the Earl of Oxford to England. Only Oxford caused any trouble, yet even his contribution was limited, since without a dynastic contender for the throne he could arouse no significant support. It seems unlikely that English renegades would have set their seals to anything, as Louis alleged, and there is no evidence to confirm it.[37] It is striking that it was at this time that Edward was to coerce both his brothers to order. Compared with 1468, Edward's hold on his throne was secure.

Edward certainly wanted to wage war earlier. His first treaty with Brittany anticipated an invasion by April 1473, ahead of any parliamentary taxation.[38] Whatever force he could have raised then, from his own resources, would obviously have been smaller, less well equipped and less well financed than what he actually did deploy. The essence of his initial strategy was a multi-pronged attack like those of Edward III that he later abandoned. Problems in coordinating his alliances, securing funding and perhaps domestic complications – he had other things to do at home in spring/summer 1473 – progressively pushed back the invasion to 1475 when, of course, Edward found Burgundy was engaged elsewhere. This was only the final indication that the fulfilment of English war aims, and even securing the concessions that Edward had promised, were not Charles's only objectives or even top of his agenda. Edward may well have become more realistic and indeed been deterred by the difficulties he encountered. Which particular problems, prolonged logistical support over such a distance or the isolation of his forces, prompted him to drop Gascony as a possible destination for Normandy? His subsequent decision to disembark not in Normandy, but in the security of Calais, was essentially defensive.[39] Operation alone in Normandy was too risky. Therefore France was to be attacked only from one direction, the east, in conjunction with Burgundy. Other decisions were implied by his recruitment of an army of bowmen who would be exposed on their own. He intended relying on firepower over hand-to-hand fighting and required protection against attack by integration with Burgundian units and/or by shelter at vulnerable times (e.g. at night) in Burgundian towns. Perhaps Edward committed himself to the classic English combination of an aggressive strategy and defensive tactics, in which the French impaled themselves on English arrows. Such expectations were misplaced. Not only were Charles's forces absent elsewhere and hence unable to provide support, but the duke denied the English access to his towns, whilst Louis himself held back his forces rather than hazarding them in battle. Reduction of French towns and fortresses by siege was scarcely practical whilst Louis's army loomed: he had already raided into Picardy. Edward advanced only slowly towards the enemy. The contrast with the rapid marches and battles that he had forced on his Lancastrian opponents in 1471 is striking. Clearly he did not consider his army capable of operating effectively on its own. A stalemate, in which Charles withheld the support that Edward thought essential for attack and in which Louis stood on the defensive, was apparent almost from the moment of landing.

Edward was worried that Burgundian support might not be forthcoming before he set off, but planning had proceeded too far for him not to go. 'But there was no stopping the campaign at the eleventh hour,' writes Pollard.[40] On disembarkation he was joined by Duke Charles 'with a few men'. Blaming him for unpreparedness, some advised returning home at once. 'Others, of sounder mind' in Crowland's estimation:

> Who were much more concerned with glory than with their comfort, thought that the duke, in behaving as he did, had acted like a wise and supremely confident prince. He had fully realised that the king's army was sufficient, by itself, to meet any sudden enemy attack – indeed in his view it was so sufficient that if the men had been his own he would not have wished for more to carry conquest right through France as far as the gates of Rome; and *he said these very words in public*.[41]

Of course he did. Whether Charles really rated Edward's army so extravagantly is highly unlikely, but obviously he wanted whatever advantages could accrue from Edward's expedition at no cost to himself. Evacuation of the English, from his angle, was entirely negative. Here, no doubt, Crowland is repeating the argument of both the Burgundians and the king, who had to maintain morale and momentum. It was they also, surely, who advanced the decidedly secondary argument that potentially damaging competition for billets and so on between the two armies was averted by the absence of Burgundian troops. On Charles's advice, Edward advanced slowly through Burgundian territory to St Quentin. Edward's relative inactivity suggests that he was uncertain what to do on his own. Moreover he had other difficulties. The Bretons stood still and the Count of St Pol defaulted. Still in Burgundian territory, Edward could neither live off the land nor plunder. Hence (Crowland tells us) his troops spent all their wages and needed their second instalment several months ahead of schedule. Richmond shrewdly asks, 'Did he stop the fighting before it had begun for the money?'[42] Whilst winter was still some months away, Edward would need to conquer towns himself as winter quarters. Ross summarizes the situation thus:

> There seemed to be every prospect that the English might be left to fight the French alone, something which Edward had always wished to avoid. The French were numerically

far superior, and the English troops were not the seasoned
warriors trained in continental warfare who had been
available a generation previously. No doubt these were the
arguments of discretion rather than valour.[43]

Whilst clearly Edward could not conquer France in a year,
especially in his cautious frame of mind, Louis potentially had much
to lose in terms of both material loss and popularity from a prolonged campaign. If the campaign continued – and Edward had
funding for a year – fighting, damage and expense was bound to
follow and it was even possible that Charles might become engaged.
Commynes credits Louis with the initial overtures, even before the
English had embarked,[44] but Edward was evidently receptive. He
abandoned all his original war aims: the conquest of France, revenge
on Louis, the employment of younger sons and the removal abroad
of unruly elements. He had little to offer except his own withdrawal,
which was what Louis especially wanted; his title to the Crown of
France was not up for offer – he did not dare surrender that – and he
did not ask for territory. Louis seems to have given him what he did
request – safe withdrawal, a truce, a lump sum of £15,000 and a
substantial pension of £10,000, a trade agreement and the betrothal
of Elizabeth of York to the Dauphin Charles. Such terms salved
Edward's pride and could be presented extremely positively, as
Crowland reports.

> These arrangements were considered, for many reasons,
> appropriate to the time and the condition of the men …
> and were accepted and praised by everybody, bringing the
> war to an end … The lord king, therefore, returned to
> England with honourable terms of peace: for they were
> so regarded by the upper ranks in the royal army though
> there is nothing so holy or proper that it cannot be
> distorted by ill-report.[45]

We have already seen how the English henceforth described
Elizabeth as dauphiness and the pension as tribute. To secure their
favour, Louis paid fees to some of the peacemakers among Edward's
councillors. Not everyone agreed with the treaty. Some of the
English wrongly thought the terms 'mean or dishonourable',
Crowland tells us, presumably those who also distorted it by ill

report, and many others at home rightly objected that 'so much treasure' had been 'so uselessly consumed'.[46] Obviously Charles the Bold disapproved of a treaty that (however excusably) breached his own agreement. Some Englishmen may have wanted to fight on, perhaps including Edward's brother, Gloucester, though we cannot know their plans. Others, especially those suborned by Louis, were fearful of being held to account, perhaps by parliament, more likely by the people. The decision to make peace had been formally agreed in as impressively attended a council of war as Edward could muster and the decision was recorded in a minute. Lord Howard secured a registered copy (exemplification or *inspeximus*) of this and also had it enrolled on the patent roll, demonstrating thereby that it was a corporate decision that had involved the king. 'No-one would have known whose heads were safe among the counsellors,' Crowland reports, 'especially those who, moved by the friendship or gifts of the French king, had been influential in making peace on the terms already described'. Howard had been councillor, negotiator and pensioner alike.[47]

Obviously Edward had qualms too, acting vigorously to keep order amongst the soldiers who returned penniless and remitting the final instalment of tax. Since the second half-year's pay was not required, he may even have ended up in pocket. It is unlikely at this stage (if ever) that Edward considered, with Chrimes, that 'he had carried appreciably further the principal aim of his domestic policy – the better endowment of the Crown. It was realism with a vengeance, even if Niccolo Machiavelli was as yet only six years of age'.[48] Actually Edward was unhappy with the result too, which he blamed on Charles: hence his angry and impulsive offer to join the French against the duke, which Louis ignored.[49] Louis's priority was to remove the English army from France, which he achieved at an easily affordable cost. The terms were indeed, Pollard notes, 'substantially those that he had offered Warwick in 1467',[50] admittedly for an offensive alliance. Louis saw the pension and marriage, it later emerged, as options rather than commitments. For Edward, the Treaty of Picquigny acknowledged that he could not reconquer his French heritage in the foreseeable future; that charge passed down by his father would not be fulfilled. Did it also mark Edward's recognition that his own title could never be made good and that Valois rule was permanent?

Modern historians today, with hindsight and a different set of values, view the Crown of France as an impractical aspiration with little to commend it. Edward and England were fortunate to be spared prolonged conflict, taxation and mortality, to little if any discernible public benefit. In retrospect we can perceive that France had recovered to become a great European power in a different league from England. By modern standards, it was the war that was a mistake and the peace is to Edward's credit. Such perceptions were not apparent to the English at the time and the arguments are anyway alien to the fifteenth century. Edward possessed a title that he wished to assert – may have felt honour-bound to implement – and that he was also expected to retrieve. He failed. Obviously Edward did not achieve all of his war aims. By fifteenth-century standards, the whole affair was an inglorious fiasco and Edward emerged seriously tarnished. He was no chivalric hero. The bold intentions that he had proclaimed had been dependent on international support that was not forthcoming and had been exposed as impractical. Edward appears to have learnt painfully that England alone could not conquer France. Indeed he dared not even engage the French army on his own. Even the supreme effort of 1475 was insufficient. He had learnt also that the English parliament could never (or would never) raise enough money for a sustained conflict. If he did not actually renounce his title to the French Crown, Edward effectively re-categorized England as a second-rate northern power, better able to irritate the French – as the Scots tormented the English – than seriously to threaten them. Yet the Picquigny campaign was not a disaster. Peace had been restored all round, not just with France. The Channel was secured. Edward's pension, though trivial by French standards, was a major contributor to his own revenues. Moreover, the Yorkist regime was not destabilized, disorder did not break out at home and relations with parliament were not decisively soured. Far from being bankrupted, he seems to have ended somewhat in credit. Any loss of prestige had no apparent domestic drawbacks. Even by fifteenth-century standards and even if unintended the achievements outweighed the downside.

1475–83

Picquigny left England at peace with all major European powers. Promoting such amicable ties was an important element in Edward's foreign policy, to be sealed by matrimonial alliances involving his numerous daughters. Several were negotiated, but the two most important – of his daughters, Elizabeth and Cecily, to the future kings of France and Scotland – had failed before his death and none was actually to take place. There are grounds for wondering whether precedence over international relations was actually given to the advancement of his daughters, whose combined portions in his 1475 will were set at the enormous sum of £20,000, payable after his death. It is certainly true that he sought to avoid paying dowries to his international partners for the entirely understandable reason that he lacked the means. Commynes's observation here is not unfair.[51] That Edward also wished to avoid committing himself to military or financial assistance to any of his neighbours ultimately denied him the international weight to which he seems to have aspired. Nothing could be bought with nothing. 'Eventually Edward allowed his own avarice and Louis's diplomatic skill to render him little more than a passive spectator of developments on the Continent and unable to exploit them to his own advantage'.[52]

The Picquigny settlement was presented as a triumph. Edward valued both the marriage – the best that any princess could aspire to! – and the pension. It set the terms for England's future relations with France and Burgundy, even after the circumstances had been radically changed by the death of Charles the Bold (1477), the succession of Mary of Burgundy and Louis XI's attack upon her. The obliteration of Burgundy, which would have denied Edward any allies against a resurgent France, was decidedly not in England's interests. Could England safely permit Louis to occupy the whole of the southern shore of the Channel? By intervening in 1477–8, Edward might have prevented and certainly diluted Louis's aggression and an English prince, Clarence, might have become Duke of Burgundy. Later, after Mary's marriage to the Archduke Maximilian of Habsburg, Edward could have provided the assistance that was so urgently needed. Edward was well aware of the worth of his backing, negotiating various concessions, but he would not supply the practical support that they required. Louis resisted further concessions for non-intervention. Edward did not want to lose the fruits of Picquigny; nor did he wish to embroil himself in a continental war, which he had learned in 1475 he could not afford; and, moreover, much of the manpower and money that he would need was committed to his war against Scotland. Though the king's credit was good, it was not inexhaustible, and it is understandable that Edward declined to take this route. If he could not decide, perhaps it was because he did not want to decide and was never forced to choose. Although evidently not the only factor in Edward's effective neutrality, the Picquigny settlement, from Louis's angle, served its purpose: Edward allowed Louis a free hand with Burgundy. It appears a classic case of the tail wagging the dog: the real and long-term interests of England sacrificed to ephemeral short-term gains.

Edward's avarice, which made preservation of his pension a priority, was based on sound calculations of what he could and could not afford. Such calculations have generally to be abandoned when essential interests are at stake. Earlier in Edward's reign security had often been allowed to override financial considerations. Were essential English interests at stake or permanently lost? The Treaty of Arras in 1482 that ended the Franco-Burgundian war had surrendered to Louis the Burgundian provinces of Artois and Picardy to the north and Burgundy itself to the south, thus substantially and permanently extending the kingdom of France. Yet the Burgundian state was not obliterated. Conquest of all the Low Countries had never been part of Louis's essential war aims and much of the modern Netherlands had been what he was willing to concede to England in the 1460s. Louis was content to settle for what were massive territorial gains and to leave the economic powerhouse of the north in Habsburg hands. Edward's intervention was therefore not needed to prevent the obliteration of Burgundy, which remained available (in Habsburg hands) as an ally for his successors; nor had French control of the Channel coast any real disadvantages since the French did not exploit it. The logical consequence, French annexation of England, was not on the agenda of Louis before or after 1482, nor was it envisaged by his immediate heirs. It is therefore hard to see that Edward's inaction and ineffectiveness had seriously damaged English interests. Keeping out of the continental war, which Edward certainly intended, was an unalloyed good, which it is no anachronism (*pace* Ross)[53] to recognize.

That said, Edward's French and Burgundian policy seems to have excited derision abroad and it certainly did collapse. Louis won his war. Neither he nor Maximilian needed English support any more and Louis decided to stop paying for it. He broke the matrimonial alliance and stopped paying the pension. 'Louis XI had got the better of him,' wrote Chrimes.[54] Louis calculated that Edward could not take effective countermeasures. Louis's action was a savage blow to Edward's standing both at home and abroad. It really stung Edward, who thought himself betrayed – a lengthy declaration to that effect was printed and circulated.[55] He wanted vengeance, reported Crowland.

> The bold king was determined to give everything for
> revenge. Parliament was again summoned and he
> disclosed the whole series of great frauds and won over
> everyone to assist him to take vengeance as often as
> opportunities of the time and circumstances might
> permit.[56]

Evidently Edward was not prepared to lose everything. Parliamentary backing was secured in principle for war some time in the future, when circumstances were more propitious. Really Edward had no plan. Without allies and much greater funds he realized that he could not wage war with France. 'Yet in an assessment of Edward's foreign policy it does not matter how serious his intentions were,' wrote Richmond. 'That he and others believed he might have to invade France for a second time in eight years is proof enough of the failure of his policy between Picquigny and Arras'.[57] Yet the propitious times were only just around the corner, as Louis died in the summer and left behind a young son. A French minority and regency offered renewed scope for troublemaking and blackmail. Sadly England could not take advantage of it, as Edward IV predeceased Louis and England's minority was succeeded by the unstable rule of the usurping Richard III. If 1482–3 was Edward's lowest diplomatic point, it was also a passing phase. Again, there was no permanent impact on England's diplomatic stature.

Scottish relations had been subordinated to other priorities in both 1465 and 1474, when long truces had confirmed the status quo. In 1474 Edward had also betrothed his daughter Cecily to the Scottish heir. The status quo had required him to accept Scottish occupation of Coldingham and Roxburgh, previously often in English hands, and even Berwick, which had been surrendered by Margaret of Anjou. By 1479 Edward thought this no longer necessary: apparently he perceived Berwick, the only part of Henry VI's kingdom that he had not recovered, to be a blot on his record. Edward could now afford a Scottish war and was prepared to contemplate one, although he thought it would not be required. Edward's ultimatum presumed that the Scots would give way peacefully and also that the matrimonial alliance could be preserved.[58] It was a serious mistake. The Earl of Angus raided Bamburgh at once, war broke out and continued up to the king's death. James III's offers to negotiate were rebuffed. Edward planned to take command himself, but failed to materialize. He was not needed in person, but unfulfilled expectations of his leadership obstructed the war effort. 'What paralysed the English invasion plans in 1481 were Edward's own delays and his final decision not to lead his army in person'.[59] A more sustained effort was made in 1482, when Gloucester briefly occupied Edinburgh and Berwick indeed fell, but Edward was unable to bring the war to a satisfactory end: by a decisive victory, since the Scots did not field an army against him; by negotiation, since James III was insufficiently in control; or by a change of regime, since the disloyal Alexander Duke of Albany lacked sufficient support within Scotland. The war was expensive. Probably Edward spent whatever surplus he had accrued, was obliged to collect the outstanding instalment of tax remitted in 1475 and found himself burdened, as Crowland reports, with the very considerable costs of another Calais in Berwick.[60] Of course Berwick was an important symbol that was stressed in Edward's epitaphs. Nor should we ignore how important northerners thought the Scottish conflict, how many of them were created knights and bannerets on campaign,[61] nor how strongly they were attached to Gloucester.

Berwick apart, a somewhat mixed blessing, the Scottish war was an unnecessary burden that drained the king's coffers and stymied his foreign policy. He could not fight on two fronts. 'The entanglement with Scotland was a major misjudgement which greatly weakened his position in relation to continental powers'.[62] But perhaps Edward regarded it as more than the sideshow to continental developments, suggests Griffiths,[63] that French sources and subsequent historians have tended to presume. Was it rather the

Franco-Burgundian conflict that left Edward with a free hand in Scotland? Perhaps Berwick was indeed the finest jewel in his crown. Its recapture certainly completed his reconquest of England. Its recovery moreover proved permanent.

Clearly Edward aspired to prominence on the international scene and even to recovery of the Crown of France or former English territories there, at least sporadically, perhaps only up to 1475. Almost throughout his First Reign, however, preservation of his throne against domestic foes took priority. He had to accept until 1468 that he could not recover Jersey or Harlech, and even had to leave the recovery of Berwick until 1482. At least four times he was outmanoeuvred by Louis XI, who prevented him invading France (1468), had him dethroned (1470), secured his evacuation (1475) and isolated him (1482). The disaster of the readeption was, however, quickly overturned. Against Edward must be held his failure to fulfil his father's charge to reconquer France. It must be said for him, however, that conquest even of a part was no longer within England's power. France was much stronger by his death and prevailed in its rivalry with Burgundy. Edward came to recognize the reality of the next two centuries – that England was far from the equal of France – yet he was able to influence French and Burgundian foreign policies and to extract valuable concessions for non-intervention. If Edward's aspirations were perhaps unduly optimistic and his frustrations and humiliations only too apparent to contemporaries, nevertheless securing international recognition, almost universal peace and retaining his throne were substantial achievements that were beyond Henry VI, Edward V and Richard III. His reign witnessed the restoration of normal international relations after the Hundred Years War.

8

The 'New Monarchy': government and finance

Everyday government

The government of Henry VI, so the Yorkists had claimed, was partial, corrupt and ineffective,[1] and his kingdom was lawless[2] and needed reforming, which York offered to undertake himself. None of this emerges from the records. What they reveal is the orderly functioning of a mature and reliable administrative system that continued to operate without interruption through all the political disturbances and civil wars. The administrative and judicial routine of the principal departments of state, the royal courts, council and parliament, persisted unabated. Central institutions repeated their demands on the localities. As ever, backwoodsmen enlisted royal power wherever advantageous. Commands, commissions, tallies and writs were still despatched to every part of the kingdom. Criminal trials were transferred, reviewed and serviced at the king's bench. Sheriffs, aulnagers, customers, farmers and local ministers were called to account. Suitors constantly conveyed petitions to king and council for rewards and for remedies, and sued their neighbours in the central courts. Bureaucratic procedures were highly developed in England's central departments. There were uniform systems of unpaid local government that operated in every English county, town and manor. That some of these functions were in the private hands of earls palatine, in Chester, Durham and Lancaster, in those of Welsh marcher lords or many lesser franchise-holders, mattered less than that they were all subject to the same expectations, all administered the king's law and kept the king's peace, and all were ultimately answerable to royal oversight. What Edward IV inherited intact was thus a massive central government machine and several extensive networks of local agents, all in efficient working order if possibly not always able to enforce their decisions, which he was able to continue and into which he was expected to breathe new life. 'There proved to be little wrong with English institutions', wrote Wolffe, 'which vigour in the king could not put right'.[3]

Edward IV did more than merely continue and revive old systems, so some of the principal critical scientific historians supposed. Bishop Stubbs was not being complimentary when he contrasted 'Yorkist backsliding' with 'Lancastrian constitutionalism'. Edward IV, he supposed, was not a partner of parliament, but an autocrat who impeded progress.[4] His contemporary John Richard Green went further. The Wars of the Roses destroyed not only the power of the nobility, but also traditional protections against arbitrary taxation, legislation and imprisonment. The resultant royal despotism, to which he gave the name 'New Monarchy' and which he dated to 1471–1509, was founded by Edward IV.[5] The term New Monarchy thus originally enshrined a political shift towards absolutism.

As such, it is unsustainable. Edward could be autocratic and high-handed, oppressive to individuals, and doubtless left some on the receiving end of his decisions aggrieved, but a despotic system is hard to find. Perhaps Edward IV would have liked to be a despot. Certainly he persuaded Crowland (and, more recently, Stratford) that he was one,[6] but his autocracy was tempered by persons and circumstances. He ruled with (and perhaps subverted) rival powers rather than subjected or overthrew them. Parliament met infrequently, but for longer sessions. It was never abandoned. It was because Edward was conscious of his weakness that he avoided confrontations with parliament, nobility and populace. He did not want showdowns. Certainly he did not destroy the power of the old nobility, as Chapter 10 reveals; if that ever occurred, it was after his death. Perhaps again he tightened his grasp on his own finances, on justice, and on the peripheries, but to a much lesser extent than Henry VII. If a real break occurred, whether under Henry VII or Henry VIII, it is difficult to regard Edward IV as more than a precursor.

The New Monarchy has also had another meaning: a new way of governing that came in round about 1500.[7] Although never a term commended by the Tudor historian Professor Elton, it may correspond to what he meant by the emergence of the modern state as explored by Dr Gerald Harriss and Dr Penry Williams in a notable controversy forty years ago.[8] It amounted to an all-embracing concept of sovereignty that overrode lesser loyalties and powers everywhere within the kingdom; kings that were autocratic and despotic; effective agents – a modern bureaucracy, recruited from the middle classes – at the king's command; and reformed royal financial and consultative systems. It is thus a combination of ideology, procedures and coercive implementation. That the modern state did indeed emerge, on the continent and in England, is common ground. When it arose is not. Lander, for instance, postponed it to the seventeenth century. Elton placed it in the 1530s, the achievement of Henry VIII's minister Thomas Cromwell. Harriss and Williams demonstrated considerable continuity from the middle ages rather than change.[9] England had long been a unitary state with a national bureaucracy. Elements certainly existed under Edward IV. Beginnings of some developments, such as conciliar justice, can be located then. That Edward self-consciously set out to change much appears unlikely. Any New Monarchy in this sense is irrelevant to Edward IV.

However the New Monarchy could have a narrower, administrative meaning than this. It is three-quarters of a century since A.P. Newton drew attention to Henry VII's use of his chamber as his principal treasury.[10] Since then, J.R. Lander has rehabilitated the Yorkist council, B.P. Wolffe Edward's management of his estates and his finances in general, J.G. Bellamy his administration of justice and P.M. Barnes his control over potential lawbreakers. It was of such specific developments, not a political despotism, that S.B. Chrimes was thinking in 1964 when he located the New Monarchy not in the reign of Henry VII, but that of Edward IV.[11] In all these ways, Edward IV was the initiator and precursor, albeit tentatively, pragmatically and generally in reaction to events rather than because of any clear-sighted plan. What he achieved, moreover, fulfilled in small ways aspects of the programme of reform that his father had led.

At the most basic level it is apparent that Edward IV ruled much as other late-medieval English kings had done. It was for him to make the key decisions – and unlike Henry VI he did indeed make them – whether initiated by himself, emanating from within the regime or reaching him as petitions, complaints or parliamentary bills. We know that he received and decided bills daily.[12] Seldom did he act alone. He was always immersed in his upper household, surrounded by knights, esquires, yeomen and chaplains only too willing to tender advice, and certainly with the secretarial and financial expertise and records of his signet office and chamber to hand. The loss of the relevant archives allows us only sporadic shafts of light from Richard III's signet register, out letters of the signet in *John Vale's Book*, exemptions for the chamber despatched to the exchequer, and from the provisos to acts of resumption.[13] Much was also handled by his council, which met several times a week, usually without the king but always subject to his direction and veto. The council was primarily a group of civil servants, who coordinated and monitored the central departments, marshalled evidence, prepared responses and organized, heard complaints and repressed disorder much as it had always done. It was Lander's achievement to demonstrate that the drying-up of earlier types of conciliar record did not involve a decline in the council's activity and importance. He showed just how wide-ranging its activities were, how sustained and decisive it could be, and how subservient it always was nevertheless to the royal will.[14] Great councils and parliaments were especially formal, well-attended and powerful councils, capable of delivering legislation and taxation attainable no other way, but also capable of thwarting the king's wishes. Edward worked quite well with parliament and succeeded in extracting from it most of what he wanted, except taxes. If parliament was managed and was not asked for too much, clashes could be avoided, but its complaints had to be taken seriously.

Overall Edward was effective rather than different as a decision-maker. Any novelty in his government lay in three key areas – finance, the administration of justice and management of the localities – all of which had been areas of weakness under Henry VI. 'Edward's modern reputation rests squarely on his work as a renovator of the royal authority,' wrote Professor Ross, a sceptic, 'as a king who brought wealth to the Crown and to his people, as a strong man who kept the peace of the realm'.[15] Justice is discussed in Chapter 9 and territorial reordering in Chapter 11. Finance is discussed below.

Making ends meet

Advanced though the exchequer had been in the twelfth century, and much though it had expanded, reformed and evolved into a large and elaborate institution, it was decidedly out of date by mid-fifteenth-century standards. Antique, unchanging and apparently unchangeable procedures in handling income and making payments, in accounting and in managing the Crown estate may have prevented peculation as intended, but did not deliver to the king enough cash, where or when he needed it. Moreover, Henry VI had been hopelessly in debt, to the tune of £372,000 in 1450. If much of this debt stemmed ultimately from the unsuccessful war in France, normal expenditure alone exceeded the derisory revenues of the Great Slump *c*.1440–80. The customs were especially ill affected. Income for years ahead was assigned to repaying debts. Edward IV dared not disavow his predecessor's debts nor indeed his own, but he was ill placed to repay them. Regular expenditure of about £50,000 a year was surely only just covered by an income less than half that of Richard II.[16] It was a disastrous combination.

The obvious remedy was higher taxes, but the notion of subsidizing normal expenditure was unacceptable to the taxpaying public. The political theory of the time did entitle the king to financial support in emergencies, such as defence of the realm, when necessity could be pleaded. These were the 'great and urgent causes' to which Edward alluded in his speech to parliament in 1467. At such times, subjects were obliged to support their monarch. This could take the form of direct taxes. Four times Edward levied such taxes for waging wars, two of which did not happen and a third of which was prematurely curtailed. Moderate in scale (a full tenth and fifteenth brought in only £31,000), direct taxes were available only when parliament was in session and were too slow to realize in crises. Often money was borrowed on the security of future taxes. Hence, against the northern Lancastrians early in the 1460s for example, Edward also sought forced loans that were repayable later. He could also exact forced gifts, the deplorable 'benevolences' that he supposedly invented in 1474: 'a new and unheard-of imposition of a gift', wrote Crowland, 'whereby everyone was to give of his good will what he wished, or more accurately, what he did *not* wish'.[17] Theoretically, subjects had no right to refuse. Crowland was wrong about the lack of precedents. Edward himself had repeatedly sought sums of his subjects' benevolence against the northern Lancastrians in the 1460s, to be levied by commissioners such as Alderman Sir Thomas Cook.[18] Forced loans and forced gifts dated back at least to the thirteenth century, as Dr Gerald Harriss has shown: the gift was in lieu of military service and the loan a more general obligation, both 'freely' due from subjects in the king's 'necessity'.[19] All that was novel, therefore, about the benevolences was their name. Of their unpopularity, however, we are left in no doubt: a statute of Richard III was to abolish them.

Edward did plead necessity for taxation on several occasions: in 1463, when he did not fight; in 1468 for a war against France which did not materialize, the tax funding his sister's wedding; and in 1472–5. His failure to fulfil the terms of such grants was a grievance of Redesdale's rebels in 1469 and in the parliament of 1472–5, which distrustingly sought to prevent any repetition by appropriating its grants to war and by control of expenditure through special treasurers, treasuries and provisions for refunds. Impractical, hence untenable and finally unavailing, their suspicions were fully justified by the premature and bloodless curtailment of the promised campaign at Picquigny. Small and inadequate though such taxes were, neither Lords nor Commons liked paying them. They experimented once again with new taxes in 1472–5, with income taxes (which the Lords under-assessed), and new modes of assessment designed to transfer the burden. All yielded too little. Taxpayers on the ground, so Lander argues, resisted and delayed payment.[20] Certainly during the 1460s Edward was able to apply taxes levied for war towards non-military expenses and the same may also be true of taxes raised towards the Picquigny campaign. That said, the incidence of taxation was low. The annual average of direct parliamentary taxes to the Yorkist kings was less than half that of Henry IV and Henry V.[21]

Edward had no choice therefore but 'to live of his own', from his ordinary revenues (which included the customs and aulnage on cloth), however inadequate they were. So indeed he declared in 1467, in what Wolffe has described as a personal reaffirmation of 'a Yorkist tradition of constitutional principles, which Edward IV was pledged to follow'.[22] Retrenchment, stringent economies, reduced commitments, increased receipts from old revenues and altogether new sources of income were obviously prescribed. Some at least of these measures were frankly impossible. Edward was expected to live splendidly like a king. He was in no position to avoid exceptional expenses when his throne was under attack and repeatedly he had to fund the repression of his foes. The pitiful straits to which he was driven emerged from his recognition in 1465 that recovering Berwick was beyond him. Edward's success, therefore, not just in repaying his debts, but in restoring the finances of the Crown, is remarkable. Not only did he engage in all kinds of princely expenditure to be expected of a king, to which his surviving library bears witness, but he also died rich and indeed was reputed avaricious. A prime Wydeville objective at his death was reputedly the seizure of his treasure and their success a damaging charge against them.[23] To manage all this despite such obstacles surely rates second only to Edward's achievement in retaining his throne. How was it done?

Critics of Henry VI had blamed his financial problems not on the insufficiency of his resources, but on his mismanagement of them and especially his extravagance in giving away the endowments of the Crown. Reformers such as York had repeatedly demanded that royal grants be resumed.[24] The resumption that they forced through in 1455–6 was initially so drastic that it threatened even to disendow the royal family.[25] As befitted York's heir, King Edward offered the Commons a succession of resumptions, in 1461, of all grants since 1422 (including those he himself had made), in 1465, 1467 and 1473; additionally, a host of partial ones related to particular estates and appropriations on other occasions.[26] A reduction by sixty-one in exemptions in 1473 marked a substantial resumption of grants to Warwick and his ex-Yorkist allies during the upheavals of 1469–71. 'The policies of parliamentary opposition under the Lancastrians', Wolffe resolved, 'do indeed appear to have become governmental policies under the Yorkists'.[27] Edward should therefore have enjoyed the whole of the estate of the Crown and the Prince of Wales, the Duchy of Lancaster which he annexed to the Crown, his own earldom of March, the custodies of royal wards such as the Talbot earls of Shrewsbury and the enormous forfeitures of the Lancastrians in 1461. To these further confiscations were added in every parliament down to 1478. On occasion Edward also forced his subjects to exchange their properties with his own.[28] King

Edward really did possess greater estates than any other fifteenth-century monarch and hence potentially much greater land revenues.

But these revenues were only potential, so Wolffe argued, because of the parlous exchequer system of estate management. Whatever the case a century earlier, the inquisitions on which the exchequer habitually relied to set the rents for its farms (leases) hopelessly undervalued them and ensured that most of the profit accrued to the fortunate farmers. Had this system been applied to Edward's vast landed estates, they could have contributed little to the royal purse. A much better model was the system of estate management as practised by aristocratic landlords, which Edward had encountered before his accession, and on the Duchy of Lancaster. Salaried officials were expected to realize everything set down in the rental and from other sources and were supervised by professional receivers and auditors, who, Wolffe tells us, were no 'mere rent collectors' but men 'of the highest initiative and trust', who were expected to maximize 'the king's profit and thereof yearly to make report'. Increased rents and farms were extracted whenever possible. Sometimes new rentals were drawn up, and new prosperity, such as the cloth industry at Castle Combe (Wilts), was tapped. A council of officers sitting in Cornwall was appointed by Edward in 1461 and reappointed in 1469 to make all leases on the Duchy of Cornwall estate. From the very beginning of the new reign, Wolffe has shown this to be the system that Edward applied. New receiverships for forfeited lands were created in 1461 and in 1462 all properties worth more than £2 a year were withdrawn from the exchequer summons of the pipe. The most striking instance, from 1478, was Clarence's Warwick, Salisbury and Spencer lands, worth over £6,000 a year, which was retained in hand and divided between receivers whose accounts survive among the exchequer foreign accounts. Wolffe identified John Hayes, responsible for the six south-western counties, as his representative example.[29]

Nor was Edward content with old sources of income. Wolffe itemizes additionally the king's levy in 1464 of a quarter of the income from all people holding royal lands, annuities or pensions for life and pleasure, the fruits of successive acts of resumption and from ad hoc commissions to improve estate administration, to which he might have added attempts to transmute base metals into gold, his search for new silver mines and the lucrative (but highly unpopular) recoinage of 1464. The king sold windfall profits rather than giving them away, sometimes sold lands and skimmed off profits from other favours. His French pension of 50,000 crowns (£10,000) a year from 1475 was an added bonus. Wolffe cites with approval Crowland's account of the king's plans to raise money via commercial ventures, by prolonging vacancies of bishoprics, his exploitation of his feudal rights and search for concealments, his forced gifts (benevolences) and the more effective customs administration achieved through his appointment of sharp-eyed customers extremely burdensome to the merchants throughout the realm.

Dr Wolffe also showed how such revenues were kept out of the hands of the exchequer, with its time-wasting administrative processes, and hence out of the hands of the king's creditors and at his own disposal. 'Edward IV and his advisers were in fact creating a new system of royal estate management and organisation intended to provide the king with a substantial and reliable income quite independent of what he received from the exchequer'. Edward sent a stream of missives (*brevia directa baronibus*) to the barons of the exchequer that exonerated his receivers and the chamber from exchequer audit and lodged only abridged declarations of account with them for enrolment on their foreign rolls. Large sums were also transferred from the exchequer to the chamber: nearly £13,820 a year in 1461–8. Evidently Edward had set up in his chamber 'an organization not only capable of collecting and distributing money and hearing accounts, but also of assigning money to different departments of state, without any reference to the exchequer … This was intended to ensure a speedier collection and augmentation of the royal revenues'. Staffed with a 'confident professional class of lay administrators', it generated records good enough to enable all royal grants to be checked and valued in 1467 and a full list of royal annuitants to be composed in 1482. It was in his chamber also that Edward 'made bargains for the sale of forfeitures, wardships, and the keeping of temporalities of bishoprics. Before the letters patent were issued he received payment, cash down, for his own coffers. He appointed receivers for his lands by word of mouth and letters missive'.

Economies moreover were made, nowhere more obviously nor more necessarily than the household. With the costs of the Calais garrison safely borne by the merchants of the staple under the statute of retainer of 1466, the king's principal expense was his household, the equivalent of the great spending departments of today. Bloated, wasteful and costing up to half the king's income under Henry VI, it was several times reformed, notably by the *Black Book* of about 1474 and a further ordinance of 1478, so that in his last years it cost less than 'it had ever been in the reign of Henry VI or was to be under Henry VII'. Queen Elizabeth was also somewhat less generously endowed than her predecessor, Margaret of Anjou. Edward IV was, in short, 'a king with a forceful personality, great energy and thoroughly conversant with his affairs, especially in matters of finance', and devoted great pains to such matters. This was how Edward's revenues were restored to the levels of his predecessors, solvency returned and that a surplus was amassed. It was very much his own achievement although, Wolffe notes, a limited one. Land revenues never sufficed 'to demote direct and indirect taxation as the main sources of public finance'. But Edward's financial arrangements nevertheless anticipated in every particular those of Henry VII.[30]

Ross was unwilling to accept this highly favourable interpretation. From Wolffe's work,

> the impression one derives is of a steady accumulation of the volume of land under the king's control matched by a systematic policy of much more efficient exploitation. Both these notions seem to me to be deserving of scepticism. It can, I think, be shown that Edward never had any clear policy of adding to the royal revenue by the accumulation of land, and there are grounds for questioning whether royal exploitation was very efficient in practice.[31]

Admittedly, 'in 1461 the restoration of some degree of solvency and financial credibility was a task of the greatest urgency'.[32] The king's enormous landed estate was a great advantage, but, Ross argued, Edward's intentions were not matched by performance. He established the new receiverships, but he gave away the lands. Patronage always took priority over income; so did personal expenditure. By 1464 the forfeitures had been alienated, so the king had to draw on Lancaster lands to endow his queen and brethren. He had to provide for his other sons also. Similarly, the Talbot custodies were dissipated in piecemeal grants. The Warwick–Salisbury–Spencer complex was not just the greatest example of estates kept in hand, it was the only one.[33] Carpenter pointed out that the new system required little decision, but must have 'come naturally' to a former nobleman. By itself it need not indicate 'whether, in the 1460s, it was intended as a "land revenue experiment" or made a substantial difference to the royal finances'. As no more than £2,000 a year was raised from lands in 1462–5, she argues, 'it seems unlikely that the lands were in any way crucial to Edward's financial position at this time'.[34] Had Edward been clear that his objective was raising revenue and had been consistent about it, rather than dissipating resources on wasteful patronage, Ross thought that he would have been solvent much quicker. Any 'new principles of estate management ... were not applied to the lands gained by forfeiture'. Moreover, Ross doubted whether the king's newly efficient methods increased revenues and cited specific examples of estates where they had not. There are plenty of examples of inefficiency, notably by Gloucester as chief steward of the North to the Duchy of Lancaster. Crowland's comments were 'far from providing a full picture of royal financial policies'. Big savings were however made in annuities, only £1,391 being payable from the Duchy of Lancaster in 1483 – a mere fraction of what Henry IV had paid. Undoubtedly Edward had better credit and did indeed pay off Henry VI's debts, but nevertheless Wolffe had overstated Edward's achievements. Even with the French pension, Ross estimated that after 1478 Edward enjoyed regular revenues from recurring sources of only £65,000–£70,000; with his savings from Calais, this may have been half as much again as his original regular charges, but still only about two-thirds those of Richard II. 'A relative affluence was part of Edward's strength'.[35] Henry VII in contrast was much more determined, consistent and hence successful in raising revenues. By his death, modern historians have shown, he enjoyed an income at least 40 per cent higher and engaged in meaningful subsidies to his foreign allies.

Actually Ross could have been much more critical than this and others have been since he wrote. From 1472, when his son was aged only two, Edward surrendered the whole appanage of the Prince of Wales to the boy's councillors, progressively adding the earldom of March and most of the Crown and Lancaster lordships in Wales,

which were no longer at the king's disposal and were spent in ways
we cannot now perceive. A great enfeoffment for his will and a
massive endowment for his second son were to be carved out of the
Duchies of Lancaster and York. What had he in mind for his short-
lived third son? A high proportion of forfeitures were restored to
those attainted or to their heirs. Many wardships were granted away
or sold, often in the exchequer or in lieu of repayment of debts, to
Warwick, Rivers, Herbert, Hastings and others. The wardship and
marriage even of Clarence's son and the custody of his Tewkesbury
estates was granted to Edward's stepson Dorset for only £2,000.[36]
Exchanges were often at the initiative of others than the king and
hence to their advantage, admittedly sometimes political rather than
financial. The Warwick–Salisbury–Spencer lands continued to be
administered by the same receivers who had run them for Clarence.
The treasurership of the chamber was evidently a part-time job,
which must have been undertaken generally by deputy after 1473,
when Thomas Vaughan was treasurer of the household of Prince
Edward in distant Ludlow. The acts of resumption also brought in
very little extra revenue. They were not meant to do so, but were
instead a means of recycling patronage rather than resuming
revenues. That of 1473 brought in scarcely anything but Clarence's
Tutbury and associated estates, together worth £1,350:[37] Crowland
was quite wrong to see resumption purely as a revenue-raising
exercise.[38] Crowland was wrong also about some of the other
money-raising schemes he cites: bishoprics were not kept vacant any
longer than hitherto and fines for unlicensed entry to inheritance
were not more noticeable. If the king did pursue feudal revenues, as
Somerville thought for his last years, tightened up the customs
administration and traded on his own behalf, these had no radical
impact on his receipts.[39] It is, of course, unreasonable to expect
Edward to have raised income at the time when the depression was
ever deepening. He did, however, progressively reduce the salaries of
the wardens of the Scottish marches[40] – was Gloucester's
Cumberland palatinate a further attempt at this? – and was spared
the costs not only of Calais but of Berwick for most of his reign.

Wolffe's case can be qualified in many more ways than even Ross
supposed, yet solvency, and apparently much more than solvency,
was nevertheless achieved. Crowland boasted of Edward's
splendour and so did his epitaphs. We know of the king's books, his

new works at St George's Chapel, Windsor, and his palaces, clothes, jewels and other types of courtly display. Given that Edward *was* indeed a very wealthy prince, it follows that his parsimony *must* have been evidence of avarice – a charge several times repeated and dating back to the 1460s. Crowland is not, however, a reliable guide in matters financial. Horrox has shown that Edward did not die rich. Far from leaving a stash of treasure, he left too little to pay for his funeral, his executors declined their charge, and his son's officers were reduced to considerable straits to meet the month-to-month costs of the garrison's salaries at Berwick.[41] No wonder the king lamented both the price of Berwick's capture and its running costs![42] He could not afford the Scottish war lingering on and certainly could not finance war with France too. Pollard perceptively writes:

> Political calculation as well as personal indulgence lay
> behind a splendid court and a reputation for
> magnificence. On his death there was not, as rumoured, a
> vast treasure salted away, indeed the coffers were
> virtually empty. But he successfully created the illusion of
> being wealthy. Thus while Edward did not achieve
> Fortescue's ideal of a financially independent monarchy,
> he successfully convinced his subjects that he had.[43]

Like Chaucer's Merchant, Edward IV managed to appear wealthy without the reality to back it. He always had done so. As Ross remarked, he never 'stinted himself on his personal finery'.[44] Hence he always had credit. He appreciated the political importance of appearances – an image of wealth and splendour – and was able to convince even councillors like Crowland, who should have known better. Commynes also did not suspect that Edward really lacked the money and could not have fought on into 1476. No wonder Edward so valued his French pension and sought to avoid paying dowries for his daughters – although those he prescribed of £6,666 each in his will of 1475 for three unmarried daughters at the expense of his unfortunate heir were cumulatively ruinous.

Carpenter thought Ross too harsh and took a more bullish approach to the whole issue:

> it has to be said that the whole debate has rested on the
> false premise that without financial stability there could

be no political stability and that political stability was in some way linked to independence from parliamentary finance ... However, we have seen in general terms that, even with the fall of customs revenues, there was no insuperable royal financial problem during the fifteenth century. More particularly, we have seen that Edward was already able to get the credit he needed in the 1460s, when he was still coping, mostly without parliamentary subsidy, with the mess left by Henry VI and the demands on his purse of continued internal war and threats of invasion. We have seen also that not even the direst financial crisis could bring a king down, nor the greatest affluence save him.[45]

Of course, Carpenter is right that modest deficits could be handled and that bridging loans could be arranged. It is unlikely, however, that Edward saw it like that or that he could access all the credit he desired. It was a real struggle to deal with each Lancastrian threat in the early 1460s and financial stringency may well have delayed the sustained efforts required to recover Harlech and Mont Orgueil in Jersey until 1468. His father's reburial was postponed until 1476. His poverty restricted him in 1465, when the recapture of Berwick was beyond his means, after 1475 when it limited his diplomatic freedom, and in 1483 when he could afford neither of the wars that loomed. Solvency in the short term certainly mattered to him. Edward never possessed enough funds for emergencies. Although lack of money was never the sole or decisive factor, it certainly contributed to the vulnerability of his regime to internal and external threats both in the 1460s and in 1469–71.

It has been cited as a measure of Edward IV's achievements that he fought the Scots for three years without requiring a grant of parliamentary taxation.[46] This is not strictly true, since in 1480 the king collected the final instalment of the tenth and fifteenth renounced in 1475.[47] He spent it too and had nothing to show for it at his death. Yet the first comment is suggestive. The Scottish war was a significant extraordinary cost. We may reasonably presume that it drained the king's resources from an earlier level when, we may also deduce, he was considerably in credit. That could have been on his return from France. Despite all the costs of preparation, he had been voted enough to pay for 13,000 archers for a year and escaped by paying only for the first six months. He could even have ended in profit. Louis paid him £15,000 down to go away. If Edward had been really desperate for the money then, he would surely have risked collecting that last instalment. If he finally paid off his debts in 1478, this interpretation would suggest that he drained away a surplus in his last years and ended almost precisely in balance. Even without wars, the loss of his French pension and the acquisition of Berwick, respectively bringing in £10,000 a year and taking out £6,666 13s. 4d., equated to a fall of a fifth in his income and were thus very serious.

Where this surplus originated is hard to say. 'Unfortunately Yorkist chamber finance was secret finance', Wolffe wisely observed.[48] Perhaps Edward really was able to combine maximum economy below stairs in his household with maximum magnificence where it showed. Obviously we do not know everything that he accrued. What moveables and plunder, for instance, came with forfeited lands? Sir William Plumpton was only one of those who paid fines to escape attainder. Even the 8,000 marks that Cook was fined did not pass wholly through the exchequer. What happened to the fines raised from Fauconberg's Kentish rebels in 1471? Forfeited recognizances may also have been significant. Quite a long list of minor bonuses can be listed. Edward was not above selling lands. He charged £2000 and £3,333 respectively for spouses for his queen's Grey grandchildren.[49] If Edward often appeared grasping and money-grubbing, it was not because he was stingy, but because he really needed the money. Criticism was a small price to pay for the political benefits of a consummately successful confidence trick.

Edward IV, in short, did make ends meet, an achievement matched by very few post-conquest kings, but he did so more by cutting costs and liabilities than by new revenues and new systems of financial management. Transferring resources to the chamber did give him more control over it, at the price of postponing repayment of his debts. That was also an inescapable side effect of the lavish patronage, generous provision for his blood relatives, in-laws and trusted lieutenants, and the splendid kingly style he cultivated. Solvency, though essential, was secondary to political management. *Pace* Ross, he achieved both. In Edward's favour, certain reforms sought in the 1450s, such as the destruction of Henry VI's favourites, acts of resumption and solvency were achieved. The rise of new favourites, also self-seeking, the use of patronage and resumption primarily for political rather than financial purposes and the dubious means whereby Edward raised money was not what the reformers had in mind. Perhaps, however, much of what they sought was unattainable given political, administrative and financial arrangements that remained fundamentally unchanged.

9

The king's peace

Edward the peacemaker?

England was much more criminous and disorderly during the reign of Edward IV than it is today. Public expectations have been constantly rising. Victorian historians such as Gairdner, Green, Plummer, Stubbs and especially Denton lambasted this particular era for its lawlessness, which cried out for reforms that only the Tudors were able to implement. Nevertheless, they recognized differences within the later middle ages, fifteenth century and even the Wars of the Roses. Supposedly Edward succeeded to a kingdom in which law and order had broken down, where justice was alternatively lacking or actually perverted by those in power, and where noble feuds escalated into private war in many regions of the country.[1] Lawlessness was rife. Too often Henry VI had pardoned compulsive criminals. This portrayal certainly exaggerates and incorporates elements of propaganda. Actually some feuds were settled. The courts continued to operate in what was a fundamentally law-abiding society. Such critiques, however, do accord with contemporary perceptions of chroniclers and petitioners to parliament alike, who appear to have aspired to higher standards rather than merely to nostalgic memories of mythical conditions some time in the past. Since kings were expected to keep the peace, Edward IV had therefore to restore law and order, had indeed a mandate to achieve it, and was himself frequently reminded by individual complainants, rebel manifestos, petitions and bills in parliament what was expected of him. How this result was to be achieved, given the readiness of even respectable Englishmen to resort to violence and the inadequate means of enforcement, is hard to imagine. 'Chronic violence and lawlessness', wrote Ross, 'offered a particularly intractable problem for governments without a large-scale bureaucracy, a standing army or a police force'.[2]

Although declaring a desire for justice, Edward failed to deliver, C.H. Williams reported long ago. His verdict was decidedly against. But Williams had not researched the topic as Professor Bellamy was to do in a pioneering paper that, forty years on, is still the most reliable assessment. Bellamy has argued both for Edward's endeavours and their success. Edward did take practical measures to achieve justice. Bellamy credits the king with the sort of general legal knowledge that all landholders needed to possess. Some of his actions were symbolic, such as the three days the king spent hearing cases at his principal court of the king's bench in 1461, but such personal involvement, he realized, was the most impressive evidence of genuine royal concern.

> Men were in no doubt that the royal presence was the panacea for every kind of eruption of the body politic ... Edward IV realized from the outset that an active peripatetic monarch constantly showing himself to his people and ensuring the hearing of their complaints was essential for the restoration of law and order ... Judicial itineraries like these can be exemplified right through Edward's reign, though of course the disturbances were not continuous.

Sometimes Edward interviewed doomed culprits in person. He made a point of attending a long list of important state trials – longer, indeed, than Bellamy's list and most of them, inevitably, treason trials. He himself led the prosecution against his brother Clarence. Such responsibility was normally delegated of course, to his judges and lay nobility, who presided over 'the most important judicial instrument of the Yorkist kings, the commission of oyer and terminer'. Sometimes deployed against traitors, such ad hoc commissions 'bore the brunt of the Yorkist attack on lawlessness and disorder' and (so Bellamy claims) stamped out the larger disturbances in preparation for the Tudor law of the Star Chamber. The celebrated case on which Bellamy focused in the north Midlands, the murder in a long-running feud of a single gentleman, by illustrating how mild legal scandals had become indicates how law-abiding Yorkist England really was. It also mattered, however, because the protagonists' lords – two barons, an earl and a royal duke – were potentially implicated and restrained, a result scarcely credible had Edward's commissioners not been backed by the king himself. Crises justified suspension of civil liberties in the interests of convictions through selected application of martial law, juries too easily overawed by powerful offenders were legitimately countered by resort to informers, and even torture on occasion could be justified. It was greatly to Edward's credit that he showed that the common law could be made to work, and succeeded 'in reducing endemic disorder to manageable proportions and thereby setting the stage for the final assault on local disturbance'. Regrettably there were limits to what he could achieve. Law enforcement relied on the cooperation of local notables, some of whom themselves offended. 'The crying need was for a strong body of law enforcement locally sited', which the councils of the marches and the North satisfied. 'In his provision of justice and order, Edward evidently anticipated the much more complete achievements of the Tudors'.[3]

Yet Edward himself has been blamed for much of the disorder that actually occurred. These charges fall into three categories: his cruelty towards dynastic foes; injustice in specific cases; and his failure to check bastard feudal abuses. Discussion of each of these follows.

We have seen how earlier generations of historians condemned his cruelty, which Stubbs supposed lacked even the merit of efficiency. Whereas Edward has been blamed for numerous executions and applied on occasion the law of arms rather than the common law, account needs to be taken of the context – civil emergencies, treasonable plots and foes who acted likewise whenever they could – and an altogether more bloodthirsty society in which the death penalty was the normal retribution and regarded as the necessary deterrent for commonplace crimes much less serious to contemporary eyes than sedition and insurrection. It may have been because martial law removed the need for unreliable juries that it could be preferred. The summary trial and despatch of the de Veres in 1462 achieved all the shock that Edward could have desired. In 1468 Londoners were confronted by the rapid elimination of a local celebrity, the tennis star Richard Stares; more time, fuss and uncertainty was caused by those for whom the common law had to be employed. Eliminating those Lancastrian aristocrats who left Tewkesbury Abbey under safe conduct in 1471, unjust, dishonest and sinful as it was, made good political sense. Others who no longer mattered, like the superannuated Fortescue and clerical Morton, were pardoned and set to good use. Though pardoned for his Kentish rebellion, once in the North the Bastard of Fauconberg was disposed of by the constable of England. The king did on occasion spare even dangerous enemies, such as John Earl of Oxford, and distinguished between humbler rebels, whom he hanged by the purse, and their leaders, whom he slew in battle or hanged by the neck. If the contrary part were deprived of figureheads, their cause would simply collapse. The Yorkists' 'reputation for judicial ruthlessness was not really deserved'.[4]

Second, the king's reputation for justice has been blighted by three particular *causes célèbres*, those of Sir Thomas Cook in 1468, Richard Lord Welles in 1470 and George Duke of Clarence in 1478. The discovery and publication of the *Chronicle of the Lincolnshire Rebellion* in 1847 proved Edward's execution of the treacherous Welles to be entirely justified. The Clarence case is discussed at length in Chapter 10. The notorious Cook's case is discussed here.

Cook's case

Alderman Sir Thomas Cook was a wealthy London mercer who helped raise money for the king, against the northern rebels in the 1460s and towards Princess Margaret's nuptial in 1468, but was implicated in a widespread Lancastrian plot in 1468. His story has been repeated many times. Put on trial, he was acquitted of treason, but convicted instead of misprision, knowing of and concealing the conspiracy – scarcely lesser an offence than participation – and was condemned to be fined at the king's pleasure. The king pleased to extract 8,000 marks; Cook lost his aldermanry and the queen sought, apparently unsuccessfully, to secure a further 800 marks as queen's gold. Here fact and justice fade into malevolence and injustice: Cook protested his innocence; the trial was rigged; Chief Justice Markham was dismissed for leniency; the fine was excessive; and the king, queen and the queen's parents (Earl Rivers and the Dowager-Duchess of Bedford) were primarily motivated by greed. Cook's private property both in London and at Gidea Park in Essex were pillaged, an opulent tapestry of the siege of Jerusalem being particularly noteworthy. Subsequently Cook supported the Readeption of Henry VI, deputizing for the mayor, but secured a pardon and died at peace with Edward IV. The scandal is apparently alluded to in Sir John Fortescue's contemporary *Governance of England*[5] and in annals of twenty years later, but two discrete sections of the full story – in circumstantial, partisan and virulent detail – appear only in two London chronicles of the next century, the *Great Chronicle* and *Fabyan's Chronicle*, which incorporate first-hand evidence, some of it apparently emanating from a former apprentice.[6] This tradition became the historical mainstream repeated by More and Camden, and many others. 'The truth of the whole ugly story', wrote Scofield and agreed Ross, 'seems to be that Earl Rivers and his wife, who for some reason wanted to get rid of Cook, played upon the cupidity of the king ... in order to accomplish their purpose'.[7] It remains one of the major charges of injustice and misgovernment against Edward IV.

A plot so close to home certainly alarmed the king. That three aldermen were implicated was surely a sensation in London and apparently came to notice in distant Bar of Sir John Fortescue, who alludes to a 'worthy, honest and upright knight' falsely accused of treason on the basis of a confession extracted from torture.[8] Surely referring to Cook and dating to 1468–70, this is our only strictly contemporary comment. Yet Fortescue was the Lancastrian chancellor-in-exile: his perception of honesty and uprightness may not have tallied with Edward IV's and his information may as well have come through Lancastrian sources as not. We cannot presume, as Ross and Tucker (formerly Holland) have done,[9] that Cook's propaganda was already current in 1468–9, that it adversely affected support for Edward at a time when he needed all he could get, or that it was what enabled Warwick, purporting to be a loyal Yorkist, to enter London in 1469. Although Cook undoubtedly pleaded not guilty, we cannot know whether he claimed malice before 1470–1, when he alleged it in parliament as a backer of Henry VI and deputy to the mayor.[10] Did Cook join the readeption in reaction to mistreatment by the Yorkists or is his participation evidence of continuous Lancastrian sentiment? Could the Lancastrians trust someone genuinely committed to the House of York? Whilst the two London chronicles present everything in the most unfavourable light, they can be faulted on several points of detail: Cook was convicted, not acquitted; his fine stemmed from that; it was not out of line with other sureties for good behaviour; he was allowed to pay his fine with goods, including some already seized; he was indicted by a jury, not merely betrayed by a confession; and Markham's supersession six months later may well have been unconnected. Copies of documents from Cook's own archive do reveal that his property at London and Gidea Park was seized, but they also prove that King Edward pardoned and protected Cook and that Rivers as Lord Treasurer released his property as soon as his fine was paid.[11]

Modern discussion has been enriched by the discovery of the record of the oyer and terminer commission that tried Cook.[12] It was first examined in detail by Professor J.G. Bellamy, who revealed Cook's conviction was for misprision, for which a fine was an appropriate penalty, and concluded that this was an orderly trial. 'The case against him [Edward], however, is not proven and such evidence as there is implies the procedure was lawful enough'.[13] On rereading the documents and not fully understanding them, Ross retained the old interpretation. 'Recent attempts to maintain that the whole affair was conducted by due process of law lack conviction'. Instead, Ross supposed, they showed that Londoners were unwilling to condemn Londoners, that a new jury had to be called and subjected to 'extreme pressure' even to convict him of misprision.[14] Almost at once two complementary articles confirmed Bellamy's interpretation. In a wide-ranging paper that set Cook firmly in his London context, Anne Sutton identified demonstrable errors by the chroniclers and in the regularity of the process, and pointed out that Cook was not the only defendant – 'Thomas Cook is thus stripped of his uniqueness and glamour'.[15] Although admitting that 'the formal record always appears orderly, however irregular the trial, but it comprises the indictments framed by the opposition', Hicks nevertheless demonstrated in even more detail how regular the proceedings were, explained how four juries made presentments simultaneously and were able to disagree on their indictments, and that most of the defendants admitted their guilt by absconding. Cook was unusual in that he was apprehended, stood trial and was not executed. His fine, though heavy, was within his means. 'Edward emerges quite well from the affair,' Hicks wrote.

> He had good reason to believe the accused and was
> genuinely alarmed on learning of the plot: this partly
> excuses any pressure on the juries and the justices. It did

not affect the result ... He acted with discrimination and generosity, even to Cook. If anything he was too lenient, enabling traitors to escape to fight another day. The affair was not badly handled and he does not deserve that it should be a blot on his reputation.[16]

Strangely these two papers did not settle the matter, which was re-examined somewhat unnecessarily by Dr Tucker and with the same result. Whilst suspicious of certain features of Cook's trial, she concluded that 'however keen the Crown may have been to weight the scales in its favour' and however much labouring took place, 'there is not the slightest evidence of unlawful conduct'. Our problem is that we possess no other legal record studied in such detail for comparison. Tucker was more inclined to believe in some of the ancillary abuses and the underlying cash motives and thought that the rest of London's aldermen rated Cook's offence trivial.[17] Revisiting the case in 1995, Sutton stressed that 'concealing plots against the king was bad enough to merit an exemplary fine'. That was something that even ex-mayors could not be permitted to do. 'The fine of 8000 marks was suited to the offender's wealth and station, *and* when taken with whatever destruction of property had occurred, did not sound like justice to Cook'.[18] The 'and' that I have italicized should surely read 'but'. Whether Londoners were inclined to acquit Londoners or whether Cook always thought himself hard-done-by, the old legend is now discounted. Cook, wrote Pollard in 2003, 'was lucky to escape with a heavy fine for the lesser conviction of misprision of treason'.[19] Cook's case is not a *cause célèbre* from which Edward IV emerges with discredit.

Bastard feudalism

Late Victorian and subsequent historians blamed much of the lawlessness and indeed the Wars of the Roses on bastard feudalism or 'livery and maintenance', the mechanism whereby the nobility were enabled to recruit the manpower to oppress their neighbours, raise the armies that fought the civil wars and pervert the legal system. Certainly bastard feudalism featured in many of the most scandalous cases: perhaps they became notorious primarily because they involved men of property and rank. Eradicating such evils was essential, so the Victorian historians argued, yet this was only achieved by Henry VII and his successors. By implication, therefore, this was an area where Edward IV could have done something but fell short. When McFarlane refuted the interpretations of his constitutional predecessors and approached medieval power-brokers on their own terms, it was one of his principal achievements to expose the muddled thinking that underlay their hostility to bastard feudalism. Late medieval England was an aristocratic society, within which lordship and patronage were integral: it was 'part of the normal fabric of society'. To root out such practices would have been to destroy society itself and was therefore unthinkable. Bastard feudalism moreover was a mechanism, capable of operating inoffensively, to the public good, or badly. It was never wrong itself: results depended on how it was applied. Neither was it illegal, nor indeed were many aspects that modern historians have deplored.[20] McFarlane conditioned how modern historians approach the subject. Yet rather more than a vestige of the old approach – that Edward IV needed to do something about bastard feudalism – still colours the outlook of many modern historians.

The present author has defined bastard feudalism at its broadest 'as the set of relationships with their social inferiors that provided the English aristocracy with the manpower they required'.[21] There is no easy cut-off from the feudalism of the Norman and Angevin eras and the patronage of subsequent centuries. Whilst traditional feudal ties, exchanging land for military service, were almost wholly obsolete, contracts of tenancy between lords and peasant cultivators did sometimes deliver manpower in large numbers in pursuit of private quarrels and in civil war. Also important, ubiquitous, committed to their lord and concentrated were households a dozen or even hundreds strong that every aristocrat maintained. Household servants or menials characteristically wore distinctive uniforms, livery or gowns issued to them once or twice a year by their lords. Every lord required officers to run his household and estates, and lawyers to advise him and to prosecute his lawsuits, all of them gentry by birth or courtesy. Such relations were natural, inescapable and beyond criticism at the time, if not in our more democratic, iconoclastic and egalitarian age. What has excited concern among modern historians are the various additional or extraordinary categories of retainers of the high nobility, who were not mere employees or tenants. Some were gentry, often substantial land-holders and shire officials, retained by the lord for life by annuities that may well have implied the terms explicitly stated in surviving indentures, that they were bound to serve their lord for peace and war against all comers. Others were more casually retained by gifts of livery, badges or tokens (henceforth called liveries), which were sometimes distributed wholesale in times of crisis. Theoretically, at least, the numbers in such connections were potentially greater the larger the estates and wealth of the lords. Such human resources were normally latent rather than actual. Retainers adorned their lord's splendid household, impressively escorted him as he travelled, attended quarter sessions or parliament, and dignified rites of passage such as funerals, marriages and baptisms.[22] Moreover, livery was the prerogative not just of the great, but might be worn perfectly legitimately by all kinds of people on all kinds of occasions, as the 1468 statute admitted:

> at the coronation of the king or queen, or at the
> installation of an archbishop or bishop, or the erection,
> creation, or marriage of any lord or lady of estate, or at
> the making of any knights of the bath, at the
> commencement of any clerk in any university, or at the
> making of serjeants of law, or to be given by any gild,
> fraternity, or corporate craft, or by the mayor and
> sheriffs of London, or by any mayor or sheriff or other
> head officer of any city, borough, town or port of this
> realm for the time being, during their term, and in
> performance of their office or occupation.[23]

Clearly most such functions were civil and pacific: at any time many such connections, often great, were headed by widowed ladies. On occasion and probably rarely, subgroups were applied to prosecute a lord's disputes by force and in court, to fight abroad or even to wage civil war at home.

To Denton, Plummer and their contemporaries all these applications were to be deplored. The rule of law was absolute and should not be interfered with and a monopoly of military violence properly belonged with the state. Slightly irrationally, they were highly critical of bastard feudalism, narrowly and mistakenly defined as the extraordinary retaining of the gentry with cash, because it was dishonourable and unstable. Here they were applying standards current in their own day anachronistically into the middle ages. Yet the Crown itself often relied on such connections both to raise armies for combat abroad and during the Wars of the Roses: indeed Edward IV could not have managed without. Yet some of their concerns were shared at the time by earlier generations, who had repeatedly legislated both on retaining and on the manipulation of justice. Denton itemized many of these acts. It was illegal, for instance, to retain royal judges or to bribe jurors. By the reign of Edward IV, these two interrelated areas – bastard feudalism and perversion of the law – were densely regulated by the law: how effectively, of course, is another issue. Within this legal framework, much was permitted that subsequent generations were to outlaw. Bastard feudalism was legal; so too was maintenance of lawsuits and labouring of juries. There is no reason to suppose as yet that lords and retainers were living on borrowed time, tolerated but disapproved of, and awaiting the legislation that would sweep them away.[24]

All members of both houses of parliament always possessed menial servants, and most had tenants and administrators, without which they could not manage. On them, therefore, there were no legislative restrictions, which were confined to the extraordinary retainers. At Edward's accession they were regulated by acts of parliament of 1390–1406, dating back to Richard II and the first Lancastrian. An additional act of 1429 made conviction much easier by removing the need for a jury. Only members of the House of Lords could retain, nobody below the rank of gentleman could be retained and no terms shorter than life were permitted. The one exception was legal counsel, whom everyone was free to instruct.[25] It was not specified in any of the acts, but had become normal by Edward IV's day, to promise service against all men *except the king*. That Edward's father York failed to reserve his allegiance to Henry VI in new indentures of retainer in 1460 indicates his intent to claim the throne. A similar failure by Edward's brother, Clarence, in 1478 became the basis for a treason charge.[26] Extraordinary retaining by gentry of mere peasants or artisans, or the scattering of livery badges broadcast were prohibited. Cases of such illegal retaining crop up throughout the Lancastrian era, often with reference to some provincial feud and always involving a mere handful of humble offenders in receipt of liveries:[27] from which one might deduce that it was legal retainers who did their lord's will. In practice illegal livery was probably normally prosecuted *only* when offenders had also committed other crimes. From those disputes where large numbers were indicted, the Percy-Neville feud in the North and Bonville versus Courtenay in the West Country, offenders were mainly tenants and household servants. Alternatively, since supporters surely wore their lord's badges – as during the major battles or the 2,000 Stafford knots that Buckingham had made in 1454[28] – it may have been simply superfluous to indict them for livery offences as well. Extraordinarily retained gentry appear always to have been few in number – perhaps because they were too costly? – except in the North and were also declining in numbers, to judge from the paucity of surviving indentures.[29] It may be, of course, that they were retained in other ways, through estate offices exercisable by deputy and thus really sinecures or within the household, but here the evidence is too slim to inspire confidence.

If most categories of retaining passed uncriticized and if there were so few offences against the livery laws, one might suppose that further legislation was unnecessary and improbable, but in fact this is incorrect. King Edward did do something about bastard feudalism. A possible motive not stated at the time was the Lancastrians' use of bastard feudal retainers against him, as well as his own and his allies' use of them on his behalf. We can more safely deduce that complaints about illegal livery, retaining, maintenance and a whole host of other crimes were made to Edward at his first parliament, since such enormities were cited as the justification for the set of articles that he made the Lords swear to and that he then had proclaimed. Interestingly, the bishops and abbots as well as lay peers were involved. At first sight these articles tightened the regulatory regime, but on closer inspection they seem designed merely to make it more effective. On this evidence, Edward had no objection to members of households, officers or lawyers of Lords or anyone else. He was concerned only with extraordinary retainers or what he called 'livery of company' – livery worn outside the household by retainers not falling into the permitted categories. In particular he forbade any distributions of livery to such people unless for suppressing rebellions or riots on the king's behalf. This reads like the nationalization of retaining to the service solely of the king that critics of bastard feudalism think proper. It is not clear whether Edward was assuming that commissioners of array would naturally give their own liveries to recruits or whether he was indicating that henceforth royal commissions of array would count as royal permission to distribute such liveries. Exempted from these articles was any livery issued by the wardens of the Scottish marches in England north of the Trent. This particular article appears to forbid life-retaining, but perhaps it did not, since offenders were liable to the penalties cited in the statutes, which did not prohibit this. Much later, Chief Justice Husy misremembered this article when he recalled 'divers of the lords make retainments by oath and surety and other things which were directly contrary to their said sureties and oaths'. Those excluded from one household for misconduct, explicitly (and surprisingly) for playing cards or dice out of the twelve days of Christmas, should not be received into another household without a sealed reference from their previous lord and his consent. Again one wonders where Edward's objection lay. Was it moral? Was he concerned to prevent poaching of valued servants and consequent quarrels between lords? Or did he fear the potential for further trouble of men already excluded from another household for misconduct? Backing up the threat of the statutes attached to each article was 'the king's great displeasure'.[30]

One of the most significant feuds under Henry VI that had involved the principal gentry of Derbyshire flared up anew in 1467, when Roger Vernon, the brother of Henry Vernon of Netherhaddon, the greatest of country gentry, was murdered by neighbours, tenants and menials of Lord Grey of Codnor. 'Those about the king favoured Grey of Codnor and the Duke of Clarence favoured Shrewsbury and Vernon'.[31] The feud threatened to draw in on one side Grey's lord, the king's chamberlain, Hastings, and on the other the Earl of Shrewsbury, Duke of Clarence and perhaps also Lord Mountjoy. Apart from identifying the murderers, commissioners had indicted fifty-six cases of illegal livery given by Grey, Shrewsbury, Mountjoy and two gentry. Spread over seven years and in some instances in the king's service against his northern rebels, they do not substantiate Edward's bold claim that 'divers persons in great number, not dreading those pains or forfeitures, daily offend against the form of the same'. The king stilled the dispute and bound the contending lords by sureties to keep the peace towards one another. Yet he was not satisfied with this result, most probably because it was not the illegal retainers who could be prosecuted who had committed the murder, but legal ones who could not. Hence the 1468 Statute of Livery, an official government measure that did indeed extend restrictions to prohibit extraordinary retaining altogether. Once again, household servants, officers and legal counsel were acknowledged as legal retainers. Henceforth, however,

> no person, of what degree or condition he be, by himself or any other for him give any such livery or sign or retain any person other than his menial servant, officer, or man learned in the one law or the other, by any writing, oath, or promise [and specifically not through any] retainer by indenture.

Exceptions were made once again to cover the wardens of the marches north of the Trent and others in defence of the realm, to exclude the three northern palatinates, and to permit a whole range of other ceremonial and innocuous uses.[32]

Suggestive of panic, the latter proviso of exemption indicated that it was the king's intention really to enforce the new rules, which is amply justified by the indictment the following year in the king's presence of the Dukes of Norfolk and Suffolk for giving illegal livery to one hundred and fifty-nine individuals under the 1468 statute. Apparently Edward was determined to let the law take its course: attempts by the Pastons to circumvent it were rebuffed. These two cases together involving three dukes, several other peers and two outlying provinces reveal the king apparently determined to stamp out the use of extraordinary retaining to maintain private quarrels by force even by the greatest magnates in the realm. Yet nothing more came of this measure. Professor W.H. Dunham was at a loss to explain how Hastings was able nevertheless to recruit seventy-four men by indenture from 1474, unless this constituted lawful service permitted by the act. Although Edward repeatedly forbade retaining within royal towns and Grey of Codnor was several times prosecuted for offences at Nottingham, Dunham could find very few cases under the 1468 act and none involving peers in Edward IV's reign.[33] In the short term, Norfolk and Suffolk and their men were exonerated in 1471 at the king's command, certainly for political reasons and most probably in recognition of their services

in recovering the king his throne.[34] Hastings' indentures were effectively authorized by the king, since they were contracted as steward
of Tutbury and Duffield honours, not for fees but for good lordship
in his capacity as chamberlain of the royal household, and thus to
exclude further service to the retainers' former lord, Clarence.[35]
That even during the selfsame East Anglian sessions in 1469 Sir
William Calthorpe and others were 'sworn my lord of Gloucester's
men' must surely also have been condoned by the king.[36]

It appears likely that Edward lost interest in illegal retaining
during his Second Reign, perhaps because he appreciated both how
much he needed the lords' connections for his French war and how
little problem it actually posed him. Apart from Hastings' highly
exceptional ones and those of the marcher wardens, actually no
indentures of retainer are known after 1470 and precious few for
Edward's reign as a whole.[37] Annuities continued, though it would
be hard indeed to prove that those we know about were not to
menials, officers or legal counsel. It is surprising that so few
prosecutions occurred when the 1468 statute had further simplified
the process, drastically enhanced the penalties and halved the
potential proceeds with informers – unless, of course, there were
very few offences. It looks as though the Lords agreed to the 1468
act because extraordinary retaining was no longer important to
them. Perhaps a small amount of illegal retaining aroused much
more symbolic indignation than it deserved in reality. Alternatively,
of course, the bastard feudalism that posed problems related to the
menial servants most committed to their lords and best organized by
them. Dukes surely had menials and officers enough not to rely on
extraordinary retainers. Not just Edward IV failed to ban menial
service; neither did Henry VII nor any successor. All these monarchs
confined themselves to punishing any crimes that such menials
committed.

It seems, therefore, that Edward did little that was effective to
regulate bastard feudalism, which was, however, slowly evolving of
itself. He enjoined his Lords not to receive miscreants expelled from
another household into their own. He also ordered in 1461 that:

> No lord, or other person of lower estate or degree,
> spiritual or temporal, whatsoever he be, wittingly receive,
> harbour in his household nor maintain pillagers, robbers,

oppressors of the people, manslayers, felons, outlaws,
rapists, and other notorious misdoers against the law,
unlawful hunters in forests, parks, or warrens, breakers
of ponds and other rioters, or any openly reputed as
such, till the time of his innocence be declared, upon pain
of the king's great displeasure and the peril that may
ensue thereof.[38]

Whether lords really wanted such men as menials, how effective
Edward's command was, and whether he implemented his
threatened displeasure we cannot at present know.

Surviving letter collections indicate that most perversions of
justice persisted – indeed much of the data cited by the Victorians
derived from the Paston Letters – but the only celebrated instance of
abuse was that by Clarence against Ankarette Twynho. Serious
crimes, in contrast, abounded, and notorious ones, especially in
Cornwall, are not hard to find. However, there can be no statistics
or trends for perversions of justice. Certainly there were cases of
retainers invoking the backing of their lords in wrongful causes and
disputes between underlings that drew in their superiors – once,
ironically, bringing the king's mother, Cecily Duchess of York, into
conflict with her son Richard Duke of Gloucester.[39] Lords did not
however automatically back their men against all comers in defiance
of right. Gloucester, Northumberland and Hastings drew back from
the brink and the royal council refused Sir William Plumpton's
request to intervene.[40] Lords at all levels commonly used their
authority to defuse conflict by prescribing mediation, arbitration
and settlement out of court.[41] Whatever the injustices of bastard
feudalism, local communities generally preferred peaceful (and
cheaper) settlements by agreement to violence or litigation in the
central courts. So too, undoubtedly, did Edward IV: himself an
aristocrat, he was ready to let the system work, although prepared
reluctantly to intervene when it did not. Indeed Carpenter claims, on
rather insubstantial grounds, that he was obliged to proceed directly
through his council against the worst offenders in Warwick's own
county of Warwickshire.[42]

Scarcely did Bellamy praise Edward for 'reducing endemic
disorder to manageable proportions'[43] than Ross expressed his
doubts. He conceded 'that Edward was conspicuously more

successful in preventing the escalation of disorder than Henry VI had been' and in quieting the feuds of the great. He listed, however, some grave offences, interestingly in outlying Cornwall and Lancashire, and continued laments about lawlessness, and faulted the king for 'the immunity of the powerful offender, especially those who had the king's support', such as the Wydevilles and Gloucester.[44] Perhaps Ross was unreasonable: Edward had to back somebody and improving standards of order generally was extraordinarily difficult to achieve. But that, after all, was what Bellamy had claimed.

What concerned Bellamy primarily were the king's intentions and practical evidence that he responded, through issuing commissions, personal judicial progresses and symbolic judicial acts. Only a tiny minority of offenders and litigants were touched by this. Most oyer and terminer commissions did not operate, to judge by the limited surviving returns and the paucity of cases tracked in the king's bench controlment rolls by the king's attorney-general. At most hundreds rather than thousands of offenders were indicted. Many of these involved treason. It was to counter sedition, insurrection, major feuds and disturbances, which threatened the government or local peace, for which such commissions were deployed. They were not employed against commonplace felonies and trespasses, everyday crimes including murder, economic offences or infringements of property, for which there was ample judicial provision from assizes and quarter sessions downwards that functioned without interruption throughout the reign. Most people were unaffected by them: most of those engaged in agriculture, crafts or trade were untouched by Edward's actions. Perhaps there is an exaggeration here. So vigorously did Edward react to disputes over elections and commons at the great cities of Bristol, Coventry and York through privy seal and signet letters that we may wonder whether there was also more royal intervention in lesser (and less well recorded) urban and rural communities. Yet Edward's pursuit of justice can have impacted little on the majority.

Everyone in Yorkist England was engaged at some time in lawsuits of some kind in some type of tribunal, whether criminal or civil, by martial, common, canon, mercantile, forest or customary laws, as plaintiffs, victims, defendants, witnesses, jurors, attornies or officials. It is fortunate perhaps that most of the records have disappeared. The laws were pervasive. Many cases at every level, moreover, were settled out of court, sometimes perhaps merely dropped, but often compromised or resolved through mediation and arbitration which left little imprint on our formal records. Every kind of law, court and even arbitration had its jurisdiction defined, its own rules and procedures, yet all were subject to perversion. What pressures caused even those with good cases to settle? Wherever suits were heard, there was scope for patronage, maintenance, labouring and the whole range of other abuses associated with bastard feudalism. Decidedly humble lords could support the most obscure dependants in the most local courts as the Plumptons and their connections did.[45] Bastard feudalism and its abuses reached right down the social order, beyond the levels where the term has in the past been thought applicable or particularly meaningful. Perverting the course of justice demanded the participation of neither lords nor retainers and was surely as often (and, probably, more often) undertaken by equals, by partners in crime and by fraternities from amongst the majority of the population who were never genteel nor normally retained. This litigation and perversion is largely concealed from us and almost wholly unstudied.

Understandably Edward was interested primarily in cases that concerned himself personally: sedition and insurrection. He was also influenced by complaints that were made to him, his council, and his chancellor by individuals, groups and, above all, the parliamentary Commons. Chancellor and council often, perhaps generally and perhaps increasingly effectively, provided remedies in particular cases.[46] Where groups or the Commons were involved, more determined action and even legislation was required. It appears that it was complaints in parliament late in 1472 about the depredations of Welshmen from marcher lordships within the adjoining English shires that prompted Edward to visit the region the next year and to settle his son there. The petitioners were concerned about crimes by Welshmen on them, not about crimes by Welshmen on Welshmen nor by the English proletariat on one another. That Edward moved decisively against the Herberts was for personal reasons unconnected with their oppressions.[47] Even the Commons was an élite body, made up of men of property, rank and local standing, and its concerns focused on matters that affected itself. The removal of potentially disruptive younger sons and unemployed soldiers in wars and garrisons was an argument that appealed to them in 1472. They demanded the more effective procedures for prosecuting certain types of offences that Bellamy has outlined, such as the use of JPs' certificates rather than indictments, even though they were very seldom used. Abuses of power, bastard feudal perversions of justice and unfair trading practices, where they were on the receiving end, were what concerned them – and what Edward took action to allay – not the violence, petty larcenies and economic frictions that were endemic in local communities. Even the robber community at Idle in the West Riding was brought to the attention only of Sir William Plumpton as lord by his tenants and was dealt with – or more probably ignored – by him.[48]

Edward has been credited with some effective initiatives in improving order. Top of the list, as indicated by Bellamy, was the establishment of devolved royal jurisdictions in Wales and the North.[49] Order clearly varied from region to region, Cornwall being especially bad, and the precedents of existing devolved systems of justice in the distant palatinates of Chester and Lancaster look especially intensive. Establishing Prince Edward in Wales anticipated Henry VIII's council in the marches of Wales, but that was not what it was nor what was intended. Jurisdiction was confined to the principality and the marcher lordships in the prince's own hands – admittedly a growing proportion of the total – and not those of other councillors and noblemen, with whom the king and later the prince as earls of March had reciprocal agreements as equals. Extradition and other agreements in indentures between king/prince and other lords repeated earlier initiatives and cannot be demonstrated to have had any impact: nothing appears in financial accounts of the lordships. Moreover, any cases that the prince's council received from Wales – and Cornwall, Chester and elsewhere on his estates – were heard not at Ludlow, but at Westminster, by councillors who were professional lawyers active there and who did not visit the marches. Their decisions depended for enforcement on the prince's officers. The best known and best documented suit, by Gruffydd Vaughan ap Eionion against the prince's treasurer, Sir Richard Croft, had already been frustrated by Croft once and may well have been again. However deplorable the rule of the Herberts, the authority exercised by the prince's agents is unlikely to have been different in type.[50] Similarly, the rule of Gloucester in the

North, which legitimized the authority of the lesser noblemen who served him and their settlement of disputes through arbitration, may well have contributed to local order at the price of denying alternative remedies to anybody on the rough side of their decisions. If Ross was right to doubt that such rulers were impartial,[51] perhaps it was more important that they ruled effectively. No public council with royal jurisdiction existed in the North until Richard III's reign and nothing is known of any cases it handled, if it did.

If uniformity of enforcement (rather than consent by the governed) was the prime objective, it was regrettable that kings of England depended on the cooperation of the leaders of local society in each locality, whether county or town. They had the local standing to implement the king's wishes, which they did without pay in return for appointment to royal offices that legitimated their authority. This unwritten contract enabled such local rulers to delay, impede or wholly stifle the king's wishes, sometimes where they themselves were the offenders, more often perhaps (as much later) where they interpreted it as contrary to the interests of their country. Northumberland was famously able to thwart Montagu's recruitment against Edward IV in Yorkshire in 1471. Short of dismissals, which were likely to result in office-holders less respected and effective locally than those removed, Edward was reduced to exhortations and threats. 'And also all Lords being at this present Parliament', he declared in 1461,

> have promised openly before the king in the parliament
> chamber that they and each of them shall help and aid all
> men that any such [criminals] will take and put them in
> their devoir to do the same, even if such misdoers are
> retained or appertaining to them or any of them.[52]

If it is significant or surprising that such a sworn undertaking was required, we are in no position to judge its efficacy. Neither Edward IV nor his immediate successors could do more. Moreover, he did not wish to do so. The rule of the regions serves to 'show Edward's tendency to rule wherever possible through trusted individuals rather than develop new institutions'.[53]

Edward's actions in Wales highlighted the obstacles to justice and order posed by marcher liberties and presaged the day when his grandson Henry VIII, as lord of most of the affected lordships, imposed the same judicial structures that operated elsewhere. Edward was willing, on occasion, pragmatically to override the privileges of sanctuaries and benefit of clergy, but he was not ready to reform or revoke them and probably did not even consider doing so. Henry VII, who went further, still stopped short. Edward did not take any major actions to improve public order as a whole.

When we consider Edward's achievements in this area, he seems to have had no significant impact on prevailing standards of law and order. Why should he? In the criminal activity and perversion of the law by the élite, however, a reduction may have been achieved. Edward was disinclined to proceed against those (such as his brother, Gloucester, and his in-laws) on whom he relied for political control of the regions. Although there is a false contrast between the escalating feuds in every region of Henry VI and their near absence under Edward IV, because most of Henry's feuds were resolved before his death, nevertheless a contrast is obvious; it is also striking that at least three feuds broke out into violence during the political crises of 1469–71 when Edward could not give his attention to such matters. Very few cases of notorious crime by the great were forwarded by the justices of the peace to the king's bench: Ankarette Twynho stands on her own. Some still happened and were recorded, for example, in the Paston Letters. Of course, crimes against property and persons were proportionately much more frequent and much graver than we expect today. Yet justice did operate continuously and as effectively as such imperfect systems could. Apparently the king did succeed in controlling lawlessness to the point where public complaints were at least muted.

10

Edward IV and the nobility

Aristocratic rule was normal for all historians up to the twentieth century. Historians of Edward IV's own age and three centuries after took for granted the landed wealth, great households, retainers and royal office-holding through which noble power was expressed and maintained, and felt no need to comment on it. Eighteenth-century and especially subsequent historians came to disapprove of 'the barons', their violence, factiousness and abuses of justice, and even came to approve of the annihilation of the 'old nobility' in the Wars of the Roses. Many noblemen were slain in Edward IV's wars of 1459–61 and 1469–71, and many of the vanquished and their noble houses were extinguished by the attainders of Edward IV.[1] Polydore Vergil surmises that Warwick feared the destruction of the ancient nobility,[2] which became a commonplace in the centuries that followed. It was a generalization that was not based on careful investigation of the facts and was rejected in a paper in 1875. In 1965, McFarlane himself attributed the disappearance of noble families to natural causes. What eliminated the familiar titles was the absence of male heirs. About the same time, Jack Lander analysed Edward's forfeitures in detail. Most attainders were reversed, the victims or their heirs being allowed to work themselves back, having first demonstrated their acceptance and service to the new regime. Many forfeitures were only temporary.[3]

Whilst all these arguments have much to commend them, they too incorporate a number of fallacies. The decisive phase in extinguishing great houses came after 1483.[4] *Pace* McFarlane, most of the great houses that disappeared during Edward's reign *did* possess heirs, who were not allowed to inherit. The Dukes of Somerset and the Marquis Montagu were telling instances. Lander also inadvertently misled. Although most of Edward IV's attainders were reversed, a mere handful of the attainted were restored in the 1460s, rather more after the decisive extinction of the Lancastrian royal family in 1471 – Fortescue and Morton are striking examples – but many did not owe their good fortune to Edward IV at all. The Courtenays, Hungerfords, Rooses and Cliffords had to wait until 1485 or even later. Twenty-five years is long enough for loyalty and traditions to die, must have looked permanent and was surely intended by Edward IV to be so. Lancastrians, in short, had either to cease to be Lancastrians, as the Wydevilles did, or remain dispossessed. Edward ruled the English regions through those who had fought for or acquiesced in his accession and especially through his new Yorkist nobility.

Edward IV was born into a great noble house, had many noble relatives, and expected to become a nobleman himself. He shared the education, recreations, tastes and outlook of the nobility, amongst whom he moved easily and from whom he chose his intimates and friends. The upper household amongst whom he lived was overwhelmingly aristocratic. A king was a nobleman written big. Edward had no prejudice against the nobility and ruled through them, employing them in military commands, as lord treasurers, on judicial and other commissions. Most of Henry VI's noblemen survived into Edward's reign, continued to engage in local government, and to attend great councils and parliaments. The noblemen and great houses that expired, whether through forfeiture or natural causes, were replaced. With Vergil's approval,[5] Edward dispersed forfeitures in grants to other noblemen and gentry whom he trusted. He created many new peers and promoted them and existing peers as rewards for their services. He endowed them to the level appropriate to support their new ranks. He made dukes of his sons and brothers and countesses of his sisters-in-law. The king appointed peers old and new to local office, so they could rule their 'countries' on his behalf. Only their personal commitment to King Edward distinguished his 'new Yorkist peerage'.[6] All the new Yorkist noblemen without exception were already aristocrats. They were noble cadets, heads of gentry houses and/or county families, whom Edward elevated in rank and wealth, and continued to act as such. Their personal contact with the king gave them weight politically and

made them attractive as local lords, for Edward expected them to
have retainers. Edward had no prejudice against bastard feudalism
as such, although he responded when necessary to demands that it
be restricted, and sought in certain localities, in the north Midlands
and royal towns like Nottingham, to keep outside lords off his
demesne. Edward ruled, in short, as previous kings had ruled. The
nobility were his lieutenants, some old and pre-selected by heredity,
others whom he had raised from his trusted intimates, which all
kings did. Perhaps he had more scope for choice, because of the
forfeitures of 1461 and later, and because some of his earlier
choices, like Fauconberg and Stafford of Southwick, died and had
to be replaced. No hereditary system is static. Edward possessed a
nobility of variable age and ability that was constantly changing
with mortality, minorities and majorities, with inheritance and
division between coheirs. He had to live and work with it and could
not normally change it. When he did in his last years, as we shall
see, his actions were resented and proved impermanent.

Edward IV and traitors

Edward IV ruled initially through loyal Yorkists, amongst whom he
distributed his forfeitures and on whom he bestowed his offices. He
appreciated the need, however, to broaden his support from a faction to embrace the nation as a whole. 'It was the combination of
old and new nobles that formed the basis of Edward's rule, but he
also needed the unregenerate Lancastrians'.[7] Those who suffered
forfeiture in 1461 were already dead or still in arms against him.
Lords Rivers, Scales and Grey of Codnor, who had fought against
him, were allowed to submit, were received into his allegiance and
escaped forfeiture. Sir William Plumpton was fined instead. Another
act provisionally attainted named individuals if they did not submit
by a specific day. Many attainted Lancastrians ceased to resist and
lived peacefully in England. If some, like Henry Clifford and
Edmund Roos, were not restored, presumably because they offered
neither potent threats nor valuable service to Edward, others were
allowed to serve him and were rewarded with pardons, reversal of
their attainders and restoration of their lands, though seldom all at
once, as Lander showed.[8] Whatever the original intent of
parliamentary attainders that purported to be permanent, by

dispossessing Edward's grantees such restorations demonstrated that title to attainted property was insecure, especially when the original beneficiary had died. Almost always the original victim or his heirs survived. Furthermore, attainder dispossessed the heirs of those attainted, who had committed no offence themselves. Such heirs were felt to have been wronged, in an era when inheritance was regarded as a sacred right. Thus they continued to enjoy the sentimental attraction of erstwhile servants and tenants, and also the advocacy of mothers, cousins and other kinsmen amongst the nobility. Some recipients of forfeited land wasted the capital assets. Yet others, such as Edward Grey of Groby and later Richard Duke of Gloucester, compounded with the attainted, selling their rights or surrendering some property in return for a secure title in the remainder. Pembroke and other hopeful fathers hoped to provide for their children by marrying them to the heirs of attainted estates and securing their restoration: in Pembroke's case at the expense, principally, of Clarence and the Nevilles. Warwick had done the same when he married his sister to the heir of the Earl of Oxford. Supposedly others, in contrast, sought forfeited property by having the current tenant or claimant attainted, as Stafford of Southwick was alleged to have done with the Courtenay heir in 1469.[9] Such uncertainty and speculation added extra scope for disputes over land and inheritance. Edward IV appreciated this, on occasion perhaps encouraged it, and had the role of final arbiter. Much manoeuvring and negotiation seems to have taken place outside our records and Edward, if involved at all, may have merely confirmed the results.

Though the Lancastrians were defeated, Lancastrianism survived. Left to itself, it might have died out naturally over a generation or so, but Edward could not afford to wait so long. Lancastrianism was not a passive creed. Diehard Lancastrians did not accept their defeat as final. Throughout Edward's First Reign, Henry VI constituted an alternative. Even in the Tower after 1465 he possessed supporters still committed to resist, invade and foment conspiracies. To make himself secure, Edward sought to root them out by force and by negotiated extradition with those who harboured them, at great expense in time and money and with limited success. To accept their submissions, to receive them into his allegiance, to restore their standing and possessions (always the essential price for any deal), to divide and weaken the Lancastrians and perhaps also to win their service to himself was a policy more attractive to Edward, if not to his Yorkist adherents. A succession of reverses, personal poverty and discomfort, separation from and the sufferings of women and children were disincentives for Lancastrians to continue resistance. Conciliation and compromise were particularly desirable for Edward in the far North. There all the natural leaders were Lancastrians, there the military, financial and logistical effort was most insupportable, and there foreign help was most readily available. The nearby Scottish border offered immunity from Yorkist countermeasures. Conciliation there could not only have ended the war, but healed the wounds. The potential advantages certainly justified the risk. 'Winning over former Lancastrians,' says Carpenter, was a 'laudable aim'.[10] Hence Edward received into his allegiance Sir Ralph Percy, Sir Ralph Grey and even the Duke of Somerset, restored their possessions, made the first two constables of castles and fêted the duke at court. Measured by results, the policy failed, all three rebelled again and were executed. Others defaulted too: Pollard adds Oxford, Courtenay and Hungerford.[11]

Edward has been much criticized for pursuing this failed policy. *Gregory's Chronicle* was scathing. 'There now followed one of those political blunders which mars Edward's record as a statesman,' pronounces Ross. 'Nothing in the record of either Somerset or Percy seems to justify Edward in placing such trust in them; and events proved how serious had been his miscalculation'.[12] How serious was it? Edward had to recapture the Northumbrian castles all over again. This argument, however, presumes that there were no advantages in short-term gains – the immediate capture of castles, the denial of the support of these leaders to the rebels, relief of military and financial strains and the propaganda coups that such desertions represented! If Percy failed him, Edward nevertheless needed the Percies in the far North and restored Ralph's nephew to the earldom of Northumberland only six years later. Somerset was head of a Lancastrian royal house and hereditary foe of the House of York. The costs were small and the potential gains large. 'To King Edward the submission of 2 so eminent persons appear'd welcome as a victory'. Others might have followed. If desperation drove Somerset and Percy to submit, it was 'now upon a false hope of fairer weather [that they] fled there again. For it is a ridiculous cunning to Historians to ascribe the actions of great men profitably to policies', Habington sententiously pronounced.[13] So too, three centuries later, argued Carpenter:

> He was pardoned and restored to his lands and titles. This was by no means as foolish as has been suggested, but was all of a piece with the need to bring Edward's former enemies to his side. If Somerset came, then many others might follow. In the same vein, Sir Ralph Percy was pardoned again and given command of both castles. Somerset himself helped take Alnwick again early in 1463 ...[14]

Pollard suggests that 'the policy of reconciliation helped the new regime to survive its fragile first years'.[15]

Moreover, failure is relative. If Oxford and Latimer rebelled again in 1470, it was for Warwick and Clarence. Tresham and many other erstwhile Lancastrians returned to active Lancastrianism only when Henry VI was king again. Sir Thomas Hungerford, if actually guilty, illustrates the desperation of those who were denied restoration. If Lancastrian loyalism remained the key obstacle, as Carpenter and Hicks have suggested,[16] perhaps also Yorkist objections – the attempted lynching of Somerset at Northampton being the extreme example! – made submission too painful. If there were risks, Edward had to take them. *Gregory's Chronicle* speaks for those Yorkists who still nourished personal enmities against the Lancastrians and who feared the fruits of their victory would be diluted by restorations. Edward needed to be more statesmanlike. And after 1471 there were no such risks in reconciliation in the few instances where Edward chose to exercise it.

Edward IV always regarded himself as a legitimate king and therefore expected subjects to recognize and obey him. Lancastrian rebels were executed at intervals throughout his First Reign both as punishments for them and as deterrents to others. He took treachery, like that of Somerset, and ingratitude, like that of Cook, most seriously. His vengeance and bloodlust, however, were not unrestrained. Lesser men, the rank and file of the Lincolnshire and Kentish rebels, were forgiven and/or fined. He usually (but not always) acknowledged the rights of wives, widows and dowagers. On occasion he relieved those lacking jointures.[17] He was prepared to negotiate with Clarence and Warwick in 1470 and to assure them of his grace provided they submitted unreservedly as true subjects should, but not to offer guarantees. The Yorkist ladies negotiated a deal between Edward and Clarence the next year, which may have been essential for his victory and which certainly facilitated it. At Clarence's urging, Edward also offered terms to Warwick in 1471, which the earl declined.[18] Edward's extermination of the Lancastrian royal family and captured aristocrats in 1471 after Tewkesbury, some as traitors and others as irreconcilable enemies, was an act of policy that apparently overrode the rights of sanctuary that he had explicitly promised to observe. Oxford's life was spared, but he was perpetually imprisoned. The most exemplary instance of royal justice and Edward's use of terror, however, was the destruction of his brother, Clarence, in 1478.

Edward IV and Clarence[19]

George Duke of Clarence was Edward IV's next brother and briefly heir to the throne. Declared of age at sixteen and generously endowed, he resented his brother's plans for him, married a great heiress in Warwick's eldest daughter and rebelled three times with Warwick in 1469–70, when he helped restore Henry VI. Evidently dissatisfied with the result and suborned by his York kinswomen, Clarence joined up again with Edward IV and helped put him back on his throne in 1471. Nobody has ever doubted that Clarence was wrong to rebel, that he was ungrateful, treacherous and obviously perjured several times, that his reputation was rightly smirched and that contemporaries must have thought his damnation was assured. If not forgotten, his offences against his brother were nevertheless pardoned and he resumed his former station. Their reconciliation necessarily had to put bygones behind them, forgive past treasons and allow the royal brothers a new beginning. It required of Edward a fresh start with Clarence. Subsequent disagreements over the Warwick inheritance, in which Edward IV reneged on his original disposition and took Gloucester's side, caused considerable friction and resentment. Not only had Clarence to surrender much of the inheritance, but he was also deprived of north Midlands lordships on which he had based his power. Whilst the Pastons connected Clarence's objections with continuing Lancastrian disturbances in

1472–3 and Carpenter has added others in 1477,[20] there is no evidence or likelihood that they were correct. During these years Clarence operated like any other magnate, attending parliament and leading a company in Edward's French invasion. Carpenter, on dubious grounds, thinks him an ineffective ruler of the West Midlands.[21]

Following the death of his duchess in 1476, Clarence was proposed as husband to Mary Duchess of Burgundy, a match which Edward scotched. Relations between the brothers thereafter were very poor. On the unlikely charge of poisoning his duchess, Clarence had her handmaiden Ankarette Twynho seized, tried and executed in 1477: arbitrary abuses of power that unquestionably breached the law. Clarence's own esquire, Thomas Burdet, the chaplain, Thomas Blake and an astronomer, Master John Stacy, were accused of conspiring the king's death by necromancy. They were indicted, tried and condemned by an authoritative commission in what contemporaries regarded as a proper legal process and were executed. The necromancy story was forgotten or not generally believed by the beginning of Henry VIII's reign, at least as regards Burdet, when Sir Thomas More alludes to an alternative explanation.[22] Unsubstantiated, apparently unsubstantiable, and most probably therefore a myth, More's story, as expounded (and expanded?) by the Elizabethans, Holinshed and Stow, and repeated thereafter, attributed Burdet's fate to what was technically treason by words: Burdet's complaints at Edward's killing of a favourite deer in his own park at Arrow (Warks)! King Edward arrested Clarence, apparently for perversion of justice, whether for speaking up for Burdet or the Twynho outrage, and staged the duke's judicial trial in the 1478 parliament that concluded in Clarence's attainder and execution. Probably Clarence was indeed executed by drowning in malmsey wine.

Clarence was tried for treason. We know the charges because we possess the act of attainder against him that parliament passed and Edward signed. A lengthy document, which appears to mingle fact and innuendo, it cannot be substantiated in any detail, though certain aspects could possibly have been construed as treason at the time: an exemplification of a Lancastrian act making Clarence the heir; indentures of retainer that did not reserve allegiance to the king; and Clarence's paranoia about the king's intentions for him.

The act does not report any new plot, threat to the king or anything else to justify Clarence's destruction, but it does deplore (in personal terms that are recognizably Edwardian in vein) his ingratitude to the king. Complaints about 1469–71 related to conduct that had been pardoned[23] and were strictly irrelevant. The act was not a source used by historians at the time – even by Crowland, who was present at the trial – or much into the modern era to account for Clarence's fate, which was generally explained in other ways. Mancini attributes the trial to the queen's fear of the duke, but says he was charged with imagining the king's death by sorceries.[24] It was Edward's frustration of his brother's remarriage that engendered the mutual animosities that were inflamed by intermediaries, reports Crowland, and Clarence's defence of his client Burdet, executed for sorcery, offered the occasion for the duke's arrest. Edward declared it 'a most serious matter, as if it were in contempt of the law of the land and a great threat to the judges and jurors of the kingdom'.[25] With reference to the actual trial, Crowland had nothing to say about the charges, which however he disbelieved. Sir Thomas More offered four options, only one treasonable: the enmity of duke and king, the envy of his enemies, the jealous slanders of the queen and Clarence's own aspiration to the Crown.[26] Although he had enquired widely, Vergil was baffled and offers three alternatives. Crowland's explanation of Clarence's arrest is summarized, but not accepted; equal weight is given to the rumour that it was because of the prophecy that Edward would be succeeded by someone whose name began with G – as in George Duke of Clarence, but also Gloucester. Vergil concludes 'that he was cast away by envy of the nobility'.[27]

All the principal narratives therefore doubt the justice of the trial: 'Whether the charge was fabricated or a real plot concealed,' queries Mancini. The trial was shocking, Crowland makes clear, with only the king prosecuting and the duke defending. So-called witnesses inappropriately doubled as accusers. Crowland did not believe the charges to be proved even though parliament, where he himself was present, 'formally condemned' the duke. 'Were he faulty, were he faultless,' quipped More; 'by right or wrong,' says Vergil.[28] All four deplore the destruction of a brother. Two, Crowland and Vergil, say that the king afterwards regretted it.[29] Whether written at the time or soon after, all our sources condemn Clarence's fate.

That Clarence was unjustly treated was the message transmitted to future generations, from Vergil and Hall via Holinshed and Stow to Shakespeare, Heywood and Habington. It was certainly the message of Shakespeare, who presents him as the victim of his brother Richard, bent on the Crown. Shakespeare's Richard predictably casts the blame on the queen. It was he who Shakespeare presented despatching Clarence ahead of the death and the reprieve of Edward IV. Shakespeare's Edward bewailed Clarence's death, remembering his brotherhood and services ahead of his fault, mere thought, for which he did not deserve to die. 'Ah, poor Clarence!' he cries. 'Simple, plain Clarence,' says Gloucester.[30] Yet it is 'false, fleeting, perjur'd Clarence', the shriek of the shade of Edward of Lancaster, the greatest foe of the House of York, that has proved memorable and continues to colour the duke's memory.[31]

Similarly Heywood stresses Clarence's loyalty to the princes, the G prophecy and blames Gloucester.[32] That Burdet was wrongly treated was apparently a commonplace that was elaborated by John Stow. The *Mirror* tells the story at much greater length: 'How George Plantagenet third son of the Duke of York was by his brother King Edward wrongfully imprisoned and by his brother Richard miserably murdered'. Clarence's earlier treasons are admitted and excused. 'For I was witless, wanton, fond and young'. Although Clarence was suborned by Warwick, he had been badly treated by the king. Coming to his senses and with no future under the Lancastrians, Clarence was reconciled with his brothers. All was well. But then he was:

> Imprisoned first, accused [me] without cause,
> And done to death, no process had by laws.

And all because of the prophecy that G 'Of Edward's children should destruction be', which the poet ridicules over many stanzas.[33] Perhaps having read Crowland, he knew of Clarence's Burgundian marriage, thwarted by the king, and of the false charges against Burdet, who was so obviously innocent 'as is a babe':

> So that I could not but exclaim and cry
> Against so great and open an injury.

Hence Clarence was arrested, exposed to further tales cooked up by Gloucester, and subjected to a form of trial:

And covertly within the Tower they called,
An inquest to give such verdict as they should.
Who what with fear, and what with favour thralled,
Durst not pronounce but as my brethren would.
And though my false accusers never could
Prove aught they said, I guiltless was condemned.
Such verdicts pass where justice is contemned.

Thus drowned I was, yet for no due desert,
Except the zeal of justice be a crime.
False prophecies bewitched Edward's heart.
My brother Richard to the crown would climb.
Note these three causes in thy rueful rhyme
And boldly say they did procure my fall,
And death, of deaths most strange and hard of all.[34]

The pro-Ricardian Buck compares Richard favourably with the 'sullen and mutinous disposition' of Clarence and acquits him of Clarence's destruction, which arose from the duke's own treasons and ingratitude which 'so extremely provoked the wrath and hatred and indignation of the king his brother against him as that no man had hope to gain any grace for him'. He recites Clarence's offences in 1469–71 – actually water under the bridge after their reconciliation in 1471! – but he had charged Edward with the bastardy wrongly attributed (by Morton!) to Richard. Hence Clarence perished due to 'the king's deep and implacable displeasure conceived of his brother ... And the king had so great fear of him that he never thought himself secure until he was dead'.[35] Buck relies on good sources, the act itself (via Stow), Crowland (unacknowledged) and Vergil, but the record certainly does not read as he says and Crowland did not intend presenting the trial as Buck interprets it. Buck was ahead of his time, however, and furthermore akin to some modern historians in his support for Clarence's destruction.

Habington was no fan of Clarence, whom he thought inconsistent and weak, and understood how each act of opposition, though legitimate, could be construed as treason, yet he acquitted him nevertheless. 'We cannot judge him of any evil action', although 'he suffered as if he actually had sinned'. Burdet's trial was itself irregular. In Clarence's absence (in Ireland, Habington wrongly

supposed), Burdet was 'apprehended, indicted, arraigned and executed all in space of two days'. The 'inconsiderate words' that he
uttered on hearing of the king's killing of the 'white buck in his
parke', that 'he wished the head and hornes and all in the king's
belly', really meant that he wished them 'in his belly who counselled
the king to kill it'. Habington had no patience with the necromancy
charge, approved of Clarence's protest and thought his action quite
insufficient for his arrest and execution. Having perused the actual
act of attainder for himself rather than relying on Stow's misrepre-
sentation, Habington found that it contained 'crimes enough to
make his death have appearance of justice', although his conviction
required the king's promotion, Gloucester's secret plotting and the
urging of the Wydevilles. The whole episode was extraordinary and
implied that nobody could oppose the king's actions even by words.
It was indefensible even amongst those

> who most favoured the king. At home it was generally
> condemned, both with regard of the manner [malmsey
> wine], it being prodigious to be drowned without water
> upon dry land, and the quality of the person. He being
> the first brother to a King in this country that ever were
> attainted ... Where for the death of a younger brother,
> upon bare suspicion, the king could know no precedent
> than the Turkish government.[36]

Nothing could be worse than Turkish! A faction claimed credit,
Habington reported, from which he deduced that Clarence was condemned for his offences a decade earlier with Warwick, supposedly
wiped clean, rather than anything new. Habington was inclined,
however, to downplay criticism of the king, since it was really the
fault of the queen's faction.

Clarence's fall, adjudged Hume a century later, was 'an act of
tyranny, of which Edward was guilty in his own family, has been
taken notice of by all writers, and has met with general and deserved
censure'. It originated in a conspiracy against him by his enemies,
the queen and Gloucester, who proceeded initially against his
friends: Thomas Burdet, who rightly objected when the king killed
his buck, was tried and beheaded in consequence; and likewise John
Stacy, who 'lay under the imputation of necromancy with the
ignorant vulgar'. When Clarence protested at 'these acts of tyranny',

again rightly, he offended the king, who put him on trial. 'Many rash expressions were imputed to him, and some too reflecting on Edward's legitimacy', conceded Hume, 'but he was not accused of any act of treason'(!) and may indeed have been denied a fair trial, 'since the liberty of judgement was taken from the court, by the king's appearing personally as his brother's accuser, and pleading the cause against him'. Whilst the alternative explanation, the prophecy of G, was conceivable 'in those ignorant times', it was probably invented later, after Gloucester's murder of the princes.[37] For Stubbs also 'the death of Clarence was but the summing up and crowning act of an unparalleled list of judicial and extra-judicial cruelties which those of the next reign supplement but do not surpass'.[38]

Yet these are the extremes. No modern historian, of course, accepts that sorcery or prophecies were effective, even if contemporaries did, and hence all reject not just the prophecy of G, but also the guilt of Burdet. To Gairdner it was 'a natural sense of justice' that prompted Clarence to protest, and to Ramsay it was 'as in honour bound', yet 'still very imprudently' that Clarence acted.[39] Burdet suffered, Stratford and Pollard agree, as a warning to Clarence. Although decidedly hostile to 'a busybody of the worst type [like Clarence], quite incapable of seeing the effect and appearance of his own actions', and questioning his sanity regarding the Twynho trial, Stratford was unconvinced by Clarence's guilt but not of the inevitability of his conviction, since Edward could tolerate no parties.[40] If Bellamy demonstrated that there was nothing unprecedented in the procedure of Clarence's trial,[41] yet the duke's conviction is certainly no evidence of his guilt. Hicks has demonstrated how carefully the show trial was staged to ensure a guilty verdict.

Yet most modern historians depart from this historiographical tradition and indeed from our contemporary narratives. They continue to hold against Clarence his conduct in 1470–1, for which they feel he should have been 'chastened' and sidelined. He should not have defended his right to the Warwick lands inherited by his duchess. Dockray refers to 'his chronic inability to realise how lucky he had been'.[42] Yet the brothers had been reconciled. Clarence had helped his brother back on to his throne. He had been reconciled with the king. He had been forgiven and formally pardoned. Both brothers intended a fresh start to be made and old coals should not therefore have been raked up in 1478. After 1471 he had lost ground materially. He was deprived of much Warwick inheritance that he had been granted – the so-called 'reconciliation and settlement' engineered by the king was all one way – and of his great honour of Tutbury; *pace* Dockray, these were both genuine grievances,[43] which, however, in no way justified the treasons of which neither Edward nor modern historians have found convincing evidence. Modern historians have no time for Clarence, whom they find foolish and inept. Regarding the proposal that Clarence should marry Mary of Burgundy, 'Edward IV *naturally* would have none of such a scheme for the vast aggrandizement of his totally unreliable brother George ...,' wrote Chrimes.[44] Why not? Likewise the duke's measured protest through a spokesman on behalf of Burdet, which so many past historians honoured him for and indeed thought him obliged to make, is regarded as suspicious (because his spokesman *may be* the Dr Goddard who proclaimed Henry VI in 1470), potentially seditious and even, according to Dockray, 'frenzied'![45] Have we lost sight of the culture of honour to which Clarence's gesture belonged and to which Gairdner and Ramsay, for instance, still subscribed?

Obviously Clarence inconvenienced Edward – oppositions do, even today, and have still to be tolerated. Late-medieval kings had to live with and work with the magnates that they inherited and could not arbitrarily rid themselves of them except extremely rarely and then only by the formal judgement of peers that was not normally so blatantly fixed. Clarence's act of attainder is undoubtedly 'alive with his overwhelming irritation at his brother's behaviour',[46] an irritation fuelled by the proximity and passions of the blood. If Clarence was thought to be a threat, there appears to be no evidence why. If Clarence was a nuisance, apparently the main argument for his destruction by Edward, so were many other disorderly noblemen, for whom confinement, recognizances and so on were established modes of management. If all our scholarship cannot substantiate any of the charges against him, to prove either his guilt or that they amounted to treason, almost all modern commentators acquiesce nevertheless in his destruction and even applaud it. 'An apologist for Edward might argue that the king put justice before the blood of his own family,' suggests Bellamy –

although no historian has ever taken that line – 'but a cynic would say he took advantage of a wonderful opportunity to remove a perpetual menace and simultaneously to advertise his own concern for the law'.[47] That he was 'mischievous' suffices for Richmond. Clarence did not fit into the regime, says Carpenter, and his non-treasonable acts were justification enough. The duke's destruction was 'a political necessity' to both Gairdner and Ramsay, and justified by 'reason of state', says Pollard. Even if there were insufficient proofs and fratricide was to be deplored, Dockray agrees with Lander, Clarence had thoroughly deserved his fate![48] What is also clear is that Clarence's conviction is no proof of guilt. 'The proceedings of the parliament were a show trial,' admits Pollard. 'It achieved its purpose, for reasons of state, of finally ridding the king of his incorrigible brother ... In truth the whole story of the destruction of Clarence does not reflect well on the king, his family or his regime'.[49] If Chrimes took a more cautiously negative stance, that 'the charges ... were carefully formulated, and it is hard to say that they were not substantially a true bill', he nevertheless deplores the result. 'A severe lesson' might have been enough; Edward could have stopped short of fratricide. 'But he did not; he was too powerful now for anyone to restrain him; he could not even restrain himself. He was to regret his action in his own life-time'.[50] Clarence's treatment flouted even contemporary standards of justice.

Our most modern historians thus seem to have completely lost sight of the able prince depicted by Crowland and Mancini, who thought him neither a fool nor inept. 'The three brothers', reports Crowland, 'possessed such outstanding talent'; 'besides he possessed such mastery of popular eloquence', opines Mancini, 'that nothing upon which he set his heart seemed impossible to achieve'.[51] We do not actually possess any evidence other than that already cited to indicate that Clarence was foolish or incompetent, as Stratford long ago observed.[52] What little evidence we have reveals him acting the conventional part of a great magnate.[53] We do know that he was popular.[54] Standards of political expediency are nowadays applied to Clarence that are applied to nobody else. They are completely alien both to contemporaries, to whom Clarence's destruction was a scandal, and for centuries of subsequent historians. The standards that Edward lived by made his action into a sin, indeed several sins. Even if *raison d'état* is sufficient justification in our post-

Machiavellian age and even if fifteenth-century kings applied it in practice, it was not permitted by the Christian values applicable at the time. Modern approval of Clarence's destruction is not strictly anachronistic, but perverse, since the standards we apply are not our own. Few, if any, of these modern historians would approve the death penalty even for the worst criminals in our own day and yet they apparently advocate it in an age that they characteristically condemn as unduly violent. We cannot disregard the historical fact that Clarence was thought to be innocent at the time; nor that his trial contravened, as Crowland supposed, contemporary standards of justice; nor that his fate flouted (as fratricide obviously did) normal expectations of brotherly relations; nor that it reveals Edward at his most blatantly unjust and arbitrarily tyrannical. 'Edward IV alone was responsible for what happened,' wrote Ross. 'No one can seriously deny that the king bore the ultimate responsibility'.[55] The king certainly led the prosecution. At the time he wanted to dispose of Clarence even though it appears unlikely that he thought him a traitor. That he afterwards regretted Clarence's death indicates, as Vergil supposed, that Clarence was the victim of a factional feud, most probably directed by the Wydevilles,[56] and therefore that the king was not the prime mover, but was manipulated into destroying his brother.

Clarence's fall is something new. Parallels with the mysterious deaths in 1397 and 1447 of two other royal uncles and dukes of Gloucester are not exact, for in neither case did a king actually dare to bring them to trial and neither was the current king's brother. To this extent Clarence's fate prefigures the judicial murders of Henry VIII. Does it also foreshadow the essentially factional murders of Anne Boleyn, Thomas Cromwell and so many others? If, moreover, it was intended to secure the succession for Edward V, it failed, and indeed removed an obstacle to usurpation. Clarence had to be removed if Gloucester was to succeed: no wonder so many have thought that this was why it happened. Clarence's case, in short, does deserve to remain a blot on Edward's reputation.

Carrot and stick

If Clarence could fall, so could anyone. Henceforth, says Crowland, deeply disapproving, the king feared nobody and there was nobody that the king would not confront with his offences to his face.[57] Clarence's fall had a deterrent effect. Crowland's observation is fascinating, since it suggests that the king hitherto had tiptoed around, evading confrontations with the great, and that thereafter he dared anybody who would not knuckle under to rebel. None presumably did.

There is much more evidence that Edward used patronage as a source of political control than coercion. He had so much patronage at his disposal: he was well placed to offer carrots to actual and potential servants, to entice and to reward, not merely moderately but lavishly. He certainly discriminated in what he bestowed, was not above disappointing expectations, but certainly allowed some individuals to accrue more over time than he ever intended or really desired. Normally such grants were permanent, for life or in tail; if intended for future service also, they were nevertheless secure and could not easily be revoked. But many consisted of forfeitures, which might be reversed. Hence recipients were balanced against the attainted and both parties pressured to demonstrate that their service was more valuable. Moreover, all such grants – and any others too – were subject to resumption by the four general acts of 1461, 1465, 1467 and 1473, and by a number of more limited ones. In order to retain what they already held, royal patentees had to secure exemptions from each act, which the king reviewed and initialled himself. They had to prove the continued relevance and value for money of what they already held. They continued to hold it less in reward for the past than in expectation of the future. The king could review what he had given and revise his disposition. Grants that had descended to heirs were revoked. Performance came into play and penalties for default. The stick accompanied the carrot, coercion supplemented patronage. In 1473, and perhaps on the other occasions too, the current occupants were interviewed personally by the king and were made to confess what they had received, which was checked against the signet records, and were told what they might keep and what they must surrender. Then they submitted precisely worded provisos of exemption that the king signed. Whilst most kept everything, some lost it all and others had their holdings pared back, amongst them the superseded chancellor Archbishop Neville.[58] When Clarence's honour of Tutbury was resumed, much else was exempted. King and duke, we may presume, had an unpleasantly frank discussion, in which Edward imposed his will and Clarence had no choice but to comply. That was in 1473. Edward could always, on this evidence, browbeat and override his greatest subjects. Warwick's possessions may not have been resumed, but on occasion alternative grants to others superseded them.

Henry V and Henry VII are known to have made extensive use of recognizances 'for good behaviour' to coerce their subjects into compliance with the royal will on pain of dire penalties. Lander argued that this was refined into a system by Henry VII that enabled him to override potential dissent. There is some evidence of such practices in Edward's reign also, applied at a routine level by the royal council and more specifically against particular individuals. Such bonds played a part in the forced exchange of lordships and the exclusion from Wales of the second William Herbert.[59]

As we have seen, Edward generally and genuinely tried to restore law and order elsewhere and to maintain it. The 1450s, which historians think was particularly disorderly, were coloured by disagreements amongst the aristocracy – what Bellamy called 'gentleman's wars' – and Storey found an 'escalation of private feuds' into private and eventually civil war. Quite a long list can be compiled. Mainly originating in disputes over inheritances or local ascendancy, they grew because King Henry VI lacked the authority to impose his will. Most ended naturally in the 1450s and others were decided by force between 1459 and 1461 – neither Bonvilles, Courtenays, nor Percies survived and Warwick's victory excluded all his rivals from their inheritances. No comparable ones emerged. It may be significant evidence that royal control was effective that Norfolk's attack on Caister, the Berkeley–Lisle and Harrington–Stanley disputes boiled over when royal authority was temporarily suspended. When Clarence intervened in the Caister dispute on behalf of the regime, he found himself no substitute for the king when Norfolk declared that 'he will not spare to do as he is purposed for no duke in England'. Embedded in the national struggle – and resolved by it – were Warwick's personal differences with Herbert and Welles's with Burgh. In his Second Reign, Edward did stop the rivalry of Gloucester and Northumberland and did impose settlements on the Harrington, Norfolk and Warwick inheritances, not necessarily justly, but effectively. What evidence there is, therefore, suggests that Edward was able when he chose to impose his will throughout his reign.

What is doubtful, however, is how consistently he did so. The retentive memory for faces and circumstances that Crowland records of Edward IV was of great use for this kind of man-management. The tight personal review of provisos of exemption, however, was immensely time-consuming, especially at such a busy time as a parliamentary session, and was probably also highly stressful for all parties and cannot have been repeated very often. It was a way of creating space for newcomers, but Edward cannot often have wished to discard the old. Most patentees did retain their offices and grants: it was the threat, not the reality, that reinvigorated service. More commonly he allowed inheritances to run their course rather than diverting them, more often selling or granting marriages to third parties than selecting the spouses themselves.

Apart from the examples cited, he did not often coerce the great. It is easier to list three occasions when Edward declined to intervene. When Suffolk destroyed the Pastons' house at Hellesdon, the ruins of which he had been shown, Edward declared that it might have merely fallen down:[60] a feeble excuse not to act, because he did not wish for a showdown with a duke who was his brother-in-law on behalf of suitors whose thanks mattered little to him. He was not prepared either to force the Duke of Norfolk to restore Caister Castle (Norfolk), which he had wrested from the Pastons by force. The duke's services to the king in 1470–1 outweighed his offences against the Pastons in 1469, when he was indicted for illegal livery, for which both he and his retainers were excused.[61] Third, when Sir John Risley planned to buy a house from Gloucester late of the Countess of Oxford, he asked King Edward 'to give him good counsel whether he should surely do yea or nay'. 'Meddle not,' replied Edward,

> for though the title of the place be good in my brother of Gloucester's hands or in any other man's hands of like might, it will be dangerous to thee to buy it and also to keep it and defend it, saying then also … that the said lady was compelled and constrained by the said Duke of Gloucester to release and forsake her right in the said place.[62]

Edward knew of the gross injustice that Gloucester had done to the countess, but was not prepared to intervene. Whatever he may have avowed, he did not in practice enforce the same standards on the high nobility as everyone else. Justice was not his sole objective. His provision for his closest kinsmen in his last months rode roughshod over rightful heirs.[63] He may well not have dared to cross Gloucester in the North, as Pollard has argued.[64] The evidence therefore does not support Crowland's portrayal of a king in complete control, still less Carpenter's eulogy of his 'perfect instinct for the vital kingly balance between justice and mercy'.[65] Edward coexisted with his greatest subjects and allowed them considerable latitude before he interfered. Any framework that he prescribed, a novelty in Carpenter's eyes, was broad indeed.[66] Edward's territorial reordering of the kingdom, however, is considered in the next chapter.

11

Territorial reordering

Changing the noble map of England

Bastard feudalism supplied the manpower that enabled lords to 'rule' their 'countries'. The land that underpinned such connections and hence local power structures, was inherited from generation to generation. Inheritance meant that kings normally had to work with such noblemen; they could not usually choose them. McFarlane's work has prompted historians of Edward IV to investigate the distribution and exercise of power in the regions. They have few precedents. Amongst contemporaries, Crowland realized that Richard Duke of Gloucester drew his power from the North and that it was his northern followers who overawed London in 1483. Mancini referred to the Gloucester estates, without any notion where they lay.[1] Kendall was breaking new ground in 1955 with his chapter on Gloucester as 'Lord of the North', which has become *de rigueur* for biographers of Richard III, not all of whom share his enthusiasm: Ross, Horrox, Pollard and Hicks are examples.[2] They appreciate that Gloucester was no innovator, but rather the inheritor of the power of the Nevilles, of Warwick the Kingmaker in the previous generation. The defeat and forfeiture of the Lancastrians in 1461 offered Edward IV exceptional scope to redraw the map of English landholding and regional power. Whether he perceived his opportunity quite like that is doubtful. Ross, to some extent, and Carpenter, Horrox, Lowe and Pollard believe that he engaged self-consciously in territorial reordering on several occasions. There were five principal exercises: in 1461, 1464–5, 1469–70, 1471 and 1483. Most estates and local power structures remained untouched throughout.

The First Reign

The new king found himself possessed of a very substantial landed
estate falling into five principal categories: the lands of the Crown,
the queen, and the princes of Wales; the Duchy of Lancaster; his own
Duchy of York and Earldom of March; Lancastrian forfeitures; and
some royal grants that had been resumed, most notably the honour
of Richmond. Edward clung on to the princes' lands, had the Duchy
of Lancaster vested permanently in the Crown and retained his
Earldom of March; the rest of his father's estates was settled on his
mother or allocated to pay York's debts. Theoretically, at least, all
these possessions were permanent endowments of the Crown. In
practice, however, Edward gave many of them away, some for short
terms and others apparently permanently, although circumstances in
due course reversed all these alienations. Estates affected were the
whole county of Chester (1464), the Gournay lands of the Duchy of
Cornwall (1464) and many Duchy of Lancaster honours and lordships. As late as 1482 the Lancaster lordship of Kidwelly was gifted
to a stepson. Others in the East Midlands were settled on his second
son in his will of 1475. Edward was also prepared, on occasion, to
grant important offices, such as the shrievalty of Cumberland and
justiciarships in Wales, in tail male.[3] None of these dispositions
endured. Lands resumed in 1461 were few, but the forfeitures were
extremely extensive, even though the property of Lancastrians slain
before 30 December 1460 was exempt and some other offenders
were forgiven or allowed to purchase immunity. The offices of the
Lancastrians were also available for redistribution. Yet many of these
had already been filled by the Yorkist government in 1460, Warwick
and other Nevilles being particular beneficiaries, and Edward as king
honoured these dispositions.

In the interests of rewarding loyal Yorkists, creating vested
interests in his regime and reinforcing his hold on the localities,
Edward granted away almost all these properties and posts in the
first year of his reign to his loyal partisans. Since inquisitions *post
mortem* had not yet been held (and were often never arranged), he
was not sure what he had to give or how forfeitures were
encumbered, for example, by rights of dower and jointure. Within
broad frameworks, therefore, the initiative was taken by petitioners,
who asked for what they wanted and often had to return for more

precise patents later. Some requests, perhaps many or most, were refused, but we know only of instances where actual patents were cancelled or superseded. Whilst some were substantial, it does not appear that wholesale grants were made to anyone in any region, even Warwick having aspirations that were disappointed. His family did not, for instance, secure *all* the Percy and Clifford lands in the North, nor was Warwick able to advance himself in South Wales, where William Lord Herbert was the king's chosen agent. Over time, Warwick's brother, John, was advanced to the Earldom of Northumberland (1464) and Herbert to that of Pembroke (1468) in reward for good service against the Lancastrians. Originally merely Warwick's deputy, John Neville grew through conspicuous service into a significant magnate in his own right, whilst Herbert expanded beyond South Wales when the king's officers in North Wales fell short. Herbert held only a few lordships of his own and his income of £2,400 fell well below that of the greatest magnates; however, he held more royal offices in Wales than any single individual before Buckingham in 1483.[4] The Nevilles' domination of the North, where Warwick was briefly lieutenant of all the marches, and the West Midlands, and Herbert's rule throughout Wales from 1468 were the only truly regional hegemonies. Warwick, before 1467, and Herbert, from at least 1465, wielded most influence with the king at court. Edward's other new favourites, Humphrey Stafford of Southwick (Earl of Devon, 1469) and Richard Earl Rivers were never endowed on this scale; his brother, Clarence, was too young to be really effective in the north Midlands during the First Reign. Royal patronage and hence power, though confined to loyal Yorkists, was spread quite widely and, Herbert apart, created no new magnates of the front rank. The acts of resumption that enabled Edward to review his patronage at intervals did not, in practice, greatly augment his resources. Edward's territorial dispositions at the beginning of his reign served their purpose: only in 1469 did the Yorkist regime rupture.

An important element here was Edward's provision for his family. Like all kings Edward had to make such provisions and like all kings he found it difficult, all the more so because of the scale of endowment he thought appropriate. Of course, Edward had always intended to provide for his brothers, elevating both to royal dukes straight away and earmarking properties for them, but in both cases other exigencies took precedence. The boys were, after all, still too young to enjoy the income or act politically. Their grants, like all others, were depleted by restorations, the essential price for conciliation, and prior titles proved by others. In 1464–5, when Edward had to find resources for his family, much of these had to come from the Duchy of Lancaster. This was true of much of the minimum endowment of £4,500 that he found for his queen. Edward was highly unusual, however, in the weight he attached to his close family, his siblings, legitimate offspring, sisters-in-law and stepchildren. Grants to Clarence in 1464 of the whole county of Chester and all the Lancaster lands in Derbyshire and Staffordshire anticipate the £3,766 achieved and the £4,400 forecast in 1467.[5] Clarence was to have six times the 1,000 marks (£666 13s. 4d.) endowment of an earl that was all that Edward III had provided from his own purse for his three younger sons or that Henry VI had found for his Tudor half-brothers. It was three times the standard endowment for a duke provided for Richard II's youngest uncles and Henry V's own brothers on their promotions. Edward IV's touchstone, in short, was not the qualifying revenue for a duke – enjoyed, for example, by his brothers-in-law, Exeter and Suffolk – but that of the greatest of magnates, such as his father, York, Warwick and Buckingham. No king since Edward I had attempted to endow his cadets on anything like that scale, though several had married into comparable wealth. Not just his heir, Clarence, but also his third brother, Gloucester, was to be endowed equally lavishly. Edward's prospective son-in-law, George Neville, Duke of Bedford, and his two younger sons, both created dukes, were surely intended to receive the same. He alienated Lancaster honours to Clarence, Gloucester and his son Richard.

Marriage to Elizabeth Wydeville, Edward had also decided, entailed providing for her family nobly, if not on quite the same scale. Earl Rivers received offices sufficient to support his new earldom and Elizabeth's brother, John, and sisters were provided for by marriages. If the endowments themselves came free, in three cases Edward settled forfeited property on the married couples. Three fathers-in-law received earldoms. Evidently Edward thought it unacceptable that any of his queen's sisters should be less than a countess, although several had to wait for their new fathers-in-law to die. Evidently Edward set out the parameters, Rivers undertook the detailed negotiations and the king implemented. Was it his estimation of his dignity – or the queen's persuasions – that commenced the process? Royal wardships were also bestowed on these sisters-in-law and Herbert's children – politically rather than as sources of income. The marriages provided for his elder stepson, Thomas Grey, were accompanied first by an earldom and then a marquisate. The sumptuary act of 1483 preferred the royal family over mere dukes.[6]

Supplying Edward's new family with the endowments that the king thought they deserved imposed great strains on his resources. No wonder that he, like them, preferred to fund it at no expense to himself, from inheritances rather than insecure forfeitures. It is in Edward's favour that this family policy connected more of the nobility to the Crown, stressed its exalted status and perhaps contributed to the prestige of the monarchy. The rewards of Clarence and York, in the short term at least, far exceeded any services they could offer. Later both Clarence and Gloucester were to use their power against the Crown. As for the king's sisters-in-law, the families into which they married were mostly loyal Yorkists and/or related in some degree to the Crown – the FitzAlans, Bourchiers, Greys of Ruthin and Herberts. No doubt they wanted the matches – and the concrete gains that these assured – but there was no political advantage to the king in binding them more tightly to the Crown, however cheaply. Edward was no stronger in consequence. Resentment followed when the bridegrooms grew up. All without exception found themselves inevitably excluded from the inner royal family and the circles of power as the king's own burgeoning litter took priority. Advancing the Wydevilles in the 1460s distorted the marriage market and excluded the legitimate expectations of others, notably those of Warwick for his daughters. It was Warwick and other Nevilles who suffered most directly when the king substituted a match with his stepson to that agreed with George Neville for his niece, Anne Holland; Hastings' daughter (also Warwick's niece), moreover, had been promised the queen's eldest son, Thomas Grey.[7] The balance of judgement about the Wydeville marriages is therefore adverse.[8]

Warwick's first coup eliminated Edward's three favourites, Devon, Pembroke and Rivers. Back in control in 1469, Edward had no choice but to reconcile himself with his ex-captors and leave them in possession of almost all the lands and offices they had accrued before their uprising. They lost what they had granted to themselves. We cannot tell whether Edward intended revenge, but certainly he denied Warwick his political objectives and the power in Wales that he hankered after. Moreover, the king chose to create a new territorial nobility to counteract and divide Warwick. Gloucester filled the gap in Wales until the younger William Herbert came of age. He also received Lancaster honours in the north-west. John Stafford was created Earl of Wiltshire. The most important elements were the restoration of Henry Percy as 4th Earl of Northumberland, restitution to him of northern lordships held by Warwick, his brother, John Neville and Clarence, his appointment as warden of the East March, again in place of John Neville, and the latter's compensation with a marquisate (Montagu), Courtenay lands in the West Country of equivalent value to the Percy ones that he lost and the promotion of his infant son, George, to the dukedom of Bedford on his marriage to Princess Elizabeth.[9] Clearly Edward IV believed in the sort of monopoly game beloved of modern historians, that noble pieces could be moved at will round the board: strangely, since he knew at first hand the strength of family and regional traditions, that bastard feudal loyalties took time to embed and that they could not be switched on and off. How could he suppose a northern nobleman like Montagu, who had secured all he ever wanted, would content himself with property in another quarter of the realm or with the prospects of a son unable ever to accede? What made him suppose that he could thereby erase Montagu's ties to his elder brother? What caused him to place his own security on him? No wonder Montagu belittled his compensation and drove the king into exile. It was pointless to irritate Warwick without securing real gains and to reorder territory without effectively redistributing power. The new earls could not replace the old. Although Edward drove Warwick into exile, his success owed nothing to his territorial reordering, which was almost devoid of positive effects.

The Second Reign

Edward's victory in 1471 gave him another chance to sort out regional power structures – another opportunity for territorial reordering – which he took. This time he made a better job of it. The outlines are clear enough. His brother, Gloucester, was given hegemony over the North. The council of the Prince of Wales, eventually dominated by the Wydevilles, was given oversight of Wales. His chamberlain, Lord Hastings, had 'rule' of the north Midlands and the Stanleys of the north-west; and, according to Carpenter, his stepson, Thomas Grey, Marquis of Dorset, dominated the West Country.[10] There were also victims: Clarence in 1471 (the Gournay lands), 1473 (Tutbury) and, by attainder, 1478; the Herberts (1479); Berkeley, Howard and Westmorland (1483). Even Clarence's dominance of the West Midlands, based on his duchess's Warwick inheritance, may have been regarded by Edward only as temporary! There and elsewhere, the king ruled through a much enlarged royal affinity.[11] Agreement that some of this was what happened is qualified by disagreement on other issues. Did the king deliberately plan for these results? Did these arrangements operate to his advantage (and the public interest) or the benefit of his agents? Was the king actually in control? Was it a stable system? Was it new and innovative? Did this reordering contribute to the collapse of the Yorkist regime after his death? Emphatically affirmative answers to all these questions except the last are given by Carpenter, and in most cases agreed by Horrox and Lowe.[12] Emphatically no, answers Hicks on all issues, with agreement at certain points from Pollard and Richmond.[13] There are differences in emphasis and in detail. This section revisits each of these questions except the last, which is reserved for Chapter 12.

Carpenter, Horrox and Lowe present Edward IV's territorial dispositions as planned. Gloucester's dominance of the North is best known. 'What was good for Gloucester was good for royal authority,' writes Horrox. 'This assumption shaped Edward's policy of establishing regional hegemonies and it was vindicated by Gloucester's control of a notoriously difficult region'. 'Whereas in the 1460s', argues Carpenter, 'Edward was not yet ready to take the disordered regions dominated by royal estates personally in hands', this was exactly what he did after 1471.

> The royal family itself was tightly knitted into this rule. The Woodville base in Wales was not their own, but created for his own use by the king, even if he was prepared to give his in-laws a certain amount of latitude in their use of royal power … The east and north

midlands were eventually put under Hastings' command ... It may well be that Edward never regarded Clarence's presence in the area [the West Midlands] as more than a stop gap.[14]

Could the case for deliberate and self-conscious decision-making at the top, the insertion of local viceroys and removal of local magnates, to which the rulers of every community complied, be more cogently or explicitly made? Is it credible? Did Edward IV view ruling in exactly the same terms that historians six centuries later have retrospectively rationalized? If regional policy requires a list of aims and principles set out in advance, at an absolute level these cannot have existed. The act attainting the traitors of 1469–71 was delayed until 1475 and was far from comprehensive, Lander showed, because of rival interests, negotiations and intervening changes over time. Edward had intended to attaint Warwick and Montagu, but did not.[15] Thereafter, as we shall see, there were adjustments. He had intended the younger Herbert earl to succeed to his hegemony, but instead demolished it.[16] Provisions for the king's younger son and stepsons were repeatedly ratcheted up until Edward's death. That said, the king formally decided, undoubtedly. Whether, however, it was he who planned it all or whether he was pressured by other interests is much less certain. The regional policy that modern historians have ascribed to Edward is retrospective. It assumes that what actually happened was pre-planned and that development was to cease in 1483. Change, with or without the usurpation, was bound to continue.

Let us commence with the rule of the North as described so cogently by Horrox.

It was royal backing which turned Gloucester's territorial influence into a regional hegemony ... As duke of Gloucester, Richard was the effective and trusted servant of his brother Edward IV, and their relationship is a copy-book example of the mutual advantages of good service, with Edward augmenting the power which Richard placed at his disposal. Gloucester was a linchpin of English royal authority ... The north moreover, was not only united, but united behind the king since Gloucester was pre-eminently the king's man. This was a

major achievement, and can be considered the
outstanding success of Edward IV's regional policy.[17]

The starting point was Warwick's three lordships of Middleham,
Sheriff Hutton (Yorks) and Penrith (Cumberland), which were
granted to Gloucester in 1471. He did not at this stage receive
Warwick's other lands in the North, such as Barnard Castle
(Durham) and Cottingham (Yorks), nor the northern forfeitures that
the earl had held. What Gloucester was given were the Neville lands
that Warwick held in tail male and of which his brother, Montagu,
was heir. He was not given the lion's share of the estates of the earl
and countess, which were heritable by his daughters, all of which
were held on 16 April 1471, two days after Barnet, by his other
brother, Clarence, who was married to Warwick's daughter, Isabel.[18]
No doubt it was a condition of the reconciliation of king and
Clarence (and doubtless of Clarence's military services *after* Barnet)
that he would retain his expectation of his wife's inheritance. At this
point, the whole inheritance was forfeited. Although his title was by
royal grant, Clarence wished to prevent the other daughter, Anne
Neville, putting in a half share and sought to put her away, allegedly
as a kitchen maid, much as Edward III's son, Thomas of Woodstock,
sought unsuccessfully to do with Mary Bohun, or a host of others
who relocated nieces and sisters-in-law to nunneries. A further development was the decision to resettle all parts of the inheritance not by
forfeiture and royal grant but by inheritance, which involved barring
the countess of Warwick and the heirs of Montagu and reserving
reversionary rights, which Gloucester later had amended.
Territorially this meant that Gloucester's possessions were extended
to include other Yorkshire properties and Barnard Castle in County
Durham, where he became the dominant magnate. This had not been
Edward's original intention. It was the result, among other factors in
and after 1472, of Gloucester's abduction of Anne, the enforced
partition of the Warwick inheritance and the allocation of the
northern estates to Gloucester.[19] *Pace* Horrox, Richard *was* primarily
'a hereditary northern magnate, whose estates made him an independent regional force'.[20]

What Edward initially envisaged was for Gloucester to be warden
in the West March, and Northumberland to be warden of the East
and Middle Marches in Northumberland. Outside the marches, each

held royal offices in particular localities; again *pace* Horrox, the chief
stewardship of the duchy and chief forestership, which Gloucester
held, did not override their more local counterparts. Gloucester did,
however, encroach on Northumberland's patch and, in particular,
retained John Westerdale, who was then the earl's undersheriff in
Northumberland. Northumberland objected and on 13 May 1473
the king's council at Nottingham ruled in his favour, that Gloucester
should not retain any more Percy men. At this point, therefore,
Edward insisted that these two great magnates must respect each
other's spheres of responsibility. Subsequently, on 28 July 1474,
Gloucester retained Northumberland in an indenture that acknowledged the earl's autonomy, but encompassed the Percy affinity within his own.[21] That was a change. Other northern noblemen followed
until Gloucester was lord, directly or indirectly, of almost every
significant northerner. As regards lands, 'from 1471, it seems,
Edward felt that he had fulfilled his responsibilities to his brother,
had given him enough, and there were to be no more unconditional
gifts of land'. Step by step, however, Gloucester gradually added to
his offices and responsibilities, securing, for instance, the shrievalty
of Cumberland, then extending the appendant perquisites and
finally, in 1483, obtaining the whole county as his palatinate. Further
northern properties were acquired by royal grant or by exchange
with Sir William Stanley or the Crown. Whatever the revenues of the
properties exchanged, whether actually more or less valuable, and
however advantageous these changes were to the Crown, in almost
all cases we possess the petition that Gloucester presented to achieve
the result. Some reallocations from Clarence's rights that Clarence
would have opposed were Gloucester's reward for his support at
Clarence's trial and perhaps his price for his support. Gradually,
Gloucester extended his possessions, offices and power in the North
and the king gave his consent.[22] Each instance, in Horrox's words,
'was Edward's tacit approval of the use his brother made of his
northern power'.[23] But Edward did not will Gloucester's regional
hegemony or deliberately plan it. He had wanted a condominium –
but he was happy nevertheless with the result. He appointed the duke
as lieutenant against the Scots in 1480/1 and then in 1483 approved
a palatinate and rights of conquest in Scotland for him. Horrox is
right that Gloucester's influence at court and capacity to deliver royal
patronage to northerners contributed to the extent and appeal of his

lordship. No doubt, also, Gloucester's power was reassessed, 'the king's perception of his role developing as the duke matured', but this was not merely a matter of perceptions and semantics, rather of who took the initiative, who was in control and what royal reservations Gloucester effectively overrode. By the 1480s, Pollard argues, it was the duke and not the king who was shaping policy towards the North and with Scotland.[24] A regional policy that the king recognized and approved after it had happened was not a royal programme at all.

Much the same applies to the rule of Wales. In 1471, following a brief interlude under Gloucester, the 2nd Earl of Pembroke entered his father's estates (and presumably his hegemony). Simultaneously, Edward IV created his infant son Prince of Wales, Duke of Cornwall and Earl of Chester, granted him the appurtenant lands, and also conceded the actual revenues, to be managed for him by a council that he appointed. This is not very different from what happened with earlier princes of Wales, of whom the Black Prince and the future Henry V were in time able to handle their affairs themselves. Revised arrangements in 1473, including the afforcement of the council with lawyers and an ordinance for the prince's household, did not require the prince to settle in Wales. Given that his coffer had three keys, one held by the queen, this was actually quite inconvenient. What appears to have happened is that in 1473, in response to complaints in parliament about the state of the marches, king and court visited Shropshire and Prince Edward was left behind at Ludlow, a temporary sojourn that repeated Edward's own experience as a youth and that in time became semi-permanent. The king sought originally to achieve order by bilateral contracts between himself as Earl of March and other marcher lords, which was still his plan in 1476 when, in fact, the prince deputized for him. In the next stage, in 1479, Prince Edward became Earl of March. It appears, therefore, that the prince's establishment acquired governmental functions extending beyond the prince's estates, which the king found convenient, and its geographical scope was progressively expanded to include the Earldom of March, Duchy of Lancaster lordships in Wales and the Herbert lordships in Pembrokeshire. The original council was a representative body, which included both the king's brothers and central officials, who may have attended when it met at Westminster. Those councillors who were royal judges remained at Westminster and officiated there. The prince's tutor,

Earl Rivers, was frequently absent abroad and day-to-day tuition was apparently overseen by Bishop Alcock. The move to the marches, which effectively excluded many councillors, and Rivers's realization of the political potential of the office, meant that in time the prince's affairs came to be managed by the Wydevilles, in particular his uncle and his half-brother, Lord Richard Grey. The Wydevilles, through the medium of the prince, were the route to preferment in Wales, on his estates and from the king.[25] Although the Wydevilles were always present, Lowe was wrong to say that they dominated from the start. That was the result.[26] Again, Edward IV did not foresee or plan much, or perhaps *any*, of what happened, but was happy with the consequences. It was Rivers who commanded the Welsh contingents in the Scottish war.

The Stanleys, Hastings and Dorset are each rather different. The king was the principal landholder and palatine earl in both Cheshire and Lancashire, but was an absentee. The Stanleys dominated both counties, where they were significant landholders and held the principal offices; somehow they escaped committing themselves fatally to Warwick in 1470–1. Intruding Gloucester into the honours of Halton (Ches.) and Clitheroe (Lancs) had brought him into conflict with the Stanleys. The duke did not return in 1471 and he was otherwise restricted to the western fringes of Lancashire. Gloucester's 'failure to achieve similar dominance in Lancashire', opines Horrox, 'strongly implies that the king had chosen to support the Stanleys instead'.[27] A different threat was posed by Edward Prince of Wales, on whose behalf the Stanley offices were resumed. They secured an act in 1472 that restored them to possession. Surely the correct reading here is that the Stanleys were already so dominant in the north-west and resisted intrusion so vigorously that Edward was obliged to give way, taking Gloucester and the prince with him? That Stanley became steward of the king's household from 1471 was because the king needed to tie him to his regime. This influential role certainly helped Stanley resolve the Harrington inheritance dispute in *his* favour, not Gloucester's. By 1483, his brother, Sir William, lord of Chirk by exchange with Gloucester, was steward to the prince.[28] If their power can be depicted as local rule by the royal affinity, nevertheless the Stanleys were primarily north-western magnates who reinforced their regional hegemony with royal authority and favour. Again, Edward did not will the end, but found it easier to recognize realities and quell disorder by retracting his original actions.

Hastings, the king's chamberlain, was granted extensive forfeitures in the East Midlands, where he built Ashby St Leger and Kirkby Muxloe castles in Leicestershire. He was drawn into the north Midlands in 1472 when Clarence, in need of support at court, made him steward of his honours of Tutbury (Staffs) and Duffield (Derby.). When these were resumed in 1473, the king continued the arrangement, additionally inducing the principal gentry to contract as retainers with Hastings. Whilst they were unpaid, they hoped for access to royal favour, and were prevented from retainer by other lords. Hastings did not, therefore, rule the north Midlands – he was anyway an absentee – but prevented other lords (perhaps especially Clarence) from intruding into the region.[29]

The king's stepson, Thomas Grey, Marquis of Dorset, was also a potential ruler, never actual. He had expectations of the midland barony of Ferrers of Groby, but he looked for preferment to his wives, Anne Holland and Cecily Bonville. The title of Earl of Huntingdon that came to Anne suggests a future in the East Midlands, which did not happen, and most of Cecily's entitlements in the West Country had yet to fall in. Dorset was not granted any of Clarence's West Country lands nor the Gournay lands: the marriages of his son, Thomas, to the Exeter inheritance and of a daughter to Clarence's son offered prospects, not yet reality.[30] If anyone 'ruled' the West Country after 1478, it was Lord Dynham. Neither Hastings nor Dorset, in short, really ruled whole regions; Dorset may have had aspirations, but Hastings, most probably, did not.

It was the standing of local notables who held royal office that made royal authority a reality everywhere, in so far as fifteenth-century government was ever effective. 'Effective royal authority', Horrox explains, 'required that men of local standing should be willing to put their knowledge and influence at the king's disposal; that they should become the king's servants as well as his subjects'. Their service in their localities – and the hegemonies in whole regions of Edward's Second Reign – 'provided stability', even 'in a regularly unsettled area … This contributed to the king's ability to call on the support of men other than his acknowledged servants'.[31] Royal office legitimized the authority of local notables. Potent though they were, all such officers were themselves liable to crimes,

disagreements, feuds, oppressions and perversions of justice, and
were likely to be subject to many forms of investigation, oversight
and correction invoked by lords, judges, rivals, complainants and
petitioners, as well as victims. Giving Gloucester, the Wydevilles and
the Stanleys a free hand in their regions may have imposed effective
control, but it may also have permitted all these abuses to persist or
even be practised by them. They monopolized office, retained the
officeholders, oversaw the operations of local bureaucracies and
courts, and offered the principal (and, indeed, sole) route to the
king, his council and central government. Occasionally they appear
arbitrating disputes, intervening and making ordinances in towns,
and implementing the king's wishes, in person or by delegation.
Sometimes they claimed to be acting on the king's behalf as well as
their own. Much, indeed, was delegated and is concealed from us.
We know from a single surviving petition that Gruffydd Vaughan ap
Eynion thought himself oppressed by the prince's treasurer, Sir
Richard Croft of Croft Castle; that a petition to the prince's council
in distant Westminster had produced a directive to Croft that he
ignored; and that Croft, secure in his local office and favour with
the prince, continued his oppressions.[32] Was Croft any better than
the Herberts whom he replaced? Was the new in-faction any better
than that it had supplanted? No, surely, was the verdict of those
who complained about Wydeville oppressions after their fall.
Although admittedly irritating, Sir William Plumpton could not
persuade the royal council, king's chamberlain or the Duke of
Gloucester to pressurize Gloucester's retainer, Northumberland, at
Knaresborough (Yorks) where the earl was the king's officer.[33]
What, then, in the earl's heartland of Northumberland itself? Did
Gloucester's deals with the lesser nobility of the North leave them to
do as they wished, free not only of royal intervention but his own?
Probably, yes. If their regimes were popular with some, surely with
others they were unpopular, partisan and irremediable? Did these
rulers exercise a filter and implement only those commands of
which they approved, as later justices were to do? We cannot tell.
Pollard is much more guarded than Carpenter when assessing the
impact on public order.[34] Edward did intervene independently of his
son and was dissatisfied with his regime at Coventry.[35] We should
not presume that the king approved everything done locally in his
name, even by his close family. If not actually planned by him, or

not all at once, this territorial reordering served what Edward saw as his interests. He was happy to work with the victors and to exploit their hold on the localities. They delivered the manpower he wanted. Local problems remained local: they were stilled or resolved locally, not necessarily justly, and did not have national repercussions.

No wonder that Gloucester, the Wydevilles and the Stanleys valued their regional hegemonies and maximized them. Royal authority, royal rewards and royal patronage for their followers fulfilled the aspirations of Gloucester and the Stanleys and reinforced their local empires. Gloucester, Stanley and Hastings were able to count the king's affinity in the localities as their own. 'By 1483 the duchy connection was Gloucester's as well as the king's'.[36] The Wydevilles had access to much greater revenues, local authority and political backing through their management of the resources of Edward IV's two sons. They used royal retainers for purposes that served *their* interests rather than those of king and prince. Those who served the prince – and thus the Wydevilles themselves – were committed to Edward V's accession and their continued management of his affairs. The prince's friends, friends of Wydevilles, were their friends; foes of the prince and the Wydevilles were their foes. This should have mattered locally. Perhaps it mattered centrally, in factional politics at court, in council or at Clarence's trial in parliament. Yet their allegiance and primary loyalty was to the king: such connections were no threat to Edward while he lived, and Horrox sees any distinction between Gloucester's authority and that of the king as meaningless before 1483.[37] After Edward had died in 1483, royal servants in the escort of Edward V were treated by Gloucester as Wydeville partisans, and others loyal to Edward IV (and, for all we know, Edward V) turned out in the northern army that overawed London on his behalf. Pollard has even argued that it was Gloucester who directed Edward's Scottish policy, fomenting war, commandeering national resources and Edward's backing.[38] Since Edward initiated the war, his opportunity to recapture Berwick and remove the principal stain on his escutcheon, this is unlikely. If true, however, handing over responsibility for the western borders and Scottish affairs to Gloucester in 1483 could have been Edward's solution, though one destined to fail whenever the problems outgrew Gloucester's resources and impinged on areas beyond his palatinate. Any appeals from within it to the king as 'fount of justice' would have had the same effect. But actually the purpose of the new Cumberland palatinate remains difficult to assess.

At all times and in all areas most members of local aristocratic societies and most of the key players in local power structures were there of right, by inheritance over generations, established and accepted. Clarence in the West Midlands and Gloucester in the North, as sons-in-law of Warwick, fall into this category. The territorial reorderings that we have been discussing involved the termination of existing players and their replacement by new-comers, who sought not to join local society but to dominate it. Such intrusions could destabilize local society and power structures, and often did. It was the insertion of Gloucester into the north-west that inflamed the Harrington-Stanley feud, into the north-east that brought conflict with Northumberland, and it was the conversion of Prince Edward's estates into a power structure that brought trouble with the Herberts, perhaps merely temporarily, as all these disputes were resolved in contrasting ways: Gloucester was withdrawn, peace was imposed and the original power-brokers were excluded.

We should also remember that there were victims of such territo-rial reorderings. Clarence had been confirmed in his possessions in 1471 and allowed to acquire his wife's inheritance, yet these promises were withdrawn in three stages: perhaps the Gournay lands lost to the prince in 1471 were not very important to him, but the north Midlands lordships certainly were that he lost in 1473 through a general act of resumption that targeted him alone, and so too was half the Warwick inheritance, partitioned in 1474–5. In two cases, Edward's new territorial dispositions benefited. One cannot wonder that Clarence was resentful. His resentment contributed to his disastrous final denouement, which appears a short-term deci-sion rather than part of a considered plan. His son remained to inherit what was still a great estate destined to dominate the West Midlands. Though husband to a Wydeville, the younger William Herbert was excluded from Wales for several years, had resumed the offices entailed on his father for his services and was obliged to exchange his lordships of Pembroke and Haverfordwest for manors of lesser value and no interest in Somerset and Devon. His comital title was changed from Pembroke to Huntingdon. Temporarily excluded, Herbert did not surrender his Welsh ambitions.

Buckingham, also husband to a Wydeville, certainly had aspirations in Wales that the prince's regime thwarted. As for Edward's final redirection of the Mowbray and Exeter inheritances, these were at the expense of the hitherto loyal Howard, Berkeley and Westmorland. It is surely no accident that Buckingham, the Herberts, Howard, Berkeley and Westmorland are to be found backing Richard III. King Edward imposed his will, rode roughshod across the claims of hitherto loyal supporters and secured parliamentary sanction for his actions, but he did not extinguish their claims. In a hereditary system, rights of inheritance could not be discarded. Temporarily disappointed, magnates nursed their claims until they could be made good. They could not have expected their opportunity would come so soon.

The new hegemonies were not stable. Where derived purely from office, not heritable land and heritable loyalties, they were no stronger than the lives of the current tenants. The Wydevilles' rule in Wales was decapitated on 30 April at Stony Stratford: there is no sign that anything residual could be conjured up in Wales against Richard III thereafter. It was Herbert who ruled South Wales for King Richard. Henry VII's promise to marry Elizabeth of York seems to have recruited few Welshmen in 1485. All offices and all power were transferred to Buckingham. It was also to Buckingham that the retainers of Hastings, essentially the frontman to a deceased king, transferred on his death. Hereditary grants promised permanence beyond the lives of the current holders, who thus exercised more lasting control. Hence such titles were sought and sometimes conceded, even though (as we now know) they were subject to review or cancellation when favour was lost or the original grantee passed on. The Stanleys and Gloucester are different. Both had deep hereditary roots within their localities. The Stanleys survived and Neville sentiment still existed at Middleham as late as the Pilgrimage of Grace. Richard tried to enhance family traditions through his two colleges at Middleham and Barnard Castle. Both depended on continued royal office-holding, which perhaps could not be denied them as long as they still held their lands. But the fertility and mortality that brought great estates together could also wrench them asunder. Partition and extinction was to be expected. Thirty generations on, the Stanleys still remain. In Richard's case, however, the hereditary core to his estates was unsound. He held the Neville lands because rival Neville claimants were excluded. In and after 1478 he sought to cover himself, unsuccessfully. When George Neville died on 4 May 1483, Richard's title to the Neville lordships diminished to a life estate: Richard Lord Latimer was the heir. When his own son died in 1484, Clarence's son became heir apparent. Gloucester's hegemony, in short, was curtailed to his own lifetime.[39]

Did Edward know this? Certainly he was aware of Gloucester's risk. Such vagaries were to be expected and not to be deprecated. That Gloucester was especially trustworthy did not mean that Edward's successors would find his heirs as trusting and would continue him in offices tenable only for life. The arrangements in the north Midlands and Wales were never more than short term, to last only until Hastings died and Edward V acceded. Edward deliberately chose to grant Hastings the stewardships of the north Midlands honours for life only, not the honours themselves. What he did intend to be permanent was the grant to his stepson, Richard Grey of the Lancaster lordship of Kidwelly that infringed Prince Edward's hegemony. No new institution called the Council of Wales was created. However convenient the arrangements, Edward was not self-consciously creating a new way of governing. Nor did he expect his dispositions to survive, but to be recycled. Stability was not to be expected, nor was it necessarily desired or desirable.

Edward's capacity to think territorially did, on occasion, mean that local potentates were removed willy-nilly from their preferred localities. When young Gloucester was relocated from Wales and the north-western palatinates to Yorkshire and the West March, he had no choice and was much the better for it, whereas Clarence certainly resented his abrupt transfer from the north Midlands. Also unwilling victims of Edward's strategic planning were Warwick's brother, Montagu, in 1470 and William Herbert II. Undoubtedly the latter also found his new-found earldom and the Gournay lands no better than the 'magpie's nest' that Montagu was fobbed off with. Moreover Edward's strategy misfired. Although temporarily suppressed and excluded, William Herbert and his heirs returned under Richard III, just as Northumberland did west of the Pennines and the Howards in East Anglia. The 'territorial reordering' of Edward's Second Reign was as short-lived as that of his First Reign, with no lasting consequences.

12

The collapse of the regime

Despite the collapse of his foreign policy, Edward IV died naturally and in control, and was succeeded automatically by his son. Twelve weeks later, Edward V had been deposed. This event occurred after Edward's death, when he was no longer in control. He could not therefore be expected to do anything about it. The dominant historical tradition, from Crowland on, confines Edward's responsibilities to his reign and lifetime. He had no part in what happened thereafter. Thus Scofield's history terminates abruptly at his death. She and most other historians share the general consensus that Edward's supposed pre-contract of marriage was an invention of 1483 and that Edward had no part in undermining his son's title. To Carpenter, one of the most recent commentators, Edward left the throne secure.[1] This is the case *for* Edward IV. *Against* his innocence, we must note that Edward's most influential early historians, Crowland, Mancini, More and Vergil, all admit that the factional divisions that exploded in 1483 originated in Edward IV's reign. Crowland actually supported Hastings against the Wydevilles, Gloucester's first coup (1 May) and perhaps, at the time, Gloucester's second coup (13 June) also. It is Mancini who attributes to Gloucester a pattern of conduct – removal from court, and so on – that Crowland identified with 'idols of the multitude':[2] mistakenly, since Gloucester remained in favour, but probably part of the duke's programme of disinformation. The mainstream tradition from Rous on traced Gloucester's elimination of rivals back to 1471. Modern historians have documented the regional hegemonies, especially that of Gloucester, which underpinned the struggle for power, and some of them, notably Richmond, have held Edward IV responsible for what followed.[3] He failed to prevent the circumstances from arising that caused or were conducive to Gloucester's usurpation.

There are six charges against Edward IV – six grounds for holding him responsible in whole or in part for the usurpation of Richard III and the collapse of the dynasty: because Edward failed to contract a valid marriage – the pre-contract story – and thus his son was a bastard and unable to rule; because he failed to create a commitment to his heir and to his dynasty; because of the factional divisions that he left behind; because he created parties with vested interests who wanted Edward V set aside; because he destroyed in Clarence the obvious lord protector; and because he did not leave clear guidance on who was to rule. These factors interacted and are not easy to separate.

Everybody agrees on Edward's lechery. In 1483 Edward's marriage was questioned, because he was already married when he wed his queen, and so their son Edward V was deposed. Almost all historians in all eras have rejected the tale as false, although Buck and recent Ricardians have accepted it. If true, Edward bears a heavy responsibility for the disasters that followed. Even if not true, it was Edward's promiscuity that made the story feasible and enabled it to be used to remove his son. Obviously, however, the story by itself was not enough, especially as many disbelieved it. If there had been no pre-contract story, another pretext might have been found for the usurpation of Richard III, since there were other causes why Richard and his supporters wanted a change. Legitimate or not, once accepted as king, constitutionally Edward V was king, some argue. Not everyone, at the time or since, has agreed. If bastardy was a bar to the succession, it is not surprising that some supposed that a king subsequently exposed as illegitimate should not continue.

'Edward did not create a collective commitment to the future of his dynasty under his son and heir strong enough to survive a minority';[4] at one level, Pollard is obviously right. Edward V's reign was prematurely terminated. At another, he is unfair, because events obstructed any decisive exercise of 'collective commitment' and because Edward's dynasty comprised much more than his eldest son. The revolution of 1483 was conducted *within* the dynasty, *within* the royal family: between the young Edward V, his paternal and maternal kin and his father's courtiers. All were committed to the House of York. Edward IV and Edward V alike relocated the Crown within the Yorkist dynasty. The usurpation of Richard III was conducted within the *Yorkist* establishment; it was that *Yorkist* establishment that rejected Richard III in Buckingham's Rebellion for the *Yorkist* Edward V; and even Henry VII acceded in 1485 as a candidate of the *Yorkist* establishment, vowing to marry Elizabeth of York. Lancastrians, by then, were few and futile. Of Tudors, as yet, there were only two. Edward IV did establish the House of York as the ruling dynasty. He saw off all rivals. Loyalty to Edward V, perhaps, may not have been so strong. Yet there were many opposed to the Wydevilles, amongst them Crowland and Hastings, who backed their destruction without intending to change the king. What looks like a consensus amongst the Yorkist establishment for Gloucester as lord protector in May 1483 became a consensus against him as king in October. Thereafter, getting rid of him was more important than maintaining his dynasty. The Yorkist establishment erred in accepting Gloucester's profession of limited objectives and not foreseeing where events were heading. To be misled, deceived and outsmarted does not require that at Edward's death there was any lack of 'collective commitment' outside Gloucester's innermost circle to the succession of Edward V. Edward IV did not fail here.

Gloucester's usurpation grew out of and depended upon factional divisions that Edward left behind. At court the queen's family was at odds with Lord Hastings. Posing as the honest broker, Gloucester first backed Hastings to destroy the Wydevilles, then destroyed Hastings and out of the wreckage made himself king. Edward knew of these warring factions, several sources report, but was unconcerned since he could control them. Once he was dead, they posed serious dangers, which again Edward appreciated and sought to quell by reconciling Dorset and Hastings. Although they went through the motions, they were not sincere and reverted almost at once when setting the escort of the new king. Perhaps the Wydevilles did intend excluding Hastings from power or even destroying him as Hastings evidently feared. All medieval favourites and factions sought monopolies of power and profit. There may also have been hostility between the king's brother, Gloucester, and the Wydevilles, although this was not apparent to Earl Rivers. Crowland was one of many courtiers and administrators hostile to the Wydevilles. They opposed rule by the king's maternal relatives and did not back the queen against Gloucester after he had seized the young king at Stony

Stratford. Of course, there were always factions at court. No king could prevent them. Kings could attack the symptoms, prevent public dissension and might even, in extreme circumstances, exclude from court or dismiss the culprits, but they could not eliminate animosities, jealousies and resentments that supporters felt. Perhaps also Edward allowed such differences to escalate beyond his control. Was Clarence the victim of factional infighting? Did the Wydevilles briefly discredit Hastings with the king, with charges that he meant to betray Calais, and did Hastings slur the Wydevilles with use of torture? Both times, it appears, the plot was scotched. Clarence, of course, could not be brought back to life. What was in question was not Edward's kingship, but who benefited from it and, perhaps, who managed it. Such factional differences should not have threatened the kingship of Edward V, since the Wydevilles and Hastings alike were committed to him and neither intended to depose him. Factional divisions again were an opportunity for Gloucester to exploit.

Edward 'cavalierly' manipulated inheritances 'to benefit his own kin'.[5] Since 1461, Edward had greatly expanded his kindred. It was necessary for any king to cater for his inner family, now more narrowly defined, exalted and distinguished from mere in-laws. To do so by dispossessing others, including former partisans, was a perilous pursuit. If the prime beneficiaries were his own sons, the benefits were exercised for them initially and perhaps identified by the queen's kin. Thus Edward created vested interests opposed to the rule of the Wydevilles and hence, perhaps, to Edward V also. We have already seen how in his last years Edward enhanced his eldest son's possessions and control in Wales, and used the Norfolk and Exeter inheritances to provide for his (step)sons at the expense of the legitimate interests of important noblemen. If the new king Edward V was to be dominated by the Wydevilles, as they had planned and apparently attempted to fulfil, remedies to these grievances were highly improbable. As lord protector and king, Richard did remedy them. Whether complicit in the usurpation or merely in the fall of the Wydevilles, these grievances offered opportunities for Richard to exploit.

Destroying Clarence was another factor. Had Edward died before 1478, he would have left behind two brothers, of whom the eldest, Clarence, would surely have been lord protector unless it was decided to do without. Clarence's hereditary title took precedence over Gloucester's and his very existence was just as much a bar to Gloucester's usurpation as Gloucester's existence was to his own. Gloucester was glad of Clarence's death, perceived More, 'whose life must needs have hindered him so intending [his usurpation]; whether the same Duke of Clarence had kept him true to his nephew, the young king, or enterprised to be king himself'.[6] The evidence of 1478 is ambiguous. Nothing that survives suggests that Clarence posed much threat. He attracted no support at a state trial with a predetermined result. Faction might well have flourished under Lord Protector Clarence. Destroying him did not secure the succession for Edward V, but rather removed another obstacle to Gloucester's usurpation, which understandably neither king nor queen foresaw.

It is far from clear whether Edward nominated Gloucester as lord protector. It was the logical decision. If so, it was a mistake for which Edward cannot easily be blamed, for modern historians are generally agreed that he had no grounds to suspect Gloucester of treason and hence to guard against his usurpation. What Edward failed to recognize was untrustworthiness and cunning in his brother that nobody else perceived either. Or perhaps the queen did. The moment Gloucester staged his first coup, she presumed his intention was the usurpation and was not dissuaded thereafter, unlike almost everyone else, who thought her conduct irrational. Yet Edward did know at first hand just how ambitious and grasping, egotistical and ruthless Gloucester was: his conduct before Edward's death was on a par with what followed.[7] Prescience was never Edward's forte. That the council in London, which was dominated by the Wydevilles, sought to prevent the duke from securing power was not Edward's fault. Gloucester quickly corrected the situation by force and made himself lord protector. That Gloucester subsequently usurped the throne was not an inevitable consequence and cannot be blamed on Edward. If, however, Edward had failed to nominate Gloucester as protector, if he left no guidance behind, and if he thus precipitated the situation that was overthrown by the *coup d'état*, he was in part responsible. In neither case did Gloucester's first coup ensure his usurpation and thereafter events were clearly beyond Edward's control. Kings, even Henry V, could not determine what happened after their deaths.

What was crucial in each case – the pre-contract, factional divisions, entrenched grievances, the destruction of Clarence and Edward's dispositions during the minority – is that each was exploited by Gloucester, for whatever reason, to usurp the throne. Gloucester, historians are generally agreed, was loyal to his brother, even conspicuously loyal. Whilst scarcely lily-white, nobody has cited evidence that should have prompted Edward IV to question his loyalty. Gloucester, indeed, asserted his fidelity to Edward V as prince and king repeatedly, apparently indeed on every possible occasion and in 1477 with unnecessarily extravagant professions of humility and respect.[8] Nobody nowadays believes that he was plotting in 1471 and 1478 and disposing systematically of those with better claims. Gloucester was, after all, the youngest brother, never close and ever more distant from the throne. It is not credible, as Jones has argued,[9] that he thought himself entitled before the death of his elder brother, Clarence, if then. Gloucester could have done nothing on his own. Edward himself had never been more securely on the throne than at his death, which he had not planned. The disasters of the usurpation stemmed from events after that involuntary action, when Edward was dead, and were not his fault.

Conclusion

For Edward, it must be noted that he possessed most of the attributes expected of a late-medieval king except virtue. A good general and effective ruler, he conquered, reconquered and reunited his kingdom of England. He secured international acceptance. With France, he completely failed; but can he be blamed for not performing the impossible? Edward re-established the authority and finances of the Crown and maintained acceptable levels of order. The images he presented, of God's predestined ruler, a reformer, solvency and the conqueror of France, reinforced his position, secured loyalty, taxes and even compliance from potential foes. Apart from securing his dynasty, his vision was short term, not to reform or change any systems but to make them work, using whatever institutions and individuals that came to hand and turning a blind eye to all but the most conspicuous of their abuses. Given the difficulties of ruling or even reigning at this time, this is an impressive record.

Against Edward must be set the limits of his achievements, which depended on his own person, the errors that Ross indicated, and especially the serious miscalculations that contributed to the loss of his throne in 1470 and that of his son in 1483. Thus he fell short of contemporary expectations. If there are some instances, there are nevertheless few of serious abuse of power. If Edward also fell short of modern expectations, such as the reforms of Henry VII a generation early, the curtailing of Warwick and the curbing of bastard feudalism, these are anachronistic expectations of which he was unaware and which, most probably, would not have assisted his rule. With the Nevilles he could not have got it right. It is not his ruthlessness that is most often criticized, but his inconsistency, yet tempering justice with mercy was essential to successful governance.

Edward was inconsistent, unscrupulous and not altogether honest, yet he naïvely expected good faith from others. Justice was not for him an absolute principle. More seriously, the king lacked foresight, seems to have lacked perception into the motives of others and was several times surprised by developments that he should have predicted and to which he was forced to react. Routine and ceremonial duties were duly performed, but sustained planning and diplomatic manoeuvres did not interest him. Others did plan ahead and extracted advantages from him that he had not planned. Most of the territorial reordering of his reign was not of his devising. King Edward was managed at various times, by Warwick, the 1st Earl Rivers, Howard in 1475 and the Wydevilles in 1478, though never apparently systematically or completely, and he could be persuaded to serve the interests of others rather than his own. His brother, Clarence, was the principal victim. Here he anticipates the manipulation of his more dangerous grandson, Henry VIII. If not himself a great king, Edward was mightily effective and paved the way for more authoritative government in the future. A good king, nevertheless he could do better.

Notes

Chapter 1 Placing Edward IV in English history

1. See below, pp. 63–4.
2. Hughes, pp. ix, 83.
3. Lander, pp. 165–70.
4. Hicks, *Warwick*, p. 256.
5. Dockray, p. viii.
6. Carpenter, p. 205.
7. Hughes, *passim*.
8. *Vale*, pp. 71–2.
9. Hughes, esp. Chs 4 and 5.
10. K.B. McFarlane, *England in the Fifteenth Century* (1981), p. 240.
11. J.L. Watts, *Henry VI and the Politics of Kingship* (Cambridge, 1996), esp. pp. 108–11; Carpenter, Ch. 5, esp. p. 93.
12. The classic exposition is R.L. Storey, *The End of the House of Lancaster* (1966). Many such feuds have been studied further, e.g. R.A. Griffiths, 'Local Rivalries and National Politics: The Percies, the Nevilles, and the Duke of Exeter, 1452–5', *King and Country* (1981), Ch. 20; S.J. Payling, 'The Ampthill Dispute: A Study in Lancastrian Lawlessness and the Breakdown of Lancastrian Government', *EHR* CIV (1989), pp. 881–907.
13. *RP* V. pp. 346–9.
14. J. Hatcher, 'The Great Slump of the Mid-Fifteenth Century' in *Progress and Problems in Medieval England*, eds R.H. Britnell and J. Hatcher (Cambridge, 1996).

15. Carpenter, pp. 180–1.

16. M.A. Hicks, 'Bastard Feudalism, Overmighty Subjects and Idols of the Multitude during the Wars of the Roses', *History* 85 (2000), pp. 386–403.

Chapter 2 The shaping of Edward IV

1. Unless otherwise stated, this chapter is based on *GEC* III, pp. 257–8 (Clarence); V, pp. 694–713 (Gloucester); VIII, pp. 433–54 (March); IX, pp. 266–85 (Mortimer); and XII (2), pp. 895–909; (York) see also pedigree 2.

2. A. Allan, 'Yorkist Propaganda: Pedigree, Prophecy, and the "British History" in the Reign of Edward IV' in *Patronage, Pedigree and Power in Later Medieval England*, ed. C.D. Ross (1979), pp. 172–8.

3. A.E. Goodman and D.A.L. Morgan, 'The Yorkist Claim to the Throne of Castile', *JMH* XII (1985), pp. 61–9.

4. W. Dugdale, *Monasticon Anglicanum* (8 vols, 1846), VII, 1600–2; A.F. Sutton and L. Visser-Fuchs, *Richard III's Books* (Stroud, 1997), pp. 23, 148; '"Richard liveth yet": An Old Myth', *The Ricardian* 117 (1992), pp. 266–9.

5. J.L. Watts, '*De Consulatu Stilicho*: Texts and Politics in the Reign of Henry VI', *JMH* XVI (1990), pp. 251–66; S. Delany, 'Bokenham's Claudian as Yorkist Propaganda', *JMH* XXII (1996), pp. 83–96 at p. 90.

6. Dugdale, *Monasticon*, VI, p. 344.

7. Allan, 'Yorkist Propaganda', p. 178.

8. Dugdale, *Monasticon*, VI, pp. 348–55.

9. See M.E. Giffin, 'Cadwallader, Arthur and Brutus in the Wigmore Manuscript', *Speculum* XVI (1941).

10. Hughes, pp. 118–20.

11. T.B. Pugh, *Henry V and the Southampton Plot of 1415* (Gloucester, 1988), pp. 89–90.

12. Ibid., pp. 5, 6, 78, 81–2, 90.

13. Hughes, Chs 4 and 5.

14. Goodman and Morgan, pp. 64–6.

15. A.F. Sutton and L. Visser-Fuchs, *The Reburial of Richard Duke of York 21–30 July 1476* (1996), pp. 28–9; Jones, pp. 49–51.

16. *Vale*, pp. 180–3, at p. 181.

17. Hughes, p. 33.

18. M.K. Jones, 'Somerset, York and the Wars of the Roses', *EHR*. CIV (1989), pp. 289–308.

19. Sutton and Visser-Fuchs, *Reburial*, pp. 28–9.

20. *Vale*, pp. 185–9; Hicks, *EPC*, pp. 197–203.

21. *Vale*, pp. 187–9.

22. Sutton and Visser-Fuchs, *Reburial*, pp. 28–9.

23. Hicks, *EPC*, p. 214.

24. Ibid., p. 214.

25. *RP* V, pp. 373–8, 380–1.

26. T.B. Pugh, 'The Estates, Finances, and Regal Aspirations of Richard Plantagenet (1411–60), Duke of York', *Revolution and Consumption in Late Medieval England*, ed. M.A. Hicks (Woodbridge, 2001), pp. 82–3.

27. Hughes, p. 124.

28. Lander, p. 104.

29. *RP* V, pp. 462–7, 484–5; Hicks, *Rivals*, pp. 359–62; 'An Escheat Concealed: The Despenser Estates in Hampshire 1400–61', *Hampshire Studies* 53 (1998).

30. *Vale*, p. 178.

31. This material is more fully discussed by Hughes, *passim*, Chs 4 and 5; Allan, 'Yorkist Propaganda', pp. 177–8.

32. Hughes, p. 83.

33. *RP* VI, p. 204.

34. A. Gross, *The Dissolution of the Lancastrian Kingship* (Stamford, 1996), p. 17.

35. British Library Harleian Roll 7353, as interpreted by Hughes, *passim*.

Chapter 3 Alternative images of Edward IV

1. Hughes, *passim*.

2. Gregory's, Warkworth's, Stone's and Fabian's chronicles are

respectively: *Historical Collections of a Citizen of London*, ed.
J. Gairdner, Camden Society new series XVIII (1876); *Death
and Dissent: The Dethe of the Kynge of Scotis and Warkworth's
Chronicle*, ed. L.M. Matheson (Woodbridge, 1999); 'Annales
Rerum Anglicarum' in *Letters and Papers Illustrative of the
Wars of the English in France*, ed. J. Stevenson, Rolls Series II(2)
(1864); *Chronicle of John Stone*, ed. W.G. Searle, Cambridge
Antiquarian Society octavo series XXXIV (1902); *New
Chronicles of England and France*, ed. H. Ellis (1811). Fabian
has also been wrongly identified as author of *The Great
Chronicle of London*, eds A.H. Thomas and I.D. Thornley
(1938).

3. For Gregory, see A. Gransden, *Historical Writing in England* II
(1982), pp. 230–1; for Warkworth, J.A.F. Thomson,
'Warkworth's Chronicle Reconsidered', *EHR* (2001), pp.
657–64; for Worcester, K.B. McFarlane, 'William Worcester: A
Preliminary Survey', *England in the Fifteenth Century* (1981);
and for the chronicles now, M.-R. McLaren, *The London
Chronicles of the Fifteenth Century* (Woodbridge, 2002).

4. *Ingulph's Chronicle of the Abbey of Croyland*, ed. H.T. Riley
(1859); Kingsford, pp. 376–8; *Three Fifteenth Century
Chronicles*, ed. J. Gairdner, Camden Society new series XXVIII
(1880).

5. 'John Benet's Chronicle for the Years 1400–62', ed. G.L. and
M.A. Harriss, *Camden Miscellany* XXIV (1972); *An English
Chronicle of the Reigns of Richard I, Henry IV, Henry V, and
Henry VI*, ed. J.S. Davies, Camden Society LXIV (1856); *Death
and Dissent*.

6. The authoritative treatment is now McLaren, *Chronicles*.

7. *The Crowland Chronicle Continuations 1459–86*, eds N.
Pronay and J.C. Cox (1986).

8. L. Visser-Fuchs, 'Edward IV's Mémoire on Paper to Charles,
Duke of Burgundy: The so-called "Short Version of the
Arrivall"', *Nottingham Medieval Studies* XXXVI (1992); *The
Arrival*; 'Chronicle of the Rebellion in Lincolnshire, in 1470',
ed. J.G. Nichols, *Camden Miscellany* I (1847).

9. *The Coronation of Elizabeth Wydeville, Queen Consort of
Edward IV*, ed. G. Smith (1934); *Excerpta Historica*, ed. S.

Bentley (1831); Kingsford, pp. 379–88; *Illustrations of Ancient State and Chivalry*, ed. W.H. Black (Roxburghe Club, 1840); A.F. Sutton and L. Visser-Fuchs, *The Reburial of Richard Duke of York 21–30 July 1476* (1996); 'Royal Burials of the House of York at Windsor', *The Ricardian* 143 (1998); 'Laments for the Death of Edward IV', *The Ricardian* 145 (1999).

10. *Chronicle of the First Thirteen Years of the Reign of Edward IV*, ed. J. Halliwell, Camden Society VI (1839), pp. 46–51; *Vale*, pp. 212–22.

11. D. Mancini, *The Usurpation of Richard III*, ed. C.A.J. Armstrong (2nd edn, Oxford, 1969); *Three Books of Polydore Vergil's English History*, ed. H. Ellis, Camden Society XXIX (1844); T. More, *History of King Richard III* (1963).

12. T. Basin, *Histoire de Charles VII*, ed. C. Samaran (2 vols, Paris 1933–4); *Histoire de Louis XI*, ed. C. Samaran (2 vols, Paris, 1963–6); P. de Commynes, *Mémoires*, eds J. Calmette and G. Durville (3 vols, Paris, 1923–5); J. de Roye, *Journal*, ed. B. Mandrot (2 vols, Paris, 1894–6); J. de Waurin, *Recueil des Croniques et Anciennes Istoires de la Grant Bretaigne*, eds W. and E.L.C.P. Hardy, V, Rolls Series (1891); A. Goodman and A. Mackay, 'A Castilian Report on English Affairs, 1486', *EHR*, LXXXVIII (1973); L. Visser-Fuchs, 'English Events in Casper Wenreich's Chronicle 1461–95', *The Ricardian* 95 (1986).

13. *Ingulph's Chronicle*, pp. 423–4, 426; *Death and Dissent*, pp. 93, 105–6.

14. *Death and Dissent*, pp. 93, 94, 105–6; *Warkworth's Chronicle*, pp. 46–51; *Ingulph's Chronicle*, p. 445.

15. *Death and Dissent*, pp. 95, 97–8, 102.

16. Ibid., p. 95.

17. Waurin, *Croniques*, v. 456; Mancini, pp. 60–1; *Chronicles of the White Rose of York*, ed. J.A. Giles (1845), p. 16; Vergil, pp. 117–18; More, p. 65; see below, p. 111.

18. *Calendar of Milanese State Papers*, pp. 113–14, as interpreted by Hicks, *Edward V*, pp. 46–7; Mancini, pp. 60–2; More, pp. 60–5.

19. *Ingulph's Chronicle*, pp. 440, 445.

20. 'Annales Rerum Anglicarum', pp. 783, 785, 786.

21. Crowland, pp. 114–15.

22. *The Chronicle of the Rebellion in Lincolnshire*, pp. 5, 9–10.

23. *Arrival, passim.*

24. R.H. Robbins, *Historical Poems of the Fourteenth and Fifteenth Centuries* (New York, 1959), pp. 226–7; *Death and Dissent*, pp. 115, 122.

25. Mancini, pp. 62–3.

26. *Arrival*, pp. 31–40.

27. This is discussed below, p. 193.

28. See below, pp. 140–1; Crowland, pp. 136–9.

29. Ibid., pp. 148–51.

30. Mancini, pp. 58–9; Commynes, II, pp. 241, 245–7.

31. Mancini, pp. 58–69; More, pp. 3–5; Crowland, pp. 146–7.

32. More, p. 2.

33. Ibid., p. 4; A.F. Sutton and L. Visser-Fuchs, 'Laments for the Death of Edward IV', *The Ricardian* 145 (1999), pp. 513, 516–17; Mancini, *Richard III*, 58–9.

34. Crowland, pp. 138–9, 146–9; 'Laments', pp. 514, 516; Mancini, *Richard III*, pp. 58–9.

35. 'Laments', p. 51.

36. *Death and Dissent*, pp. 94, 96, 100, 117–19, 121; Crowland, pp. 136–9.

37. Mancini, pp. 66–7; Crowland, pp. 138–9; 'Laments', p. 514; More, p. 5.

38. Mancini, pp. 58–9, 64–7; More, p. 97.

39. More, p. 4.

40. Ibid., pp. 4–5, 10–13.

41. Lander, p. 161.

42. Ross, *Edward IV*, p. 433.

43. Ibid., pp. 433–4.

44. Commynes, I, p. 192.

45. Ibid., II, p. 202.

46. Ibid., I, pp. 193, 197; II, 64, 70; III, 334.

47. Ibid., I, p. 197.

48. Ibid., I, pp. 197, 200.

49. Ibid., II, pp. 10–17; see also II, 27–8.

50. Ibid., II, pp. 11, 15, 32, 39–82, 231.

51. Ibid., III, p. 231.

52. W. Fulman, 'Historiae Croylandensis Continuatio', *Rerum Anglicarum Scriptores Veterum* (Oxford, 1684), pp. 449–552.

53. Ross, *Edward IV*, p. 430.

54. Kingsford, pp. 182–3; A. Hanham, *Richard III and his Early Historians 1483–1535* (Oxford, 1975), p. 74; Ross, *Edward IV*, p. 430; Gransden, *Historical Writing in England*, II, p. 265; Crowland, p. 95; A.J. Pollard, 'Review Article: Memoirs of a Yorkist Civil Servant', *The Ricardian* 96 (1987), p. 382.

55. N. Pronay, 'The Chancellor, the Chancery, and the Council at the end of the Fifteenth Century', *British Government and Administration*, eds H. Hearder and H.R. Loyn (Cardiff, 1974), p. 102.

56. Ibid., pp. 102–3; Crowland, p. 66.

57. Gransden, *Historical Writing in England*, p. 251.

58. Pollard, 'Memoirs', p. 382.

59. Crowland, p. 8.

60. Kingsford, p. 183.

61. Pollard, p. 311.

62. Crowland, pp. 124–7, 136–9, 142–3, 148–51.

63. D. Williams, 'The Crowland Chronicle 615–1500', *England in the Fifteenth Century* (Woodbridge, 1987), p. 384.

64. Crowland, pp. 112–14, 116–17, 122–3.

65. Ibid., pp. 116–17, 146–9.

66. Ibid., pp. 134–9, 158–9, 170–1.

67. Ibid., pp. 112–13.

68. Ibid., 122–5; *Three Fifteenth-Century Chronicles*, p. 184.

69. Crowland, pp. 134–5.

70. Ibid., pp. 136–7.

71. Ibid., pp. 112–13, 190–1.

72. Ibid., pp. 114–15.

73. Ibid., pp. 116–17.

74. Ibid., pp. 134–5, 138–9, 143–4, 148–9.

75. Ibid., pp. 152–3; see also below, Chapter 7.
76. Ibid., pp. 150–3.

Chapter 4 The degeneration of Edward IV

1. Lander, pp. 160–1.
2. Crowland, pp. 180–3.
3. Ibid., pp. 184–5.
4. Vergil, p. 154.
5. A. Hanham, *Richard III and his Early Historians 1483–1535* (Oxford, 1975), pp. 148–51.
6. Vergil, pp. 109–72, esp. 109–10, 117–18, 124, 133, 139, 167–8, 172.
7. Hughes, p. 3; for what follows, see also the comments in Hanham, *Richard III*, pp. 159–60.
8. More, esp. pp. 4–5, 7, 64–5.
9. Ibid., p. 39.
10. Ibid., p. 15.
11. Ibid., pp. 69–72.
12. *Hall's Chronicle*, ed. H. Ellis (1809), pp. 257–332, esp. 260–2, 277, 292, 300, 302.
13. T. Heywood, *The First and Second Parts of King Edward the Fourth* (1842).
14. W. Shakespeare, *King Henry VI Part II*, act V scene 1.
15. W. Shakespeare, *King Henry VI Part III*, ed. A.S. Cairncross (1964), esp. act I scene 2, act III scene 2, act V scenes 6 and 8.
16. W. Shakespeare, *King Richard III*, ed. A. Hammond (1981), acts I and II.
17. *Mirror for Magistrates*, ed. L.B. Campbell (San Marino, 1938), pp. 197–390, esp. 206, 208–9, 222, 225, 227, 236–390. For further discussion, see below Chapters 6 and 9.
18. G. Buck, *History of King Richard III (1619)*, ed. A.N. Kincaid (Gloucester, 1979), pp. 17–18, 21, 31, 52, 175–8, 184, 186. For his nephew's abridgement, see G. Buck, *History of Richard III*, ed. A.R. Myers (Gloucester, 1973).

19. Habington, *passim*.

20. Lander, p. 162. For what follows, see D. Hume, *History of England* (1778), II, pp. 451–9.

21. H. Walpole, *Historic Doubts on the Life and Reign of Richard III*, ed. P.W. Hammond (Gloucester, 1987), p. 13.

22. M.A. Hicks, 'Bastard Feudalism: Society and Politics in Fifteenth Century England', *Rivals*, pp. 3–5; *Bastard Feudalism* (Harlow, 1995), pp. 15–16.

23. J.R. Green, *A Short History of the English People* (1878), pp. 555–7, 561–2, 569–71; *History of the English People* II (1878), pp. 27–8; see also Lander, p. 162.

24. W. Stubbs, *A Constitutional History of England during the Middle Ages*, III (Oxford, 1880), pp. 208ff., esp. 236–7, 251, 293, 295.

25. J. Gairdner, *History of the Life and Reign of Richard III* (Cambridge, 1898), pp. 1–42 at 2, 26; Dockray, p. XXXIX n. 41. Hughes seems to be reading between the lines rather than literally, Hughes, p. 7.

26. J.H. Ramsay, *Lancaster and York*, II (Oxford, 1892), pp. 268–472 at 453.

27. L. Stratford, *Edward the Fourth* (1910), *passim*.

28. Dockray, p. XXX.

29. Scofield, II. pp. 19, 123–4.

30. Ibid., *passim*.

Chapter 5 The rehabilitation of Edward IV

1. J.P. Cooper, Introduction, in K.B. McFarlane, *The Nobility of Later Medieval England* (Oxford, 1973); *The McFarlane Legacy: Studies in Late Medieval Politics and Society*, eds R.H. Britnell and A.J. Pollard (Stroud, 1995), *passim*; Hicks, *Rivals*, pp. 6ff.

2. V.H. Galbraith, 'A New Life of Richard II', *History*, XXVI (1941–2), pp. 222–39, esp. 229–30.

3. M.A. Hicks, 'Bastard Feudalism, Overmighty Subjects, and Idols of the Multitude', *History* 85 (2000), pp. 386–403.

4. Dockray, p. xl, n. 50.

5. A.R. Myers, ed., *The Household of Edward IV* (Manchester, 1959); D.A.L. Morgan, 'The King's Affinity in the Polity of Yorkist England', *Transactions of the Royal Historical Society* 5th series 23 (1973); see also A.R. Myers, *Crown, Household and Parliament in Fifteenth Century England* (1985), Ch. 9.

6. Lander, Chs 7 and 8; for Wolffe, see below note 13.

7. For example, A.R. Myers, 'Parliament 1422–1509' in R.G. Davies and J.H. Denton, *The English Parliament in the Middle Ages* (Manchester, 1981); Lander, Chs 5 and 10; M.A. Hicks, 'The 1468 Statute of Livery', *HR* LXIV (1991).

8. J.G. Bellamy, 'Justice under the Yorkist Kings', *American Journal of Legal History* IX (1965).

9. A.R. Myers, 'The Character of Richard III', *History Today* IV (1954); P.M. Kendall, *Richard III* (1955).

10. Hicks, *Rivals*, Chs 2, 7, 8, 9, 10; E. Powell, 'After "After McFarlane": The Poverty of Patronage and the Case or Constitutional History', *Trade, Devotion and Governance*, eds D.J. Clayton, R.G. Davies and P. McNiven (Stroud, 1994); Carpenter, *passim*.

11. Lander, *passim*, at pp. 104, 163, 170: see also *idem, Conflict and Stability in Fifteenth-Century England* (1969); *Government and Community: England 1450–1509* (1980).

12. Myers, *Household; Crown, Household and Parliament*, Chs 9, 11, 12.

13. B.P. Wolffe, 'The Management of English Royal Estates under the Yorkist Kings', *EHR,* LXXXI (1956); *The Crown Lands 1471–1536* (1970); *The Royal Demesne in English History* (1971), Ch. 6.

14. S.B. Chrimes, *Lancastrians, Yorkists and Henry VII* (1964), *passim*.

15. Ibid., pp. 111, 124, 125.

16. Ross, *Reign*, p. 49; *Edward IV*, p. XXV. These two works taken together with Ross, *Richard III*, are quoted and discussed in the sources for the next three paragraphs.

17. R.A. Griffiths, 'Foreword to the Yale Edition' in Ross, *Edward IV*, pp. IX, X.

18. Dockray, pp. XXXII–XXXIII.
19. Most of the material cited is readily located in Hicks, *Clarence*; *Edward V*; *Richard III*; *Rivals*; and *Warwick*.
20. Horrox.
21. Carpenter, Chs 8 and 9, at pp. 173, 180–1, 191, 193–4, 196–7, 199, 204–5.
22. Dockray, p. xl n. 50.
23. *Vale*, pp. 43–72, esp. 43–4, 46–7, 49, 67, 71.
24. Griffiths, Foreword, pp. IX–XXIII.
25. Pollard, Chs 10 and 11, at pp. 319–20.
26. Dockray, p. XXXVI.
27. Hicks, *EPC*, p. x.
28. Hughes, p. xii.
29. Ibid., *passim*.

Chapter 6 Edward's first reign

1. Ross, *Edward IV*, pp. 70–1, Appendix iii.
2. Ibid., p. 63.
3. Chrimes, pp. 99, 124.
4. Ross, *Edward IV*, p. 71.
5. Pollard, p. 274.
6. Ross, *Edward IV*, pp. 82–3.
7. The fullest recent survey is in Hicks, *Edward V*, pp. 37–47.
8. As shown above, p. 59.
9. Vergil, p. 114.
10. *Hall's Chronicle*, ed. H. Ellis (1809), pp. 262–4.
11. W. Shakespeare, *Henry VI Part III*, ed. A.S. Cairncross (3rd edn, 1965), act III scene 2; act IV scene 1.
12. Habington, p. 32.
13. G. Buck, *History of King Richard III (1619)*, ed. A.N. Kincaid (Gloucester, 1979), pp. 176–9.
14. J.H. Ramsay, *Lancaster and York*, II (Oxford, 1892), p. 306.
15. Chrimes, p. 92.
16. Ross, *Edward IV*, pp. 85–90; *Reign*, p. 50.

17. Carpenter, p. 170; Dockray, pp. xxxiv, 7, 40.

18. Pollard, pp. 275–6.

19. Dockray, p. 41.

20. Lander, pp. 107–16.

21. T.B. Pugh, 'The magnates, knights and gentry', *Fifteenth-century England 1399–1509: Studies in Politics and Society*, eds S.B. Chrimes, C.D. Ross and R.A. Griffiths (Manchester, 1972), pp. 92–3.

22. Ross, *Edward IV*, pp. 92–6.

23. Hicks, *Clarence*, pp. 34–5, 38; *Rivals*, p. 215.

24. 'Annales Rerum Anglicarum', *Letters and Papers Illustrative of the Wars of the English in France*, ed. J. Stevenson, Rolls Series II(2), p. 786.

25. Pollard, p. 276.

26. 'Annales Rerum Anglicarum', p. 786; Hicks, *Edward V*, pp. 132, 134.

27. Crowland, pp. 114–15.

28. Chrimes, p. 99; Ross, *Edward IV*, p. 105; Hicks, *Clarence*, p. 41; *Warwick*, pp. 258–9; *Edward V*, p. 49; Pollard, p. 277; Dockray, pp. 7–8.

29. Hicks, *Edward V*, pp. 52–3.

30. See above, p. 108.

31. See above, p. 50.

32. See below, Chapter 7.

33. Carpenter, p. 163.

34. *Vale*, pp. 135–8.

35. *Warkworth's Chronicle*, pp. 46–51.

36. Ross, *Reign*, pp. 51–2.

37. Ross, *Edward IV*, p. 115.

38. Hicks, *Clarence*, pp. 38–9, 43.

39. Hicks, *Warwick*, pp. 2, 5; L. Visser-Fuchs, 'Warwick, by Himself": Richard, Earl of Warwick, "The Kingmaker", in the *Recueil des Croniques d'Engleterre* of Jean de Waurin', *Publications du Centre Européen des Études Bourguignonnes (xive–xvie)* 41 (2001).

40. See above, Chapter 4; Hicks, *Warwick*, pp. 3–5.
41. Chrimes, pp. 88, 91.
42. Carpenter, p. 181.
43. Pollard, pp. 275, 290.
44. Dockray, p. 30.

Chapter 7 The king's wars

1. Ross, *Edward IV*, p. 364.
2. M.A. Hicks, 'A Minute of the Lancastrian Council at York, 19 January 1461', *Northern History* XXXIV (1998).
3. Hicks, *Warwick*, p. 243.
4. Ibid., p. 247.
5. Dockray, pp. 7–8.
6. Ross, *Edward IV*, p. 111.
7. Hicks, *Warwick*, p. 263.
8. Ross, *Edward IV*, p. 112.
9. Scofield, I, pp. 450, 453–4.
10. Ross, *Edward IV*, p. 113; R. Vaughan, *Charles the Bold* (1973), pp. 55–6.
11. *Warkworth's Chronicle*, p. 51.
12. Chrimes, p. 111.
13. *Vale*, pp. 69, 266.
14. Jurkowski, p. 111.
15. Lander, pp. 239–40.
16. Ibid., p. 240.
17. Ross, *Edward IV*, p. 211.
18. Crowland, pp. 130–1.
19. Crowland, pp. 132–3; L. Starkey, 'Anglo-Burgundian Diplomacy 1467–85' (London University MPhil thesis, 1977), pp. 56–7.
20. Ross, *Edward IV*, p. 209.
21. Ibid., p. 207.
22. Ross, *Reign*, p. 52.
23. Ross, *Edward IV*, pp. 210–11.

24. Crowland, pp. 130–1. This is also the thrust of the seventeenth-century translation of a document (perhaps a speech or circular) included in Habington, pp. 120–7.

25. Hicks, *Edward V*, pp. 60–3.

26. Crowland, pp. 133–4; Habington, pp. 120–7.

27. Lander, pp. 228–30.

28. Ibid., p. 228.

29. Hicks, *EPC*, pp. 25–6.

30. Crowland, pp. 132–5.

31. Lander, p. 230.

32. Ibid., pp. 230–4; Jurkowski, pp. 111–18.

33. Lander, p. 231.

34. Ibid., p. 234n.

35. Ibid., p. 239.

36. Commynes, II, p. 11.

37. Hicks, *Clarence*, p. 118.

38. Ross, *Edward IV*, p. 207.

39. Ibid., pp. 207, 225.

40. Pollard, p. 303.

41. Crowland, pp. 137–8.

42. Ibid., pp. 136–9; *Vale*, p. 70.

43. Ross, *Edward IV*, p. 229.

44. Commynes, II, pp. 31–2.

45. Crowland, pp. 136–7.

46. Ibid., pp. 134–7.

47. Ibid., pp. 136–7; Commynes, II, pp. 31–3.

48. Chrimes, p. 119.

49. Commynes, II, pp. 81–2.

50. Pollard, p. 303.

51. Commynes, III, p. 334.

52. Ross, *Edward IV*, p. 250.

53. Ibid., p. 294.

54. Chrimes, p. 123.

55. *Vale*, p. 71.

56. Crowland, p. 151.

57. *Vale*, p. 71.

58. Hicks, *Richard III*, p. 77.

59. Ross, *Edward IV*, p. 282.

60. Crowland, pp. 148–9.

61. Hicks, *Rivals*, pp. 391–4.

62. Ross, *Edward IV*, p. 294.

63. R.A. Griffiths, 'Foreword to the Yale Edition' in Ross, *Edward IV*, p. xviii.

Chapter 8 The 'New Monarchy': government and finance

1. For example, *Vale*, pp. 208–12.

2. For example, R.A. Griffiths, *The Reign of Henry VI 1422–61* (1981), Chs 7, 20.

3. B.P. Wolffe, *Yorkist and Early Tudor Government 1461–1509* (1966), p. 7.

4. W. Stubbs, *Constitutional History of England during the Middle Ages*, III (1878), pp. 300–4.

5. J.R. Green, *Short History of the English People* (1978), pp. 564, 569.

6. Crowland, pp. 146–7; L. Stratford, *Edward the Fourth* (1910), p. 207.

7. Witness the useful survey in A. Goodman, *The New Monarchy: England 1471–1534* (1988), esp. pp. 4–7.

8. G.L. Harriss, 'A Revolution in Tudor History? Medieval Government and Statecraft', *Past and Present* 25 (1963), pp. 4–7.

9. The debate between Elton, Harriss and Williams is in *Past and Present* 25 (1963), 29 (1964), 32 (1965).

10. A.P. Newton, 'The King's Chamber under the Early Tudors, *EHR* XXXII (1917), pp. 348–72.

11. Chrimes, p. 125.

12. L. Clark, 'The Benefits and Burdens of Office: Henry Bourgchier (1408–83), Viscount Bourgchier and Earl of Essex,

and the Treasurership of the Exchequer', *Profit, Piety and the Professions in Later Medieval England*, ed. M.A. Hicks (Gloucester, 1990), p. 128.

13. See examples in *Vale*; *British Library Harleian Manuscript 433*, eds P.W. Hammond and R.E. Horrox (4 vols Upminster, 1979–83); B.P. Wolffe, *The Crown Lands 1471–1536* (1970); see also Hicks, *Rivals*, pp. 71–5.

14. Lander, Chs 7 and 8.

15. Ross, *Reign,* p. 55.

16. Ross, *Edward IV*, pp. 371–3.

17. Crowland, pp. 134–5.

18. *Vale*, pp. 135–8, 145–6.

19. G.L. Harriss, 'Aids, Loans and Benevolences', *Historical Journal* VI (1963), pp. 1–19, esp. 12.

20. Lander, pp. 233, 234n.

21. Wolffe, p. 146.

22. Ibid., p. 147.

23. Hicks, *Richard III*, pp. 126–7.

24. The full story is told by B.P. Wolffe, 'Acts of Resumption in the Lancastrian Parliaments', *EHR* LXXIII (1958).

25. Hicks, *Warwick*, p. 125.

26. Hicks, *Rivals,* p. 72.

27. Wolffe, pp. 145, 158.

28. Ibid., p. 154n.

29. B.P. Wolffe, 'The Management of English Royal Estates under the Yorkist Kings', *EHR* LXXI (1956), pp. 1–27.

30. Wolffe, pp. 179–80

31. Ross, *Reign*, p. 55.

32. Ross, *Edward IV*, p. 371.

33. Ross, *Reign*, pp. 55–9.

34. Carpenter, pp. 168–9.

35. Ross, *Edward IV*, pp. 380–7; *Reign*, p. 56.

36. *Calendar of the Patent Rolls 1476–85*, p. 212.

37. Hicks, *Clarence*, p. 173.

38. Crowland, p. 139.

39. Ibid.

40. Hicks, *Rivals*, p. 381.

41. 'Financial Memoranda of the Reign of Edward V', ed. R.E. Horrox, *Camden Miscellany* XXXIV (1987).

42. Crowland, pp. 148–9.

43. Pollard, pp. 310–11.

44. Ross, *Edward IV*, p. 261.

45. Carpenter, p. 201.

46. Scofield, II, pp. 386–7.

47. Jurkowski, p. 118.

48. Wolffe, p. 149.

49. Hicks, *Edward V*, p. 134; *Calendar of Patent Rolls, 1476–85*, p. 212.

Chapter 9 The king's peace

1. The classic exposition remains R.L. Storey, *The End of the House of Lancaster* (1966).

2. Ross, *Edward IV*, p. 61.

3. J.G. Bellamy, 'Justice under the Yorkist Kings', *American Journal of Legal History* IX (1965), pp. 135–155 at 136–8, 147–8, 154.

4. Ibid., pp. 140–2, 155.

5. J. Fortescue, *On the Laws and Governance of England*, ed. S. Lockwood (Cambridge, 1997), p. 33.

6. *The Great Chronicle of London*, eds A.H. Thomas and I.D. Thornley (1938), pp. 204–6; *New Chronicles of England and France*, ed. H. Ellis (1811), p. 660.

7. Scofield, I, p. 461; Ross, *Edward IV*, p. 101.

8. Fortescue, *Governance*, p. 33.

9. Ross, *Edward IV*, pp. 99–101; Ross, *Reign*, p. 51; P. Holland, 'Cook's Case in History and Myth', *HR* LXI (1988), pp. 34–5.

10. *Great Chronicle,* pp. 213–14.

11. *Vale*, pp. 154–5, 169–70. These were used in 1978 by Hicks, *Rivals*, Ch. 23.

12. PRO KB 9/319.

13. Bellamy, p. 145.

14. Ross, *Edward IV*, pp. 100–1.

15. A.F. Sutton, 'Sir Thomas Cook and his "Troubles"', *Guildhall Studies in History* III (1978), pp. 85–108.

16. Hicks, *Rivals*, pp. 419–434 esp. 422, 433.

17. Holland, 'Cook', pp. 21–35.

18. *Vale*, p. 91.

19. Pollard, p. 281; see also R.A. Griffiths, 'Foreword to the Yale Edition' in Ross, *Edward IV*, p. XIII.

20. Hicks, *Rivals*, pp. 1–7.

21. M.A. Hicks, *Bastard Feudalism* (Harlow, 1995), p. 1.

22. Ibid., *passim*.

23. M.A. Hicks, 'The 1468 Statute of Livery', *HR* LXIV (1991), p. 21.

24. Hicks, *Rivals*, pp. 3–5; *Bastard Feudalism*, Ch. 4.

25. Hicks, *Bastard Feudalism*, p. 128.

26. Ibid., p. 116; 'Private Indentures for Life Service in Peace and War', eds M. Jones and S. Walker, *Camden Miscellany* XXXII (1994), pp. 164–5; *Rolls of Parliament*, VI, p. 174.

27. Hicks, '1468 Statute'.

28. *EHD*, p. 272.

29. Hicks, *Bastard Feudalism*, p. 131.

30. *RP* V, pp. 487–8; W.H. Dunham, *Lord Hastings' Indentured Retainers 1461–83* (1955), pp. 91–2.

31. 'Annales Rerum Anglicarum', *Letters and Papers illustrative of the Wars of the English in France*, Rolls Series II(2), (1864), p. 789.

32. *RP* V, pp. 633–4; Hicks, '1468 Statute', pp. 15–28. These are also the source of the next paragraph.

33. Dunham, *Hastings*, pp. 80–9; see also J.G. Bellamy, *Bastard Feudalism and the Law* (1989).

34. Hicks, '1468 Statute', p. 26.

35. Hicks, *Rivals*, Ch. 12.

36. *Paston Letters and Papers of the Fifteenth Century*, ed. N. Davis, I (1976), pp. 400, 545.

37. 'Private Indentures', pp. 176–8; C.S. Perceval, 'Documents of Sir John Lawson, Baronet', *Archaeologia* XLVII (1992), p. 189.

38. *RP* V, pp. 487–8.

39. Horrox, p. 4; Jones, p. 8.

40. Hicks, *Bastard Feudalism*, p. 180.

41. Hicks, *EPC*, pp. 156–9.

42. Carpenter, p. 165.

43. Bellamy, p. 155.

44. Ross, *Reign*, pp. 61–2.

45. Hicks, *EPC*, pp. 155–6.

46. P.M. Barnes, 'The Chancery corpus cum causa file, 10–11 Edward IV', *Medieval Legal Records*, eds R. Hunnisett and J.B. Post (1978), pp. 430–76.

47. Hicks, *Edward V*, pp. 105–8, 113–14.

48. *The Plumpton Letters and Papers*, ed. J. Kirby, Camden Society 5th series VIII (1996), p. 55.

49. Bellamy, p. 154.

50. Hicks, *Edward V*, pp. 89, 107–14, 117.

51. Ross, *Reign*, pp. 61–2.

52. *RP* V, p. 487.

53. Ross, *Edward IV*, p. 199.

Chapter 10 Edward IV and the nobility

1. Lander, Ch. 5.

2. Vergil, p. 119.

3. T.K. Oliphant, 'Was the Old English Aristocracy destroyed by the Wars of the Roses?', *Transactions of the Royal Historical Society* I (1875), pp. 437–43; K.B. McFarlane, 'The Wars of the Roses', *England in the Fifteenth Century* (1981), p. 257; Lander, pp. 127–58, esp. 133–7.

4. M.A. Hicks, 'Richard III, The Great Landholders, and the Results of the Wars of the Roses', *Tant D'Emprises: So Many Undertakings. Essays in Honour of Anne Sutton*, ed. L. Visser-Fuchs, *The Ricardian* XIII (2003).

5. Vergil, p. 116.

6. Ross, *Edward IV*, p. 83.

7. Carpenter, p. 160.

8. Lander, pp. 133–6.

9. Hicks, *Clarence*, pp. 38–9; *Rivals*, pp. 143–4, 264; *Warwick*, p. 234; *Death and Dissent*, p. 98.

10. Carpenter, p. 159.

11. Pollard, p. 273.

12. Ross, *Edward IV*, pp. 51–2.

13. Habington, pp. 21–5.

14. Carpenter, p. 161.

15. Pollard, p. 273. Courtenay and Hungerford did not actually *rebel*; Oxford in 1469 was pro-Warwick, not pro-Lancastrian.

16. Carpenter, pp. 157, 163; Hicks, *Rivals*, Ch. 8, esp. pp. 159–60.

17. Lander, p. 140.

18. 'Chronicle of the Rebellion in Lincolnshire, in 1470', ed. J.G. Nichols, *Camden Miscellany* I (1847), pp. 13–15; *Arrival*, p. 12.

19. The fullest modern account, Hicks, *Clarence*, corrects an earlier paper in Lander, Ch. 10, and both are the principal sources for what follows. See Chapters 3 and 4 for some earlier assessments of Clarence's fall.

20. M.C. Carpenter, 'The Duke of Clarence and the Midlands: A Study of the Interplay of Local and National Politics', *Midland History* XI (1986).

21. Ibid.

22. More, p. 70.

23. *RP* VI, pp. 193–5.

24. Mancini, pp. 62–3.

25. Crowland, pp. 144–5.

26. More, p. 7.

27. Vergil, pp. 167-8.

28. Mancini, pp. 62–3; Crowland, pp. 144–7; More, p. 7; Vergil, p. 168.

29. Crowland, pp. 146–7; Vergil, p. 168.

30. W. Shakespeare, *King Richard III*, ed. A. Hammond (1981), act I, scene 1; act II, scenes 1–2.

31. Ibid., act I scene 4 paraphrasing *idem*, *King Henry VI Part III*, ed. A.S. Cairncross (3rd edn, 1964), act IV scene 4.

32. T. Heywood, *The First and Second Parts of King Edward IV* (1842), pp. 136–8.

33. *Mirror for Magistrates*, ed. L.B. Campbell (1938), pp. 220–39, esp. 220–9; see also H. Walpole, *Historic Doubts on the Life and Reign of Richard III*, ed. P.W. Hammond (1987), pp. 19–22.

34. *Mirror for Magistrates*, pp. 232–4.

35. G. Buck, *History of King Richard III (1619)*, ed. A.N. Kincaid (1979), pp. 18, 135–7.

36. Habington, pp. 191–5.

37. D. Hume, *History of England* (1778), II, pp. 489–92.

38. W. Stubbs, *Constitutional History of England during the Middle Ages*, III (Oxford, 1878), p. 236.

39. J. Gairdner, *History of the Life and Reign of Richard III* (1898), p. 30; J.H. Ramsay, *Lancaster and York* (1892) II, p. 421.

40. L. Stratford, *King Edward the Fourth* (1910), pp. 282–90; Pollard, p. 307.

41. Bellamy, p. 147.

42. Dockray, pp. 8, 96–7.

43. Ibid., p. 96.

44. Chrimes, p. 121.

45. Dockray, p. 97.

46. Ross, *Richard III*, p. 32.

47. Bellamy, p. 147.

48. *Vale*, p. 67; Carpenter, pp. 189–90; Pollard, p. 307; Dockray, p. 97; Gairdner, *Richard III*, p. 32; Ramsay, *Lancaster and York*, II, p. 424.

49. Pollard, pp. 308–9.

50. Chrimes, p. 122.

51. Crowland, pp. 132–3; Mancini, pp. 62–3.

52. Stratford, *Edward IV*, p. 289.

53. Hicks, *Rivals*, Ch. 7.

54. Crowland, pp. 146–7.

55. Ross, *Richard III*, p. 32.

56. Vergil, p. 168.

57. Crowland, pp. 146–7.

58. Hicks, *Rivals*, Ch. 3.

59. Barnes, 'Corpus cum causa', pp. 439–40.

60. *Paston Letters & Papers*, II, p. 544.

61. Hicks, '1468 Statute', p. 26.

62. Hicks, *Rivals*, p. 61.

63. Hicks, *Edward V*, Ch. 5.

64. Pollard, pp. 314–15.

65. Carpenter, p. 205.

66. Ibid., p. 188.

Chapter 11 Territorial reordering

1. Crowland, pp. 154–5; Mancini, pp. 70–1.

2. P.M. Kendall, *Richard III* (1955); Ross, *Richard III*, Ch. 3; Horrox, Ch. 1; A.J. Pollard, *Richard III and the Princes in the Tower* (1991); Hicks, *Richard III*, Ch. 2.

3. Ross, *Richard III*, p. 25; Hicks, *Edward V*, pp. 112, 127–8, 134.

4. T.B. Pugh, 'The Magnates, Knights and Gentry', *Fifteenth-century England 1399–1509: Studies in Politics and Society*, eds S.B. Chrimes, C.D. Ross and R.A. Griffiths (Manchester, 1972), p. 92.

5. Hicks, *Clarence*, pp. 172, 179–80.

6. Pugh, 'Magnates', pp. 92–3; Hicks, *Clarence*, pp. 34–6, 38; *Edward V*, pp. 123, 131–3; *Rivals*, pp. 214–15.

7. Hicks, *Edward V*, pp. 44, 50.

8. See also above p. 113.

9. Hicks, *Clarence*, pp. 55–61.

10. Carpenter, p. 183.

11. Ibid., pp. 189, 192.

12. Carpenter, Ch. 9; Horrox, pp. 69, 72, 74; D.E. Lowe, 'Patronage and Politics: Edward IV, the Wydevills, and the Council of the Prince of Wales, 1471–83', *Bulletin of the Board of Celtic Studies* 29 (1980–2).

13. Pollard, pp. 311–14; *Vale*, pp. 71–2.

14. Horrox, p. 72; Carpenter, pp. 160, 186, 189; Lowe, 'Patronage and Politics'.

15. Lander, pp. 138, 139n.

16. Hicks, *Clarence*, p. 56; *Edward V*, pp. 112–14.

17. Horrox, pp. 26, 60, 65–6.

18. Birmingham Reference Library MSS 347914, 347865.

19. Hicks, *Clarence*, Ch. 3; Hicks, *Rivals*, Ch. 18.

20. Horrox, p. 72.

21. Hicks, *Rivals*, pp. 369–71.

22. M.A. Hicks, 'Richard III as Duke of Gloucester and the North', *Richard III and the North*, ed. R.E. Horrox (Hull, 1985), pp. 13–16.

23. Horrox, p. 66.

24. Pollard, pp. 314–15.

25. Hicks, *Edward V*, Chs 3–4.

26. Lowe, 'Patronage and Politics'.

27. Horrox, pp. 30, 68.

28. Hicks, *Rivals*, p. 76; *Edward V*, p. 82; *RP* VI, pp. 46–7.

29. Hicks, *Rivals*, Ch. 12.

30. Hicks, *Edward V*, pp. 131–4.

31. Horrox, pp. 1, 5.

32. D.E. Lowe, 'The Council of the Prince of Wales and the Decline of the Herbert Family during the Second Reign of Edward IV (1471–83)', *Bulletin of the Board of Celtic Studies* 27 (1976–8).

33. *Plumpton Letters and Papers*, ed. J. Kirby, Camden Society 5th series VIII (1996), pp. 51–3.

34. Pollard, p. 313.

35. Hicks, *Edward V*, p. 110.

36. Horrox, p. 48.

37. Ibid.

38. Pollard, pp. 314–15.

39. M.A. Hicks, 'Richard Lord, Latimer, Richard III, and the Warwick Inheritance', *The Ricardian* 154 (2001).

Chapter 12 The collapse of the regime

1. Carpenter, p. 205.
2. Mancini, pp. 62–4; Crowland, pp. 146–7.
3. *Vale*, pp. 71–2.
4. Pollard, p. 319.
5. Ibid., p. 319.
6. More, p. 9.
7. As demonstrated in Hicks, *Rivals*, Ch. 13.
8. Hicks, *Edward V*, p. 59.
9. Jones, p. 77.

Select bibliography

Unless otherwise stated, all works were published in London.

Allan, A., 'Yorkist Propaganda: Pedigree, Prophecy and the "British History" in the Reign of Edward IV', *Patronage, Pedigree and Power in Later Medieval England,* ed. C.D. Ross (Gloucester, 1979).

Barnard, F.P., *Edward IV's French Expedition of 1471: The Leaders and their Badges* (1925).

Barnes, P.M., 'Chancery corpus cum causa files, 10–11 Edward IV', *Medieval Legal Records*, eds R.F. Hunnisett and J. Post (1978).

Basin, T., *Histoire de Charles VII*, ed. C. Samaran (Paris, 1933–4).

Basin, T., *Histoire de Louis XI*, ed. C. Samaran (2 vols, Paris, 1963–6).

Bellamy, J.G., 'Justice under the Yorkist Kings', *American Journal of Legal History* IX (1965).

Bellamy, J.G., *Bastard Feudalism and the Law* (1989).

Bentley, S., ed., *Excerpta Historica* (1831).

Biggs, D., Michalove, S.D. and Reeves, A.C., eds, *Traditions and Transformations in Late Medieval England* (Brill, 2002).

Britnell, R.H. and Hatcher, J., eds, *Progress and Problems in Medieval England* (Cambridge, 1996).

Bruce, J., ed., *The Historie of the Arrivall of Edward IV in England and the Finall Recouerye of his Kingdomes from Henry VI*, Camden Society I (1836).

Buck, G., *History of Richard III*, ed. A.R. Myers (Gloucester, 1973).

Buck, G., *History of King Richard III (1619)*, ed. A.N. Kincaid (1979).

Calendar of the Close Rolls 1461–85 (3 vols, 1949–54).

Calendar of the Patent Rolls 1461–85 (3 vols, 1897–1901).

Calmette, J. and Périnelle, G., *Louis XI et l'Angleterre* (Paris, 1930).

Campbell, L.B., ed., *Mirror for Magistrates* (San Marino, 1938).

Carpenter, C., 'The Duke of Clarence and the Midlands: A Study in the Interplay of Local and National Politics', *Midland History* XI (1986).

Carpenter, C., *Locality and Polity: A Study of Warwickshire Landed Society 1401–1499* (Cambridge, 1992).

Carpenter, C., *The Wars of the Roses: Politics and the Constitution in England, c.1437–1509* (Cambridge, 1996).

Chrimes, S.B., Ross, C.D. and Griffiths, R.A., eds, *Fifteenth-century England: Studies in Politics and Society* (Manchester, 1972).

Chrimes, S.B., *Lancastrians, Yorkists and Henry VII* (1964).

Commynes, P. de, *Mémoires*, eds J. Calmette and G. Durville (3 vols, Paris, 1924–5).

Davies, J.S., ed., *An English Chronicle of the Reigns of Richard II, Henry IV, Henry V, and Henry VI*, Camden Society LXIV (1856).

Davis, N., ed., *Paston Letters and Papers of the Fifteenth Century* (2 vols, Oxford, 1971–6).

Denton, W., *England in the Fifteenth Century* (1888).

Dockray, K.R., *Edward IV: A Source Book* (Stroud, 1999).

Dugdale, W., *Monasticon Anglicanum* (8 vols, 1846).

Dunham, W.H., *Lord Hastings' Indentured Retainers 1461–83* (New Haven, 1956).

Ellis, H., ed., *Hall's Chronicle* (1809).

Ellis, H., ed., *The New Chronicles of England and of France* (1811).

Ellis, H., ed., *Three Books of Polydore Vergil's English History*, Camden Society XXXIX (1844).

Fortescue, J., *On the Laws and Governance of England*, ed. S. Lockwood (Cambridge, 1997).

Gairdner, J., ed., *Historical Collections of a Citizen of London in the Fifteenth Century*, Camden Society, new series XVII (1876).

Gairdner, J., ed., *Three Fifteenth Century Chronicles*, Camden Society new series XXVIII (1880).

Gairdner, J., *The Life and Times of Richard III* (1898).

Gibbs, H.V. *et al.*, eds, *The Complete Peerage of England, Scotland, Ireland and the United Kingdom* (13 vols in 12, 1910–59).

Giffin, M.E., 'Cadwallader, Arthur and Brutus in the Wigmore Manuscript', *Speculum* 16 (1941).

Goodman, A., *The New Monarchy: England 1471–1534* (1988).

Goodman, A. and Morgan, D., 'The Yorkist Claim to the Throne of Castile', *Journal of Medieval History* XII (1985).

Gransden, A., *Historical Writing in England* II (1982).

Green, J.R., *A Short History of the English People* (1878).

Griffiths, R.A., *King and Country: England and Wales in the Fifteenth Century* (1991).

Griffiths, R.A., *The Reign of King Henry VI 1422–61* (2nd edn, Stroud, 1998).

Griffiths, R.A. and Sherborne, J.W., eds, *Kings and Nobles in the Later Middle Ages* (Gloucester, 1986).

Gross, A.J., *The Dissolution of the Lancastrian Kingship. Sir John Fortescue and the Crisis of Monarchy in Fifteenth-Century England* (Stamford, 1996).

Habington, W., *History of the Reign of King Edward the Fourth* (1640).

Hanham, A., *Richard III and his Earlier Historians* (Oxford, 1975).

Hanham, A., 'Author! Author! Crowland Revisited', *The Ricardian* 140 (1998).

Harriss, G.L., 'Aids, Loans and Benevolences', *Historical Journal* (1963).

Harriss, G.L. and Harriss, M.A., eds, 'John Benet's Chronicle for the Years 1460–62', *Camden Miscellany* XXIV (1972).

Hearder, H. and Loyn, H.R., eds, *British Government and Administration. Studies presented to S.B. Chrimes* (Cardiff, 1974).

Heywood, T., *The First and Second Parts of King Edward the Fourth* (1842).

Hicks, M.A., *False, Fleeting, Perjur'd Clarence: George Duke of Clarence 1449–78* (1st edn, Gloucester, 1980).

Hicks, M.A., *Richard III and his Rivals: Magnates and their Motives during the Wars of the Roses* (1991).

Hicks, M.A., 'The 1468 Statute of Livery', *Historical Research* LXIV (1991).

Hicks, M.A., *Bastard Feudalism* (1995).

Hicks, M.A., *Warwick the Kingmaker* (Oxford, 1998).

Hicks, M.A., *Richard III* (2nd edn, Stroud, 2000).

Hicks, M.A., *English Political Culture in the Fifteenth Century* (2002).

Holland, P., 'Cook's Case in History and Myth', *Historical Research* LXI (1988).

Horrox, R.E., ed., 'Financial Memoranda of the Reign of Edward V. Longleat Miscellaneous Manuscript Book II', *Camden Miscellany* XXIX (1987).

Horrox, R.E., *Richard III: A Study of Service* (Cambridge, 1989).

Horrox, R.E. and Hammond, P.W., eds, *British Library Harleian Manuscript 433* (4 vols, Upminster, 1979–83).

Hughes, J., *Arthurian Myths and Alchemy: The Kingship of Edward IV* (Stroud, 2002).

Ives, E.W., 'Andrew Dymmock and the Papers of Anthony, Earl Rivers, 1482–3', *Bulletin of the Institute of Historical Research* LXI (1968).

Jones, M. and Walker, S., eds, 'Private Indentures for Life Service in Peace and War 1278–1476', *Camden Miscellany* XXXII (1994).

Jones, M.K., 'Richard III and the Stanleys', *Richard III and the North*, ed. R.E. Horrox (Hull, 1985).

Jones, M.K., 'Somerset, York and the Wars of the Roses', *English Historical Review* CIV (1989).

Jones, M.K., *Bosworth, 1485: Psychology of a Battle* (Stroud, 2002).

Jurkowski, M., Smith, C.L. and Crook, D., *Lay Taxes in England and Wales 1188–1688* (1998).

Kekewich, M.L., Richmond, C.F., Sutton, A.F., Visser-Fuchs, L. and Watts, J.L., eds, *The Politics of Fifteenth-Century England: John Vale's Book* (Stroud, 1995).

Kelly, H.A., 'The Croyland Chronicle Tragedies', *The Ricardian* 99 (1987).

Kelly, H.A., 'The Last Chroniclers of Croyland', *The Ricardian* 91 (1985).

Kelly, H.A., 'Crowland Observations', *The Ricardian* 108 (1990).

Kendall, P.M., *Richard III* (1955).

Kendall, P.M., *Louis XI* (1971).

Kingsford, C.L., ed., *Chronicles of London* (1905).

Kingsford, C.L., *English Historical Literature in the Fifteenth Century* (Oxford, 1913).

Kingsford, C.L., ed., *Stonor Letters and Papers of the Fifteenth Century*, Camden Society 3rd series XXX (2 vols., 1919).

Kirby, J., ed., *Plumpton Letters and Papers*, Camden Society 5th series IV (1997).

Lander, J.R., *Conflict and Stability in Fifteenth-Century England* (1969).

Lander, J.R., *Crown and Nobility 1461–1509* (1976).

Lander, J.R., *Government and Community 1450–1509* (1980).

Lander, J.R., *English Justices of the Peace 1461–1509* (Stroud, 1989).

McFarlane, K.B., *England in the Fifteenth Century* (1981).

McLaren, M.-R., *The Chronicles of the Fifteenth Century. A Revolution in English Writing* (Woodbridge, 2002).

Mancini, D., *The Usurpation of Richard III*, ed. C.A.J. Armstrong, (2nd edn., Oxford, 1969).

Matheson, L.M., ed., *Death and Dissent: The Dethe of the Kynge of Scotis and Warkworth's Chronicle* (Woodbridge, 1999).

More, T., *The History of King Richard III*, ed. R. Sylvester (Yale, 1963).

Morgan, D.A.L., 'The King's Affinity in the Polity of Yorkist England', *Transactions of the Royal Historical Society* 5th series 23 (1973).

Myers, A.R., ed., *The Household of Edward IV: The Black Book and the Ordnance of 1478* (Manchester, 1959).

Myers, A.R., ed., *English Historical Documents, IV, 1327–1485* (1969).

Myers, A.R., *Crown, Household and Parliament in Fifteenth Century England* (1985).

Nichols, J.G., ed., 'Chronicle of the Rebellion in Lincolnshire, in 1470', *Camden Miscellany* I (1847).

Payling, S.J., 'The Ampthill Dispute: A Study in Aristocratic Lawlessness and the Breakdown of Lancastrian Government', *English Historical Review* CIV (1989).

Pollard, A.J., *North-Eastern England during the Wars of the Roses: Lay Society, War and Politics 1450–1500* (Oxford, 1990).

Pollard, A.J., *Richard III and the Princes in the Tower* (Gloucester, 1991).

Pollard, A.J., ed, *The Wars of the Roses* (Basingstoke, 1995).

Pollard, A.J. ed., *The North in the Age of Richard III* (Stroud, 1996).

Pollard, A.J., *Late Medieval England 1399–1509* (Harlow, 2000).

Pollard, A.J., *The Wars of the Roses* (2nd edn., Basingstoke, 2001).

Pronay, N., 'The Chancellor, the Chancery and the Council at the End of the Fifteenth Century', *British Government and Administration*, eds H. Hearder and H.R. Loyn (Cardiff, 1974).

Pronay, N. and Cox, J., eds, *The Crowland Chronicle Continuations 1459–86* (1986).

Ramsay, J.H., *Lancaster and York* (2 vols, Oxford, 1892).

Richmond, C.F., *The Paston Family in the Fifteenth Century* (3 vols, Cambridge 1990–6, Manchester, 2000).

Riley, H.T., ed., *Ingulph's Chronicle of the Abbey of Croyland* (1859).

Robbins, R.H., ed., *Historical Poems of the Fourteenth and Fifteenth Centuries* (New York, 1959).

Rolls of Parliament (6 vols, Record Commission, 1832).

Ross, C.D., *Edward IV* (2nd edn, 1997).

Ross, C.D., *Richard III* (2nd edn, 1999).

Scofield, C.L., *The Life and Reign of Edward IV* (2 vols, 1923).

Shakespeare, W., *Henry VI Part III*, ed. A.S. Cairncross (3rd edn, 1965).

Shakespeare, W., *History of King Richard III*, ed. A. Hammond (1981).

Smith, G., ed., *The Coronation of Elizabeth Wydeville, Queen Consort of Edward V, on May 26th, 1465* (1934).

Stevenson, J., ed., 'Annales rerum anglicarum', *Letters and Papers Illustrative of the Wars of the English in France*, II(2), Rolls Series (1864).

Storey, R.L., *The End of the House of Lancaster* (1966).

Stratford, L., *Edward the Fourth* (1913).

Stubbs, W., *Constitutional History of England during the Middle Ages* (3 vols, Oxford, 1875–8).

Sutton, A.F., 'Sir Thomas Cook and his "Troubles"', *Guildhall Studies in History* 3 (1978).

Sutton, A.F. and Visser-Fuchs, L., *The Reburial of Richard Duke of York, 21–30 July 1476* (1996).

Sutton, A.F. and Visser-Fuchs, L., 'The Royal Burials of the House of York at Windsor', *The Ricardian* 143 (1998).

Sutton, A.F. and Visser-Fuchs, L., 'Laments for the Death of Edward IV', *The Ricardian* 145 (1999).

Thielemans, M.R., *Bourgogne et Angleterre: Relations Politiques et Economiques entre les Pays-Bas Bourguignon et l'Angleterre 1435–1467* (Brussels, 1967).

Thomas, A.H. and Thornley, I.D., eds, *The Great Chronicle of London* (1938).

Thomson, J.A.F., 'Warkworth's Chronicle Reconsidered', *English Historical Review* (2001).

Vaughan, R., *Philip the Good* (1970).

Vaughan, R., *Charles the Bold* (1973).

Virgoe, R., *East Anglian Society and the Political Community of Late Medieval England*, eds C. Barron, C. Rawcliffe and J.T. Rosenthal (Norwich, 1997).

Visser-Fuchs, L., 'Memoirs of a Yorkist Civil Servant: A Comment', *The Ricardian* 99 (1987).

Visser-Fuchs, L., 'Edward IV's Mémoire on Paper to Charles Duke of Burgundy: The so-called "Short Version of the Arrivall"', *Nottingham Medieval Studies* XXXVI (1992).

Visser-Fuchs, L., '"Warwick, by himself": Richard Neville, Earl of Warwick, "The Kingmaker"', in the *Recueil des Croniques d'Engleterre* of Jean de Waurin, *Publications du Centre Européen d'Études Bourguignonnes (XIVe –XVIe)* 41 (2001).

Walpole, H., *Historic Doubts on the Life and Reign of Richard III*, ed. P.W. Hammond (Gloucester, 1987).

Watts, J.L., '*De Consulatu Stilicho*: Texts and Politics in the Reign of Henry VI', *Journal of Medieval History* 16 (1990).

Waurin, J. de, *Recueil des Croniques et Anciennes Istoires de la Grant Bretaigne*, eds E.L.C.P. Hardy and W. Hardy, Rolls Series V (1891).

Williams, D., 'The Crowland Chronicle, 616–1500', *England in the Fifteenth Century* (Woodbridge, 1987).

Wolffe, B.P., 'The Management of English Royal Estates under the Yorkist Kings', *English Historical Review* LXXXI (1956).

Wolffe, B.P., 'Acts of Resumption in Lancastrian Parliaments, 1399–1456', *English Historical Review* 73 (1958).

Wolffe, B.P., *Yorkist and Early Tudor Government 1461–1509* (1966).

Wolffe, B.P., *The Crown Lands 1471–1536* (1970).

Wolffe, B.P., *The Royal Demesne in English History* (1971).

Chronology of events

1442
28 April
Birth of Edward, son (eldest?) of Richard Duke of York, soon after titular Earl of March.

1454–5
York's First Protectorate.

1455–6
York's Second Protectorate.

1459–61
First phase of the Wars of the Roses: House of York vs regime of Henry VI (1422–61) of House of Lancaster.

1459
Rout at Ludford. Flight of the Yorkist leaders: Edward Earl of March to Calais.

1460
26 June
Landing of Edward with Yorkist earls at Sandwich.
10 July
Battle of Northampton. Yorkist seizure of Henry VI and his government.
October
York claims the Crown in parliament; the Accord recognizes his right after Henry VI's death; York's Third Protectorate.
30 December
Battle of Wakefield: York killed.

1461
2–3 February
Edward wins battle of Mortimer's Cross over the Welsh Lancastrians.
4 March
Accession of Edward IV in London.
29 March
Battle of Towton. Decisive defeat of the Lancastrians.

1461–70
Edward IV's First Reign.

1461–4
The Nevilles combat and crush the northern Lancastrians, finally at battle of Hexham.

1464
1 May
Traditional date of Edward IV's secret marriage to Elizabeth Grey (née Wydeville).
September
Edward's marriage revealed and (after debate) Elizabeth is accepted as his queen.

1465
Long truce with Scotland.

1467
Edward IV informs parliament of his intention 'to live of his own except in great and urgent causes'.
8 June
Dismissal of Warwick's brother, Archbishop Neville, as chancellor in Warwick's absence.

1468
Marriage of Edward's sister, Margaret of York, to Charles the Bold, Duke of Burgundy.

1469–71
The crisis of the reign. Second phase of the Wars of the Roses.

1469
June
Rebellion of Robin of Redesdale in Yorkshire.

24 July
Battle of Edgecote. Warwick and Clarence imprison Edward IV and seize control of the government; deaths of Edward's principal new nobility earls of Pembroke (Herbert), Devon (Stafford of Southwick), and Rivers (Wydeville). Apparent attempts to bastardize Edward IV and discredit his marriage.

October–December
Collapse of Warwick's regime. Reconciliation of Edward IV with Warwick and Clarence.

1470
March–April
Edward crushes Lincolnshire rebellion, and drives Warwick and Clarence into exile.

22–25 August
Treaty of Angers between Louis XI of France, Warwick and Henry VI's queen, Margaret of Anjou.

September–October
With French backing, Warwick invades England, dethrones Edward IV, who flees abroad, and restores King Henry VI: his readeption.

2 November
Birth in sanctuary at Westminster Abbey of Edward's son, Edward, later Prince of Wales and Edward V.

1471
March–May
Edward IV invades England, is reconciled with his brother Clarence, defeats (and destroys) Warwick (14 April) and Lancastrians (7 May) and recovers his throne.

21 May
Death of Henry VI.

1471–83
Edward IV's Second Reign.

1472–5
Edward IV plans to invade France. Diplomacy to secure alliances with Brittany and Burgundy. Protracted parliament that votes substantial taxes.

1475
c.4 July–c.20 September
Edward IV invades France.
29 August
Treaty of Picquigny.

1476
Reinterment of Richard Duke of York at Fotheringhay.

1477
5 January
Defeat at Nancy and death of Charles the Bold, Duke of Burgundy; succession of his daughter, Mary of Burgundy.
May
Arrest of George Duke of Clarence.

1478
January–February
Trial of Clarence in parliament, conviction for treason, and execution.

1480–3
War with Scotland.

1482
Edward's last brother, Richard Duke of Gloucester, briefly occupies Edinburgh. Capture of Berwick.
Treaty of Arras between France and Burgundy, shutting out Edward IV. Repudiation of betrothal of Dauphin Charles to Elizabeth of York.

1483
January
Parliament at Westminster.
Grant to Gloucester of Cumberland palatinate and hereditary wardenship of West March.
Edward IV ineffectually plots war of revenge against France.
9 April
Death of Edward IV.
10 April
Accession of Edward's son as Edward V (1483).

1483–7
Third phase of Wars of the Roses.
25 June
Deposition of Edward V.
26 June
Accession of Edward IV's youngest brother, Richard Duke of Gloucester, as Richard III (1483–5).

1485
22 August
Battle of Bosworth. Victory of Henry Tudor as Henry VII (1485–1509). Death of Richard III and end of Yorkist dynasty.

Index

Allan, Dr Alison 26, 102
André, Bernard 55
Amstrong, C.A.J. 83, 93
Arras, treaty of (1482) 35, 45, 78, 124, 144–5
Arrival, The 25, 29, 33–4, 50, 85
Arthur, Arthurian Legend 7, 16, 25, 56, 100

Barnes, Dr P. 151
Bastard feudalism 69, 71, 96, 171–84, 187, 229
Beaufort family, dukes of Somerset 8, 19, 77, 185, 189–90
Bellamy, Professor J.G. 84, 151, 166, 170,179–80, 182, 197–9, 202
Benevolences 61, 63, 72–3, 153–4
Berwick-upon-Tweed 25, 34, 37, 48–9, 51, 60, 95, 128, 146–7, 160–3, 219
Bokenham, Osbert 14–15
Brittany, duchy of 44, 24, 130, 133, 137
Brown, Professor A.L. 84
Brutus *see* Troy
Buck, Sir George 55, 65–7, 100, 195
Buckingham, dukes of *see* Stafford
Burdet, Thomas 61, 192, 194, 196–7
Burgundy, duchy of 32, 40–2, 63, 70, 97–8, 123–6, 129–30, 133, 135, 137–8, 144, 147
see also Charles, Mary, Philip

Cadwallader 16, 25
Calais 2, 8, 41, 43, 105, 123–6, 132–3, 146, 159–60, 226
Cambridge, earl of *see* Richard
Camden, William 169
Carpenter, Dr Christine 4, 7, 9, 83, 86, 93–100, 111, 113, 115, 118, 120, 159, 162, 179, 190, 192, 199, 204–5, 211, 218
Castile 5, 13, 19, 125
Charles VII (1422–61), King of France 19, 124, 127
Charles VIII (1483–98), King of France 40, 45, 140
Charles the Bold, Duke of Burgundy (d. 1477) 24, 35, 40–2, 44–5, 50, 57, 108, 114, 124–5, 128–9, 131, 134, 138–9, 141, 143
Chrimes, Professor Stanley 88–9, 101, 105, 111, 114, 118, 141, 46, 151, 198–9
Chronicle of the Lincolnshire Rebellion 24, 35, 40–2, 44–5, 50, 57, 108, 114, 124–5, 128–9, 131, 134, 138–9, 141, 143
Clare, house of 11–12, 14–15, 17–18, 102
Clarence, dukes of *see* George, Lionel
Commynes, Philippe de 29, 36, 39–45, 65, 67–8, 87, 89, 97, 111, 114, 124, 133, 137, 140, 161

Cook, Sir Thomas 31, 61, 67–8, 77, 89, 93, 104, 115, 130, 153, 161, 163, 168–71
Cornazzano, Antonio 107
Croft, Sir Richard 182, 218
Crowland Chronicle
  First Continuation 28, 30–2, 46, 48, 55–7, 114
  Second Continuation 28, 32–3, 36–9, 46–53, 55–6, 66–7, 73, 85, 87, 95, 108, 114, 128, 133, 135, 137, 140, 144–6, 153, 157, 159–61, 193–5, 199–200, 202, 204–5, 223, 225

Dauphiness *see* Elizabeth
Denton, Revd William 70, 165, 173–4
Dobson, Professor R.B. 94
Dockray, Keith 4, 76, 83, 85, 87, 93, 97–9, 112, 114, 118, 197–9
Dunham, William Huse junior 177

Edmund Duke of York (d.1402) 3, 12–13, 17
Edward IV (1461–83)
  and avarice 38–9, 51–2, 144
  and bastardy, 4, 114, 224
  and brothers *see* George, Richard
  and children, 29, 58
  see also Elizabeth, Edward V
  and damnation 58, 66–7
  and father *see* Richard
  and marriage 31–2, 63–5, 67, 77, 107–15
  and mother 3, 179
  and perjury 58, 62–3, 65, 74
  and precontract 59, 66, 79, 108, 110–11, 224, 228
  and vices 60–7, 69–70, 72, 224
  and wife *see* Elizabeth
  compared to a Turk 67, 69, 71, 196
Edward V (1483), formerly Prince of Wales 4, 26, 60, 65, 67, 147, 160, 182, 200, 211, 215–6, 219, 222–8

Edward Duke of York (d. 1415) 12–13, 17
Edward Prince of Wales (d. 1471) 3, 62, 64, 66–7, 128, 194
Elizabeth, formerly Grey (née Wydeville), queen to Edward IV 29, 60, 65–6, 74, 107–15, 158, 163, 168, 196
Elizabeth of York, queen to Henry VII 4, 26, 35, 45, 140, 143, 210, 221

Fabyan's Chronicle 28, 169
Fastolf, Sir John 8, 19
Sir John Fortescue 25, 103, 168–9, 186
Fotheringhay (Northants) 13–14, 16, 18, 26
France 10, 18–19, 32, 35–6, 41–4, 48, 74, 87, 97, 108, 123–4, 127, 138
  see also Charles, Louis

Gairdner, Dr James 70, 72–3, 165, 197–9
Galbraith, V.H. 82
George, Duke of Clarence 18–19, 24, 33, 35, 42, 45, 48–9, 52, 59, 61, 63, 65, 67, 70, 72, 74, 78, 85, 93, 96–106, 110, 113, 117, 120, 129, 137, 143, 156, 158, 160, 166, 168, 176, 178–9, 188, 190, 200–2, 207–10, 213, 217, 220, 226–8, 230
Gladys Ddu, 12, 16
Gloucester, dukes of *see* Humphrey, Richard
Gransden, Dr Antonia 46–7
Grant, Dr Alexander 111
Green, Dr J.R. 70, 71, 150, 165
Gregory's Chronicle 28, 85, 87, 190
Grey, Thomas, Marquis of Dorset 24, 64, 113, 160, 163, 209, 211, 216–17, 225
Griffiths, Professor Ralph 93, 97, 146
Gruthuyse, Louis Lord 29, 35, 134

Habington, William 55, 67–8, 110, 190, 194–6
Hall, Edward 40, 57, 62–3, 109, 194
Hammond, P.W. 85
Hanham, Dr Alison 46, 57
Harriss, Dr Gerald 93, 151, 154, 162–3, 198
Hastings, William Lord (d. 1483) 26, 39, 41, 64, 93, 160, 176, 178, 211–12, 216–17, 219–26
Hatcher, Professor John 9
Henry IV (1399–1413) 1, 3, 17, 26, 50, 71, 89, 154, 159
Henry V (1413–22) 1, 3, 8, 71, 89, 98, 130, 154, 202, 208, 215, 227
Henry VI (1422–61) 1–10, 18, 21–3, 30–1, 34, 38, 50, 56–8, 62–6, 71–2, 76, 78, 89–90, 100, 115–16, 124, 127, 147, 149, 151–3, 155, 165, 168, 174, 184, 202, 208
Henry VII (1485–1509) 4–9, 13, 47, 56, 58, 71, 83, 87, 89, 92, 103, 150–1, 158–9, 178, 184, 202, 221, 225, 229
Henry VIII (1509–47) 98, 109, 150, 182–3, 230
Herbert, William, earl of Pembroke (d. 1469) 18, 106, 108, 112, 115, 117, 120, 122, 160, 188, 202, 207, 209
William, earl of Huntingdon 202, 212, 215, 220–2
Hicks, Professor Michael 83–4, 86, 93–5, 99–100, 114, 117, 170–1, 190, 197, 205, 211
Heywood, Thomas 63, 194
Holinshed, Raphael 62, 109,192, 194
Horrox, Dr Rosemary 83, 93–5, 99, 161, 205, 211–14, 216–17, 219
Howard, John Lord 141
Hughes, Dr Jonathan 25–6, 86, 100–2
Hume, David 55, 69–70, 196–7
Humphrey Duke of Gloucester 8, 20, 23

Hundred Years War 8–10, 19–21, 43, 92, 123–47

Jones, Dr M.K. 101, 228

Kekewich, Margaret 96
Kendall, Paul Murray 84–5, 205
Kingsford, C.L. 47
Kidwelly 206, 222

Lancaster, house of, 3, 100
  see also Edward, Henry IV, V, VI
Lander, Professor Jack 22, 40, 55, 68–9, 83–4, 86–8, 93, 95, 107, 112, 114, 133, 135–7, 151–2, 154, 185–7, 202
Lionel Duke of Clarence 6, 11–12, 14, 16
Louis XI (1461–83), King of France 19, 27, 35–6, 40–1, 43–5, 68, 74, 77–8, 87, 89–90, 107, 110, 124, 128–34, 137–8, 140–5, 147, 163
Lowe, David 205, 211, 216

McFarlane, K.B. 7, 82–3, 93–4, 96, 99–100, 172, 185, 205
Mancini, Dominic 32, 34, 36–8, 45, 85, 193, 199, 223
Margaret of Anjou, queen to Henry VI 21, 30, 34, 63, 127–8
Margaret of York, Duchess of Burgundy 12,24, 57,129, 192
Markham, John, chief justice 61, 168
Mary, Duchess of Burgundy (1477–82) 35, 45, 108, 125, 143, 168, 198
Maximilian, archduke, late emperor 45, 78, 143, 145
Mirror for Magistrates 55, 64–5, 67, 117, 194–5
Montagu *see* Neville
More, Sir Thomas 29, 32, 36–7, 39, 59–62, 65, 84–5, 108–9, 223, 227
Morgan, D.A.L. 93

Mortimer family 3, 6, 11–13, 16–18, 22, 102
Morton, John, cardinal 168, 186, 195
Myers, Professor Alec 83–7, 93

Neville family 13, 24, 103–6, 111, 118, 188, 207, 209, 229
Neville, George, Archbishop of York 38, 201
  George, Duke of Bedford 208, 210, 222
  John, Marquis Montagu 10, 24, 48, 105, 109, 117, 121–2, 183, 207, 210, 212–13, 222
  Richard, Earl of Warwick, the kingmaker 2, 9, 23, 27, 31–4, 41, 43–4, 48–50, 57–8, 63 65, 68, 70, 71–2, 74–5, 77, 78, 85–7, 94–7, 103–10, 116–21, 124, 126–8, 131–3, 155, 160, 186, 188, 190–1, 194, 202, 207–10, 212–13, 229–30

Oman, Sir Charles 70, 74
Oxford, earl of *see* Vere

Paston family 73, 177, 184, 191
Péronne, treaty of (1468) 114, 131, 133–4
Philip the Good, Duke of Burgundy (d. 1467) 124, 129
Picquigny, treaty of (1475) 41, 45, 48, 60, 72, 78, 85, 89, 98, 114, 132, 134, 141–9, 154
Plummer, Revd Charles 70, 165, 173
Plumpton family 73, 163, 79, 181, 187, 218
Pollard, Professor Anthony 7, 46–7, 83, 93, 97–8, 112–14, 118, 139, 141, 161, 171, 190, 197, 197, 199, 204–5
Powell, Edward 86, 99
Pronay, Nicholas 46–7
Pugh, T.B. 17, 93, 112

Ramsay, Sir James 70, 73, 111, 197

Rapin de Thoyras 67–8
Redesdale, Robin of 31, 32, 116,154
Richard Duke of Gloucester, later Richard III (1483–5) 1, 4, 6–7, 12, 24, 26, 36, 42–3, 49, 51–2, 55–6, 58–61, 63, 65–7, 72, 82, 84–5, 89, 97–8, 108, 115–17, 129, 141, 144–5, 147, 158, 179–80, 184,188, 191, 194–7, 200, 205–10, 212–14, 218–26
Richard Duke of York 3–6, 8–9, 11–14, 16–22, 25–6, 29–30, 48, 76, 125, 155, 174, 208–9
Richard Earl of Cambridge 3, 12, 17, 22–3
Richmond, Professor Colin 5, 67, 83, 93, 96–8, 111–12, 119, 139, 145, 199–200, 211, 223
Ross, Professor Charles 40, 46, 55, 76, 83–4, 86, 89–93, 96–9, 104–6, 111–19, 129, 133–4, 139, 144–5, 152, 158, 160–1, 163, 165, 169–70, 179, 183, 205, 229
Rous, John 55, 223

Scofield, Cora L. 73–80, 84, 86, 90, 118–19, 121, 169, 223
Scrope, Richard, Archbishop of York 18, 23
Shakespeare, William 1–2, 6, 40, 57, 63–4, 82, 109–10, 194
Shore, Elizabeth 62, 65
Somerset *see* Beaufort
Stafford family, dukes of Buckingham 8, 21, 61, 175, 208, 220–1
Stanley family 44, 211, 214, 216, 218–19, 221
Stares, Richard 167
Stillington, Robert, Bishop of Bath and Wells 65, 111, 129, 131
Storey, Professor R.L. 202
Stow, John 62, 109, 194–5
Stratford, Laurence 73–5, 86, 101, 119, 197, 199
Stubbs, William 70–2, 82, 99, 150, 165, 167, 197

Sutton, Dr Anne 29, 85, 170–1

Tout, Professor T.F. 82
Troy, Trojan legends 7, 16, 23, 100
Tucker, Dr P. 171
Tudor, house of 2, 4, 6–7, 9, 26,
    71, 74, 117, 138, 167, 225
    see also Henry VII, Henry VIII
Tudor historians 55–65, 84, 119
    see also André, Hall, Heywood,
        Holinshed, *Mirror*, More,
        Shakespeare, Stow, Vergil
Tutbury honour (Staffs.) 198, 201,
    211
Twynho, Ankarette 179, 184, 192

Vaughan, Gruffydd ap Eionion
    182, 218
Vere family 31, 34, 67, 73, 121,
    138, 167–8
Vere, Elizabeth de, Countess of
    Oxford 203–4
    John de, Earl of Oxford
        (d. 1462) 188
Vergil, Polydore 29, 32, 36–7,
    56–9, 62, 66–7, 107, 109,
    114, 185–6, 193, 195, 200,
    223

Visser-Fuchs, Dr Livia 29

Walpole, Horace 69
Warkworth's Chronicle 28, 30–1,
    34, 38, 85
Warwick *see* Neville
Watts, Dr John 7
Waurin, Jehan de 29, 32
Welles, Richard Lord 33, 62, 67,
    69, 70, 163, 168, 202
Westerdale, John 214
Williams, Professor C.H. 166
    Dr Daniel 48
    Professor Glanmor 26, 102
    Dr Penry 151
Wolffe, Dr B.P. 83, 87, 90, 92–3,
    150–1, 154–60
Worcester, pseudo-Worcester,
    Chronicle 28, 32, 85, 102, 114
Wydeville family 108, 111–12,
    121, 128–9, 155, 168, 170,
    180, 187, 196, 200, 208–9,
    211, 218–27, 230
    see also Elizabeth

York, house of *see* chapter 2,
    Edmund, Edward, George,
    Richard